The Teachings For Victory

Learning From Nichiren's Writings

Daisaku Ikeda

16pt

Copyright Page from the Original Book

Published by

**World Tribune Press
606 Wilshire Blvd.
Santa Monica, CA 90401**

© 2013 by the Soka Gakkai • All rights reserved.
Printed in the United States of America.

Design by Lightbourne, Inc.
Source artwork: www.iStockphoto.com

ISBN 978-1-935523-54-3
LCCN: 2013946892

10 9 8 7 6 5 4 3 2 1

TABLE OF CONTENTS

EDITOR'S NOTE	iii
PREFACE	v
CHAPTER 1: "LETTER FROM SADO"—PART 1 OF 3	1
CHAPTER 2: "LETTER FROM SADO"—PART 2 OF 3	40
CHAPTER 3: "LETTER FROM SADO"—PART 3 OF 3	85
CHAPTER 4: "LETTER TO THE BROTHERS"—PART 1 OF 3	126
CHAPTER 5: "LETTER TO THE BROTHERS"—PART 2 OF 3	166
CHAPTER 6: "LETTER TO THE BROTHERS"—PART 3 OF 3	205
CHAPTER 7: "THE SUPREMACY OF THE LAW—PART 1 OF 3	248
CHAPTER 8: "THE SUPREMACY OF THE LAW"—PART 2 OF 3	285
CHAPTER 9: "THE SUPREMACY OF THE LAW—PART 3 OF 3	316
CHAPTER 10: "THE THREE KINDS OF TREASURE"—PART 1 OF 3	349
CHAPTER 11: "THE THREE KINDS OF TREASURE"—PART 2 OF 3	382
CHAPTER 12: "THE THREE KINDS OF TREASURE"—PART 3 OF 3	413

i

EDITOR'S NOTE

This series of lectures by SGI President Daisaku Ikeda was published in SGI-USA's *Living Buddhism* magazine from the November–December 2009 issue through the September–October 2010 issue.

Please also see *The Writings of Nichiren Daishonin*, vol.1, as follows:
- "Letter from Sado," pp.301–08
- "Letter to the Brothers," pp.493–504
- "The Supremacy of the Law," pp.612–17
- "The Three Kinds of Treasure," pp.848–53

- GZ, page number(s)—refers to the *Gosho zenshu*, the Japanese-language compilation of letters, treatises, essays and oral teachings of Nichiren Daishonin.
- LSOC, page number(s)—refers to *The Lotus Sutra and Its Opening and Closing Sutras*, translated by Burton Watson (Soka Gakkai: Tokyo, 2009).
- OTT, page number(s)—refers to *The Record of the Orally Transmitted Teachings*, translated by Burton Watson (Soka Gakkai: Tokyo, 2004).
- WND, page number(s)—refers to *The Writings of Nichiren Daishonin*, vol.1 (WND-1) (Tokyo:

Soka Gakkai, 1999) and vol.2 (WND-2) (Tokyo: Soka Gakkai, 2006).

References to dates in *The Writings of Nichiren Daishonin* are from the lunisolar calendar that was used in thirteenth-century Japan, which differs from the current Gregorian calendar commonly used in the West.

PREFACE

NICHIREN'S TEACHINGS ARE THE WELLSPRING OF VICTORY

Nichiren Daishonin's writings are a compilation of teachings for victory. They are the driving force for all success—be it winning in life and society, triumphing over negative karma or defeating devilish functions.

Nichiren Buddhism is a philosophy of inner transformation empowering people to the highest degree, enabling them to develop strength, wisdom and richness of heart. Each word and phrase of Nichiren Daishonin's writings is infused with the spirit of the Buddha to draw forth people's inherent potential. Nichiren's intense, compassionate wish as the Buddha of the Latter Day of the Law is to help his disciples and all people achieve victory in their lives. This wish resonates powerfully through each of his writings.

Nichiren's writings are a wellspring of everlasting victory, holding the key to success and prosperity for all people. As long as the SGI keeps forging ahead with Nichiren's words as its foundation, it will continue to develop and thrive forever.

This year, 2009 [when this series started], is the SGI's Year of Youth and Victory. I am happy to say that I am still enjoying the best of health. For the sake of our young people and our ongoing victory, I will take even more energetic leadership for worldwide kosen-rufu based on Nichiren's teachings. And I will continue speaking and writing about the essential Buddhist spirit of mentor and disciple for the sake of posterity. Let us study the writings of Nichiren Daishonin, the eternal scripture of the SGI, and further expand our magnificent network of people living with an ever-victorious spirit.

Daisaku Ikeda
SGI President

CHAPTER 1

"LETTER FROM SADO"—PART 1 OF 3

MY DISCIPLES, WIN WITH THE HEART OF A LION KING!

In this lecture series, I will focus in depth on those writings that the first three Soka Gakkai presidents especially found to be a source of spiritual inspiration and sustenance. The first is "Letter from Sado," which Nichiren Daishonin left for future generations out of his passionate wish to safeguard the correct teaching of Buddhism. It communicates a powerful message to his disciples.

It would be no exaggeration to say that "Letter from Sado" is the writing for the Soka Gakkai. This is because the first three presidents, with a selfless dedication to faith and united by bonds of mentor and disciple, have put the teachings of this writing into practice in their lives.

Founding Soka Gakkai president Tsunesaburo Makiguchi, when admonishing arrogant disciples, would frequently cite from this writing the line "a magpie mocking a phoenix."[1] And he made known widely the great mission of the Soka Gakkai to energetically undertake the practice of *shakubuku*,[2] which is a major focus of "Letter from Sado."

Second Soka Gakkai president Josei Toda often lectured on "Letter from Sado" in order to impress its message upon us. During the famous Osaka Campaign[3] of 1956, he also lectured on this writing at a gathering held at the Central Civic Hall in Nakanoshima, Osaka, to help spur the Kansai members on to victory.

This writing was also a source of inspiration for my own Buddhist practice in my youth. I suffered from tuberculosis, and Mr. Toda's businesses faced serious setbacks. During this bitterly trying period, I read "Letter from Sado" again and again, drawing from it the courage to struggle on and make it through each day, and ultimately to realize victory. I also put my heart and soul into lecturing on this writing. I spoke on it wherever I went in those early days of our movement.

In 1959, the year after President Toda's death, I gave a lecture on "Letter from Sado" at the Toshima Civic Hall in Tokyo, a venue that held for me many fond memories of my mentor. As Mr. Toda's disciple, I appealed fervently to my fellow members, echoing his mighty cry: "Disciples, rise resolutely to action, one and all!"

I also lectured on this letter to a group of high school division members, young phoenixes who would shoulder the future, addressing them just as I would adults. Those young people are now outstanding leaders of kosen-rufu around the world.

Passage for Study in This Lecture

This letter is addressed to Toki.[4] It should also be shown to Saburo Saemon,[5] the lay priest Okuratonotsuji Juro,[6] the lay nun of Sajiki,[7] and my other followers. Send me the names of those killed in the battles at Kyoto and Kamakura.[8] Also, please have those who are coming here bring me the anthology of non-Buddhist texts,[9] volume two of *The Words and Phrases of the Lotus Sutra,* volume four of *The Profound Meaning of the Lotus Sutra* and the commentary on this volume, and the collected official opinion papers and collected imperial edicts.

The most dreadful things in the world are the pain of fire, the flashing of swords, and the shadow of death. Even horses and cattle fear being killed; no wonder human beings are afraid of death. Even a leper clings to life; how much more so a healthy person. The Buddha teaches that even filling the entire major world system with the seven kinds of treasures does not match offering one's little finger to the Buddha and the

[Lotus] sutra. The boy Snow Mountains[10] gave his own body, and the ascetic Aspiration for the Law[11] peeled off his own skin [in order to record the Buddha's teachings]. Since nothing is more precious than life itself, one who dedicates one's life to Buddhist practice is certain to attain Buddhahood. If one is prepared to offer one's life, why should one begrudge any other treasure for the sake of Buddhism? On the other hand, if one is loath to part with one's wealth, how can one possibly offer one's life, which is far more valuable?

The way of the world dictates that one should repay a great obligation to another, even at the cost of one's life. Many warriors die for their lords, perhaps many more than one would imagine. A man will die to defend his honor; a woman will die for a man. Fish want to survive; they deplore their pond's shallowness and dig holes in the bottom to hide in, yet tricked by bait, they take the hook. Birds in a tree fear that they are too low and perch in the top branches, yet bewitched by bait, they too are caught in snares. Human beings are equally vulnerable. They give their lives for shallow, worldly matters but rarely for the Buddha's precious teachings.

Small wonder they do not attain Buddhahood.

Buddhism should be spread by the method of either shoju or shakubuku, depending on the age. These are analogous to the two worldly ways of the literary and the military. The great sages of old practiced the Buddhist teachings as befitted the times. The boy Snow Mountains and Prince Sattva[12] offered their bodies when urged that by doing so they would hear the teaching in return, and that giving one's life constitutes bodhisattva practice. But should one sacrifice one's life at a time when it is not required? In an age when there is no paper, one should use one's own skin. In an age when there are no writing brushes, one should use one's own bones. In an age when people honor the observers of the precepts and the practitioners of the correct teaching while they denounce those who break or ignore the precepts, one should strictly follow the precepts. In an age when Confucianism or Taoism is used to suppress Shakyamuni's teachings, one should risk one's life to remonstrate with the emperor, as did the Dharma teachers Tao-an and Hui-yüan[13] and the Tripitaka Master Fa-tao.[14] In an age when people confuse Hinayana and Mahayana teachings, provisional and true teachings, or exoteric and esoteric doctrines, as though unable to distinguish gems from tiles and stones or cow's milk from donkey's milk,[15] one should strictly differentiate between them, following the example of the great teachers T'ien-t'ai[16] and Dengyo.[17]

It is the nature of beasts to threaten the weak and fear the strong. Our contemporary scholars of the various schools are just like them. They despise a wise man without power, but fear evil rulers. They are no more than fawning retainers. Only by defeating a powerful enemy can one prove one's real strength. When an evil ruler in consort with priests of erroneous teachings tries to destroy the correct teaching and do away with a man of wisdom, those with the heart of a lion king are sure to attain Buddhahood. Like Nichiren, for example. I say this not out of arrogance, but because I am deeply committed to the correct teaching. An arrogant person will always be overcome with fear when meeting a strong enemy, as was the haughty asura who shrank in size and hid himself in a lotus blossom in Heat-Free Lake when reproached by Shakra. Even

> a word or a phrase of the correct teaching will enable one to gain the way, if it suits the time and the capacity of the people. But though one studies a thousand sutras and ten thousand treatises, one will not attain Buddhahood if these teachings are unsuitable for the time and the people's capacity. (WND-1, 301–02)

LECTURE

Nichiren Daishonin's Immense Compassion and Concern for His Followers

This letter is addressed to Toki. It should also be shown to Saburo Saemon, the lay priest Okuratonotsuji Juro, the lay nun of Sajiki, and my other followers. (WND-1, 301)

This passage precedes the main body of the letter and names the specific recipients for whom it is intended. In these lines, we can see Nichiren Daishonin's spirit to reach out to his followers individually.

The letter, however, as indicated at the end, is formally addressed to all of "Nichiren's disciples and lay supporters" (WND-1, 306). It was written in March 1272, during Nichiren's exile on Sado Island.[18] In the postscript, he writes, "I want people with seeking minds to meet and read this letter together for encouragement" (WND-1, 306). At the time, his followers in Kamakura had been buffeted by a storm of persecution. The Daishonin, therefore, strongly urged those with genuine faith to stay in close communication with one another and, basing themselves on his guidance, to unite solidly to triumph over their hardships.

In an article on "Letter from Sado," President Toda wrote: "What I find deeply moving when reading this writing is that, despite the fact that Nichiren Daishonin's own life was in constant danger and he was living in the direst, most impoverished circumstances, his warm parent-like affection and concern for his disciples is still abundantly clear. The image that comes to mind is one of gentle waves bathed in sunlight lapping serenely at the base of a great, indomitable rock rising up from the spring sea."[19]

Even amid his life-threatening exile, Nichiren continued to show the utmost concern for his disciples' well-being. He demonstrated a vast, unperturbed state of life. This is what President Toda compared to a great rock soaring high above the spring sea, an analogy for Nichiren's towering state of life and immense compassion. For the sake of Buddhism, Mr. Toda himself had overcome persecution at the hands of Japan's militarist authorities during World War II and had fought on to the end with the unwavering, rocklike resolve of an indomitable champion, just like Nichiren.

Challenging great hardships is what enables us to boundlessly develop our state of life. A teacher or mentor in Buddhism is someone who teaches this essential principle. What incredible good fortune it is to have such a teacher! The true way of a disciple is to repay that profound debt of gratitude. "Letter from Sado" can be read as a pledge infused with the quintessential spirit of Buddhism—namely, the shared commitment of teacher and disciple.

***

The Buddha's Serene State of Life

Send me the names of those killed in the battles at Kyoto and Kamakura. Also, please have those who are coming here bring me the anthology of non-Buddhist texts, volume two of *The Words and Phrases of the Lotus Sutra,* volume four of *The Profound Meaning of the Lotus Sutra* and the commentary on this volume, and the collected official opinion papers and collected imperial edicts. (WND-1, 301)

Nichiren Daishonin asks to be sent the names of those killed in the fighting in Kyoto and Kamakura no doubt so that he can chant Nam-myoho-renge-kyo for them. Here, we see a glimpse of his boundless compassion to pray for people's happiness throughout the three existences—past, present and future. In addition, he requests that those planning to visit him on Sado bring various reference materials, including the anthology of non-Buddhist texts, T'ien-t'ai's *Words and Phrases of the Lotus Sutra* and other documents.

In his remote place of exile, the Daishonin devoted himself with even greater passion to the important task of clarifying his ideas and setting them down with the aim of guiding all people in the Latter Day to enlightenment. Asking here to be sent various texts highlights his serene state of life entirely unaffected by his circumstances. What untold courage his followers must have derived from just these few opening lines.

The Fundamental Issue of Life and Death

The most dreadful things in the world are the pain of fire, the flashing of swords, and the shadow of death. Even horses and cattle fear being killed; no wonder human beings are afraid of death. Even a leper clings to life; how much more so a healthy person. (WND-1, 301)

By launching into the main body of this letter with the words above, Nichiren Daishonin powerfully draws attention to the concerns that weigh on all people's minds.

To fear death and cling to life is the way of living beings. "The pain of fire" indicates accidents or natural disasters, while "the flashing of swords" signifies violence or war. Nothing is more frightening than the shadow of death—the prospect of one's own demise. This is as true for animals as for human beings. If, however, we do nothing but fear death and cling to life, we cannot savor a truly profound existence. Why are we born? What is the purpose of our lives? Why do we die? Only by earnestly contemplating our own existence can we lead lives of great depth and meaning.

Nichiren takes up the subject of life and death here in order to explain to his followers, who were suffering tremendous hardships, that Buddhism exists to resolve the fundamental problems of human existence. And he further drives home to them that no matter what tempests might blow, they must never lose sight of faith, the foundation of everything.

For What Purpose Should We Use This Irreplaceable Life?

The Buddha teaches that even filling the entire major world system with the seven kinds of treasures does not match offering one's little finger to the Buddha and the [Lotus] sutra. The boy Snow Mountains gave his own body, and the ascetic Aspiration for the Law peeled off his own skin [in order to record the Buddha's teachings]. Since nothing is more precious than life itself, one who dedicates one's life to Buddhist practice is certain to

attain Buddhahood. If one is prepared to offer one's life, why should one begrudge any other treasure for the sake of Buddhism? On the other hand, if one is loath to part with one's wealth, how can one possibly offer one's life, which is far more valuable? (WND-1, 301)

For what purpose, then, should we use this life, which is irreplaceable? In "Letter from Sado," Nichiren Daishonin teaches that by dedicating our lives to the practice of Buddhism we can attain Buddhahood. To underscore the profound significance of such dedication, he first cites "Medicine King," the 23rd chapter of the Lotus Sutra. He then points to the examples of the boy Snow Mountains and the ascetic Aspiration for the Law—who both represent Shakyamuni Buddha in past existences when he was carrying out bodhisattva practice—to clarify that striving with an ungrudging spirit is the key to accomplishing our Buddhist practice.

Further, Nichiren notes that those who are prepared to give their lives will not hesitate to part with any other treasure. He is in effect saying with strict compassion to those of his followers who trembled at the thought of being persecuted and suffering such terrible consequences as having their fiefs confiscated: "Aren't these present persecutions we are facing an unparalleled chance to give our lives in exchange for Buddhahood? Since the goal of attaining that supreme state of life is just ahead, what can we possibly have to fear?"

This passage also conveys an important spirit that offers lessons for us today. One lesson, as noted above, is that simply clinging to our lives will not result in attaining genuine happiness. Establishing a fundamental purpose and pursuing the correct course in life—ready to face any hardship this might entail—enables us to experience deep joy and fulfillment. If we allow ourselves to be controlled by shallow desires and hold fast to our lesser selves at a crucial moment, then our hearts will wither, and only misery and regret will await us.

Another lesson is that the lofty state of life gained through Buddhist practice is eternal, transcending the limited nature of our present existence. By dedicating this precious lifetime to Buddhism, we are certain to enjoy abundant happiness and benefit in all future lifetimes.

Coming to see things from the perspective of the eternity of life throughout past, present and future, and also in terms of eternal happiness, constitutes a fundamental turning point for breaking through innumerable problems. Individuals gaining a correct perspective on life and death can elevate the life condition of humankind as a whole. For a philosophy to open up possibilities for twenty-first-century society, it is vital that it distinguish between shallow and profound views of life and death. As Nichiren Buddhists, we are all in the vanguard of this endeavor. Let us proudly forge ahead with this conviction.

Dedicate This Supreme Life to Buddhism

The way of the world dictates that one should repay a great obligation to another, even at the cost of one's life. Many warriors die for their lords, perhaps many more than one would imagine. A man will die to defend his honor; a woman will die for a man. Fish want to survive; they deplore their pond's shallowness and dig holes in the bottom to hide in, yet tricked by bait, they take the hook. Birds in a tree fear that they are too low and perch in the top branches, yet bewitched by bait, they too are caught in snares. Human beings are equally vulnerable. They give their lives for shallow, worldly matters but rarely for the Buddha's precious teachings. Small wonder they do not attain Buddhahood. (WND-1, 301)

Earlier, by noting that people often lose their lives in accidents or in armed conflicts—which he expresses as "the pain of fire" and "the flashing of swords" (WND-1, 301)—Nichiren Daishonin reminds us that all people treasure their own lives. In this next section, he also points out that there are many examples of people laying down their lives in accord with their society's moral conventions and values.

There are also many cases of people foolishly duped into sacrificing their lives, try as they might to protect themselves from harm. The behavior of the fish and birds described in this section are based on the insights of ancient thinkers documented in such works as *Zhenguan zhengyao* (The Essentials of Government in the Chen-kuan Era),[20] a Chinese classic on the art of leadership. "Tricked by bait" is a metaphor for how human beings—even though taking various measures and precautions to stay safe—may be swept away by immediate desires or have a lapse of judgment due to narrow thinking, leading ultimately to their self-destruction. Sadly, such human folly remains very much in evidence today.

Nichiren, therefore, counsels that rather than giving our lives—the most valuable possession of all—for "shallow, worldly matters," we should dedicate them to "the Buddha's precious teachings."

We speak of not begrudging one's life, but Nichiren Buddhism is definitely not a teaching of reckless self-sacrifice or martyrdom. Mr. Makiguchi, Mr. Toda and I—the first three presidents of the Soka Gakkai—have taken action with the resolve to advance kosen-rufu in such a way that not one member is sacrificed, and we have willingly given our all toward that end. In the future, as well, this must remain the spirit of successive Soka Gakkai presidents.

You absolutely must not throw away your precious lives. To our young men and women,

I say: No matter what painful or difficult challenges you may be facing, you must never disrespect or harm your own lives or the lives of others. Each of you is endowed with the wondrous and supremely noble Buddha nature.

In specific terms, how should we practice in order to dedicate this invaluable lifetime to "the Buddha's precious teachings"? In another writing, Nichiren says with regard to ordinary people attaining Buddhahood in the Latter Day of the Law: "As for the matter of becoming a Buddha, ordinary people keep in mind the words 'earnest resolve' and thereby become Buddhas" ("The Gift of Rice," WND-1, 1125). These words express the spirit of "not begrudging one's life" in its supreme and highest form. It is the Daishonin's emphatic declaration that ordinary people of this age can, without having to sacrifice their lives in the manner of the boy Snow Mountains, attain the same benefit that accrues to such selfless dedication through their "earnest resolve."

As Nichiren writes, "It is the heart that is important" ("The Strategy of the Lotus Sutra," WND-1, 1000). It's a matter of exerting millions of kalpas of effort in a single moment of life for the sake of Buddhism, for the noble cause of kosen-rufu. For us, not begrudging our lives ultimately means steadfastly chanting Nam-myoho-renge-kyo without any fear and wholeheartedly dedicating ourselves to showing actual proof of faith—for the sake of the world, for the sake of the future and for the sake of others.

President Makiguchi described this as "a selfless way of life of great good." Overcoming both selfishness and fear, and striving for the happiness of both oneself and others characterize such a way of life. He explained, "It is an ordinary way of life, a way of plain humanity—such that anyone who consciously experiences it and comes to realize that it is universally accessible will feel an overwhelming desire to embrace it, and, indeed, will feel compelled to do so."[21]

Therefore, he asserted that the Soka Kyoiku Gakkai (Value-Creating Education Society; forerunner of the Soka Gakkai) "was itself living proof of a life of great good."[22]

In other words, selfless dedication is found in a seemingly ordinary way of life open to anyone. A true example of such dedication can be seen in our daily efforts for kosen-rufu, exerting ourselves body and soul to encourage others and sincerely sharing the greatness of Buddhism with those around us.

***

"The Latter Day Is the Time for Shakubuku Alone"

Buddhism should be spread by the method of either shoju or shakubuku, depending on the age. These are analogous

to the two worldly ways of the literary and the military. (WND-1, 301)

In this passage, Nichiren Daishonin clarifies the Buddhist practice appropriate to the Latter Day of the Law. *Shoju* means explaining the Law according to each person's capacity. *Shakubuku* means directly teaching others the ultimate principle of Nam-myoho-renge-kyo just as it is. Here, the Daishonin says that the method of propagation chosen should depend on the age or time. Which method is suitable for a particular period can only be determined through a profound understanding of what the people and the times are seeking. The Buddhist sutras generally divide the time after the Buddha's passing into three periods: the Former Day of the Law, the Middle Day of the Law and the Latter Day of the Law.[23] In "The Selection of the Time," Nichiren says, "Let us borrow the eye of the Buddha to consider this question of time and capacity" (WND-1, 540). Determining the time in terms of choosing the right method of propagation for a certain age requires that we view things through the insightful lens of Buddha wisdom.

In a lecture he gave on "Letter from Sado," Mr. Toda discussed the passage "Buddhism should be spread by the method of either shoju or shakubuku, depending on the age," saying: "We mustn't misinterpret the meaning of the word *age*. Nichiren says that we should employ either shoju or shakubuku depending on the age or time, but many erroneously take this to mean that they can arbitrarily decide for themselves what age it is and correspondingly decide which method of propagation. For instance, they think: 'Since people in society are so critical of Nichiren Buddhism right now, let's go with shoju,' or 'Since everyone's rather quiet and not making any objection, let's employ shakubuku.' This is wrong. Age here refers to the Former Day, the Middle Day and the Latter Day of the Law ... And the Latter Day is the time for shakubuku alone."[24]

Whenever and wherever we carry out activities, we must never forget to be guided by the spirit to share Nam-myoho-renge-kyo with others. This is the way of genuine disciples of great teachers of shakubuku.

"We Must Not Let the Banner of Propagation Fall!"

The great sages of old practiced the Buddhist teachings as befitted the times. The boy Snow Mountains and Prince Sattva offered their bodies when urged that by doing so they would hear the teaching in return, and that giving one's life constitutes bodhisattva practice. But should one sacrifice one's life at a time when it is not required? In an age when there is no paper, one should use one's own skin. In an age when there are no writing brushes, one should use one's own bones. In an age

when people honor the observers of the precepts and the practitioners of the correct teaching [of the Buddha] while they denounce those who break or ignore the precepts, one should strictly follow the precepts. In an age when Confucianism or Taoism is used to suppress Shakyamuni's teachings, one should risk one's life to remonstrate with the emperor, as did the Dharma teachers Tao-an and Hui-yüan and the Tripitaka Master Fa-tao. In an age when people confuse Hinayana and Mahayana teachings, provisional and true teachings, or exoteric and esoteric doctrines, as though unable to distinguish gems from tiles and stones or cow's milk from donkey's milk, one should strictly differentiate between them, following the example of the great teachers T'ien-t'ai and Dengyo. (WND-1, 301–02)

Great sages or bodhisattvas of the past could attain Buddhahood by practicing in accord with the time, something on which Buddhism places utmost importance.

Even before the appearance of Shakyamuni and the birth of Buddhism as a formal body of teaching, we see various selfless practitioners and respected teachers, such as those cited in the passage above, giving their lives in pursuit of the ultimate truth that would lead to enlightenment. Meanwhile, in an age when the teachings of the Buddha are widely accepted in society, the practitioners of those teachings have a responsibility to set an upright example so that many others will also correctly uphold them. In contrast, in an age when the ruler rejects and represses Buddhism, its practitioners should admonish that ruler at the risk of their own lives. And in an age when, within Buddhism, the teachings become mixed up and people are confused as to which are correct, it becomes imperative to clarify the relative superiority of the different teachings.

What kind of age, then, is the present? Only with an understanding of the practice appropriate to the age in which we live can Buddhism be correctly transmitted.

Here, as indicated by Nichiren Daishonin's reference to the "great sages of old," those who accurately recognize the time and take the required action when necessary are called sages and worthies in Buddhism. What great sages of the past and teachers of Buddhism share in common is the spirit to protect the Law—the spirit to treasure the correct teaching of the Buddha above all and to share it with others even at the cost of their lives. It was because they did not begrudge their lives that they could clearly grasp what they had to do.

A fundamental requirement for Buddhist teachers or leaders is to understand the time and propagate the teaching in a manner that accords with it. The Soka Gakkai achieved great development because the leadership of its first two presidents, Mr. Makiguchi and Mr. Toda, always befitted the time. And I, as third president, while carrying on a dialogue in my heart with my mentor, Mr. Toda, have also prayed and worked tirelessly to open a way to kosen-rufu that suits the time. That is why our movement has been so successful.

In spring 1980, upon completing my fifth visit to China, I flew directly from Shanghai to Nagasaki to embark on a guidance tour of Kyushu—my first regional guidance tour in Japan since having been forced to step down as Soka Gakkai president the previous year.[25] After Nagasaki, I traveled to Fukuoka. There, I called out to my beloved disciples in Kyushu, who were deeply committed to working with me for kosen-rufu: "We must not let the banner of propagation fall! We must not let the flame of faith be extinguished!"

From Kyushu, an area that had suffered so much on account of problems caused by the Nichiren Shoshu priesthood, I launched a powerful counteroffensive, determined to keep alive the spirit of selfless dedication to kosen-rufu that is the hallmark of Nichiren Buddhism. With the awareness that this was the crucial moment to lay the foundation for the Soka Gakkai's eternal victory, the members of Kyushu stood up together with me. When disciples follow the mentor's lead in waging a struggle for kosen-rufu that accords with the time, their victory is assured. Our members in Kyushu have written just such a triumphant history.

It is now up to our successors in the youth division to solidly carry on this all-important spirit of mentor and disciple and ensure that it is passed on into the eternal future.

Practitioners of the Correct Teaching Encounter Resentment and Persecution in the Latter Day

It is the nature of beasts to threaten the weak and fear the strong. Our contemporary scholars of the various schools are just like them. They despise a wise man without power, but fear evil rulers. They are no more than fawning retainers. Only by defeating a powerful enemy can one prove one's real strength. (WND-1, 302)

This passage describes the prevailing climate of the Latter Day of the Law, an age when those who uphold the correct teaching encounter resentment and persecution.

The Tatsunokuchi Persecution[26] and Sado Exile constituted religious persecution undertaken by despotic government officials in league with aberrant priests such as Ryokan of Gokuraku-ji, a temple in Kamakura, and others in an attempt to destroy Nichiren Daishonin and his community of believers.

The "nature of beasts" refers to the essential character of the likes of Ryokan and other priests of established Buddhist schools during Nichiren's day. They despised a person of wisdom (Nichiren) and feared evil rulers (the government authorities). This was the spiritual climate in Japan that led to the harsh crackdown on the Daishonin and his followers.

Nichiren, however, boldly confronted this great persecution, declaring, "Only by defeating a powerful enemy can one prove one's real strength."

Defeating Injustice by Speaking Out for What Is Right

When an evil ruler in consort with priests of erroneous teachings tries to destroy the correct teaching and do away with a man of wisdom, those with the heart of a lion king are sure to attain Buddhahood. Like Nichiren, for example. I say this not out of arrogance, but because I am deeply committed to the correct teaching. (WND-1, 302)

"When an evil ruler in consort with priests of erroneous teachings tries to destroy the correct teaching and do away with a man of wisdom"—this describes a perverse alliance between political and religious authorities. The pattern of persecution against those who uphold the correct Buddhist teaching is the same in every age.

Amid a calamitous storm of persecution, Nichiren Daishonin forged ahead with the "heart of a lion king," refusing to retreat a single step. To have the heart of a lion king means to calmly recognize the "nature of beasts" for what it is and to defeat it. In Buddhism, lion king is another name for a Buddha. Those who stand up with this heart—or spirit—are certain to attain Buddhahood.

"Like Nichiren, for example," he says. Here, he urges his followers to take note of his example, stressing that he is not speaking out of arrogance but, rather, out of his deep commitment to the correct teaching.

We should keenly reflect on his profound commitment to the Law. When we "treasure the Law more highly than our own lives"[27]—when we overcome attachment to our lesser selves and reveal our greater selves by basing our lives on the Law—we will find the courage to confidently speak out for what is right without fearing anyone. Herein lies the essence of faith.

Since meeting Mr. Toda more than six decades ago (on August 14, 1947), I have championed the noble cause of the Soka Gakkai and proclaimed the ideals of our movement widely throughout the world, without retreating a step. I have summoned the power to do so because of my unwavering commitment to realizing the vision of my mentor, a great leader of kosen-rufu, which is a goal more precious to me than my own life. In other words, I stood up and took action with the spirit to rigorously protect the Soka Gakkai—the organization carrying out the Buddha's intent and decree—and to foster its development around the globe in accord with Mr. Toda's fervent wish.

To not begrudge one's life and to live with the heart of a lion king are like two sides of a coin. Unhesitatingly committing yourself to the Law and having the lionhearted courage to battle the enemies of the Lotus Sutra are in essence the same thing. It seems to me the key message of the first half of "Letter from Sado" is that the Daishonin's disciples should be lion kings, courageous individuals who embody the same selfless spirit as he does. Let us note how emphatically he drives this point home.

His words, "Like Nichiren, for example," represent a passionate cry to his disciples. We can imagine him calling out to the depths of their being: "Just as I defeated all devilish forces, you, too, must summon the heart of a lion king and win over all negative forces. Fight with the same spirit as Nichiren! Fight alongside me and with the same resolve!" He was waiting for dedicated disciples to stand up with the same spirit and commitment that he had.

During World War II, only Mr. Makiguchi and Mr. Toda carried on Nichiren's lionlike spirit. The priesthood, in stark contrast, succumbed to cowardly self-interest. Nichiren's legacy as a selfless lion king lives on today in the Soka

Gakkai alone. We have faithfully inherited his courageous and ungrudging spirit, and have thereby opened wide the path to worldwide kosen-rufu. Our benefit, as a result, is also immense beyond measure. With this powerful conviction, let us reach out to even more people and share with them the true greatness of the Soka path of mentor and disciple.

The Spirit To Cherish the Correct Teaching Gives Rise to Infinite Courage

An arrogant person will always be overcome with fear when meeting a strong enemy, as was the haughty asura who shrank in size and hid himself in a lotus blossom in Heat-Free Lake when reproached by Shakra. (WND-1, 302)

Nichiren Daishonin's assertions about his teaching or his practice are free of arrogance. He observes, "An arrogant person will always be overcome with fear when meeting a strong enemy." It is just as he says. The true nature of the arrogant is egotism. Being self-centered, when coming face to face with a powerful opponent, they are solely concerned with their own welfare. As a result, they are consumed by fear. In contrast, those with the heart of a lion king always live based on the Law. Because they are not obsessed with themselves, they have an endless supply of courage to take a firm stand against those who seek to destroy the Law.

Carrying Out the Practice That Accords With the Time and Capacity of the People

Even a word or a phrase of the correct teaching will enable one to gain the way, if it suits the time and the capacity of the people. But though one studies a thousand sutras and ten thousand treatises, one will not attain Buddhahood if these teachings are unsuitable for the time and the people's capacity. (WND-1, 302)

Shakubuku means, with the spirit of a lion king, to denounce error and persist in speaking the truth. Nichiren declares that as long as people have the courage to do so, then even just a word or phrase of the correct teaching will confer the benefit of attaining Buddhahood. But without this fundamental spirit—that is to say, the shakubuku spirit based on cherishing the Law—people cannot reveal their enlightenment, even if they study a thousand sutras or ten thousand treatises.

The British author G.K. Chesterton wrote, "A martyr is a man who cares so much for something outside him, that he forgets his own personal life."[28] From our standpoint as Nichiren Buddhists, that for which we care so much can mean the Mystic Law and our teachers in faith; our fellow members, our friends and loved ones, and humanity as a whole; as well as the Soka Gakkai and kosen-rufu. "Forgetting our own personal life" is comparable to not begrudging our lives, or to valuing the Law more highly than our own lives.

In a lecture, Mr. Toda once discussed the teaching of "single-mindedly desiring to see the Buddha, not hesitating even if it costs them their lives," which is a passage from the Lotus Sutra (LSOC, 271), essentially saying: "Without this selfless spirit, we could not chant Nam-myoho-renge-kyo ... I'm sure no one with whom you've shared Buddhism has praised you for doing so. Unless we have the spirit of not hesitating even at the cost of our lives, we cannot accomplish kosen-rufu. If just being called a few names or drawing a violent reaction is enough to discourage you, then you'd be better off not bothering in the first place."[29]

This was the tremendous spirit of Mr. Toda, a great leader and teacher of shakubuku. From the earliest days of our movement, our members have proceeded with courage and tireless perseverance to share the Mystic Law with others, just as he instructed.

Each of you who has engraved this spirit of mentor and disciple in your heart and is earnestly exerting yourself day and night for the Law, for society and for your fellow members is a true champion of selfless dedication who possesses the heart of a lion king. I commend you all most highly.

As long as the spirit of mentor and disciple is passed on to future generations, the Soka

Gakkai will forever prosper and grow. I emphatically state this to all my direct disciples, especially those in the youth division.

"Follow in the footsteps of the teachers who embody the heart of a lion king! Disciples, win with the heart of a lion king!"—this is the motto for the eternal victory of Soka mentors and disciples who read "Letter from Sado" with their lives.

This lecture was originally published in the January 2009 issue of the Daibyakurenge, *the Soka Gakkai's monthly study journal.*

NOTES

[1] Please see the end of "Letter from Sado" (WND-1, 306).

[2] Shakubuku: A method of expounding Buddhism, the aim of which is to suppress others' illusions and to subdue their attachment to error or evil. This refers to the Buddhist method of leading people, particularly its opponents, to the correct Buddhist teaching by refuting their erroneous views and eliminating their attachment to opinions they have formed. The practice of shakubuku thus means to correct another's false views and awaken that person to the truth of Buddhism. The term *shakubuku* is used in contrast

with *shoju,* which means to lead others to the correct teaching gradually, according to their capacity and without directly refuting their religious misconceptions.

[3] Osaka Campaign: In May 1956, the Soka Gakkai members in the Kansai region of Japan, rallying around the young Daisaku Ikeda, who had been dispatched by second president Josei Toda to support them, introduced 11,111 households to the practice of Nichiren Buddhism. In elections held two months later, the Soka Gakkai-backed candidate in Kansai won a seat in the Upper House, an accomplishment thought all but impossible at the time.

[4] Toki Jonin (1216–99): A lay follower of Nichiren. He lived in Wakamiya, Katsushika District of Shimosa Province (part of present-day Chiba Prefecture) and was a leading samurai retainer of Lord Chiba, the constable of that province. He converted to Nichiren's teaching around 1254, the year after it was first proclaimed at Seicho-ji, a temple in Tojo Village in Nagasa District of Awa Province, Japan. He was also the recipient of many of the Daishonin's writings, including "The

Object of Devotion for Observing the Mind," and carefully preserved them.

[5] Shijo Kingo (circa 1230–1300): One of Nichiren's leading followers. His full name and title were Shijo Nakatsukasa Saburo Saemon-no-jo Yorimoto. As a samurai retainer, he served the Ema family, a branch of the ruling Hojo clan. Shijo Kingo was well versed in both medicine and the martial arts. He is said to have converted to Nichiren's teaching around 1256. When the Daishonin was taken to Tatsunokuchi to be beheaded in 1271, Shijo Kingo accompanied him, resolved to die by his side.

[6] Lay priest Okuratonotsuji Juro (n.d.): A follower of Nichiren. His name would indicate that he lived in Tsuji in the Okurato area of Kamakura, but detailed information about him is not known.

[7] Lay nun of Sajiki (n.d.): Also known as the lady of Sajiki. She was a follower of Nichiren and lived in the Sajiki area of Kamakura. Information about her is scant.

[8] This refers to a revolt that took place within the ruling Hojo clan. It resulted in fighting in Kyoto and Kamakura, the imperial capital and the seat of the military government, respectively. In February

1272, Hojo Tokisuke revolted against his younger half brother, the regent Hojo Tokimune, in an attempt to seize power. Tokisuke and others, including Nagoe Tokiakira and Nagoe Noritoki, were killed on suspicion of involvement. It is also known as the Hojo Tokisuke Disturbance or the February Disturbance.

[9] This refers to a collection of writings of various non-Buddhist philosophies and teachings.

[10] The boy Snow Mountains: Shakyamuni Buddha's name in a previous lifetime when he was carrying out bodhisattva practice. The god Shakra, to test the boy's resolve, appeared before him in the form of a hungry demon and recited half a verse from a Buddhist teaching. The boy begged the demon to tell him the second half of the verse. The demon agreed, but demanded flesh and blood in payment. The boy Snow Mountains gladly promised to offer his own body to the demon, who in turn gave him the latter half of the teaching. The demon, changing back into Shakra, praised the boy Snow Mountains' willingness to give his life for the Law.

[11]   Aspiration for the Law: The name of Shakyamuni Buddha in a past existence. A devil disguised as a Brahman appeared to him and said that he would teach him one verse of a Buddhist teaching if the latter were ready to transcribe it using his skin as paper, one of his bones as a pen and his blood as ink. When Aspiration for the Law gladly complied and prepared to write down the Buddhist teaching, the devil vanished. Instead, in response to Aspiration for the Law's seeking mind, a Buddha appeared and taught him a profound teaching.

[12]   Prince Sattva: A prince who sacrificed himself to save a starving tigress, according to the Golden Light Sutra. He is identified as a previous incarnation of Shakyamuni Buddha. This story is cited in several Buddhist scriptures as an illustration of compassion. One day, when Prince Sattva was walking in a bamboo grove, he chanced upon a starving tigress that had given birth to seven cubs and was too weak with hunger to feed them. The prince presented his flesh and blood as an

offering to the tigress and thus saved her and her cubs.

[13] Tao-an and Hui-yüan: Both were Buddhist priests and scholars who lived in sixth-century China, during Emperor Wu's reign (from 560–78) of the Northern Chou dynasty. Tao-an (n.d.) submitted a treatise to the emperor, in which he asserted the superiority of Buddhism over Taoism and criticized Confucianism. Hui-yüan (523–92), later, remonstrated with the emperor when the latter threatened to outlaw Buddhism.

[14] Fa-tao (1086–1147): A priest who remonstrated with Emperor Hui-tsung of China's Sung dynasty when the emperor supported Taoism and attempted to suppress Buddhism. He was branded on the face and exiled.

[15] Cow's milk indicates the Lotus Sutra, while donkey's milk, thought to be poisonous, represents the other sutras.

[16] T'ien-t'ai (538–97): Also known as Chih-i. The founder of the T'ien-t'ai school in China. He was commonly referred to as the Great Teacher T'ien-t'ai. His lectures were compiled in such works as *The Profound Meaning of the Lotus*

Sutra, *The Words and Phrases of the Lotus Sutra* and *Great Concentration and Insight.* T'ien-t'ai refuted all the other Buddhist schools in China and spread the Lotus Sutra.

[17]   Dengyo (767–822): Also known as Saicho; the founder of the Tendai (T'ien-t'ai) school in Japan. He refuted the errors of the six schools of Nara—the established Buddhist schools of the day—and elevated the Lotus Sutra. He dedicated himself to the establishment of a Mahayana ordination center on Mount Hiei.

[18]   Sado Exile: When the authorities failed to execute Nichiren at Tatsunokuchi in September 1271, they exiled him the following month to Sado Island, which was tantamount to a death sentence. When Nichiren's predictions of internal strife and foreign invasion were fulfilled, however, the government issued a pardon in March 1274, and Nichiren returned to Kamakura.

[19]   Translated from Japanese. Josei Toda, *Toda Josei zenshu* (Collected Writings of Josei Toda) (Tokyo: Seikyo Shimbunsha, 1983), vol.3, p.252.

[20]   *Zhenguan zhengyao* (The Essentials of Government in the Chen-kuan Era): A work edited by Wu Ching, a historian of the T'ang dynasty (618–907) in China. It was widely studied by Japanese government officials during Nichiren's day.

[21]   Translated from Japanese. Tsunesaburo Makiguchi, *Makiguchi Tsunesaburo zenshu* (Collected Writings of Tsunesaburo Makiguchi) (Tokyo: Daisanbunmei-sha, 1987), vol.10, p.17.

[22]   Ibid., 21.

[23]   Three periods: the Former Day of the Law, the Middle Day of the Law and the Latter Day of the Law. Three consecutive periods or stages into which the time following a Buddha's death is divided. During the Former Day, the spirit of Buddhism prevails and people can attain enlightenment through its practice. During the Middle Day, although Buddhism becomes firmly established in society, it grows increasingly formalized, and fewer people benefit from it. In the Latter Day, people are tainted by the three poisons—greed, anger and foolishness—and lose their aspiration for

enlightenment; Buddhism itself loses the power to lead them to Buddhahood.

[24] Translated from Japanese. Josei Toda, *Toda Josei zenshu* (Collected Writings of Josei Toda) (Tokyo: Seikyo Shimbunsha, 1986), vol.6, pp.541–42.

[25] President Ikeda resigned his position as third Soka Gakkai president on April 24, 1979, and thereafter became the organization's honorary president. Earlier in 1975, he became president of the newly formed Soka Gakkai International, a position he continues to hold.

[26] Tatsunokuchi Persecution: On September 12, 1271, powerful figures in the government unjustly arrested Nichiren and led him off in the middle of the night to a place called Tatsunokuchi on the outskirts of Kamakura, the seat of government, where they tried to execute him under cover of darkness. The execution attempt failed, and, about a month later, the Daishonin was exiled to Sado Island.

[27] A rewording of a passage from Chang-an's *Annotations on the Nirvana Sutra*: "One's body is insignificant while the Law is supreme" ("Letter to Akimoto," WND-1, 1021).

[28] Gilbert K. Chesterton, *Orthodoxy* (New York: Dodd, Mead and Company, 1949), p.133.

[29] Translated from Japanese. Josei Toda, *Toda Josei zenshu* (Collected Writings of Josei Toda) (Tokyo: Seikyo Shimbunsha, 1985), vol.5, p.415.

CHAPTER 2

"LETTER FROM SADO"—PART 2 OF 3

THE DIRECT PATH TO ATTAINING BUDDHAHOOD: OVERCOMING GREAT OBSTACLES IS THE KEY TO TRANSFORMING OUR KARMA

The Passage for Study in This Lecture

Twenty-six years have passed[1] since the battle of Hoji, and fighting has already broken out twice, on the eleventh and the seventeenth days of the second month of this year.[2] Neither non-Buddhists nor the enemies of Buddhism can destroy the correct teaching of the Thus Come One, but the Buddha's disciples definitely can. As a sutra says, only worms born of the lion's body feed on the lion.[3] A person of great fortune will never be ruined by enemies, but may be ruined by those who are close. The current battle is what the Medicine Master Sutra means by "the calamity of revolt within one's own

domain." The Benevolent Kings Sutra states, "Once the sages have departed, then the seven disasters[4] are certain to arise." The Golden Light Sutra states, "The thirty-three heavenly gods[5] become furious because the king permits evil to run rampant and fails to subdue it." Although I, Nichiren, am not a sage, I am equal to one, for I uphold the Lotus Sutra exactly as it teaches. Furthermore, since I have long understood the ways of the world, the prophecies I have made in this life have all come true. Therefore, you must never doubt what I have told you concerning future existences.

On the twelfth day of the ninth month of last year, when I was arrested, I called out in a loud voice, "I, Nichiren, am the pillar, sun, moon, mirror, and eyes of the ruling clan of Kanto. If the country abandons me, the seven disasters will occur without fail." Did not this prophecy come true just 60 days and then 150 days later?[6] And those battles were only the first signs. What lamenting there will be when the full effect appears!

Ignorant people wonder why Nichiren is persecuted by the rulers if he is truly a wise man. Yet it is all just as I expected. King Ajatashatru[7] tormented his father and mother, for which he was hailed by the six royal ministers. When Devadatta[8] killed an arhat[9] and caused the Buddha to bleed, Kokalika[10] and others were delighted. Nichiren is father and mother to the ruling house and is like a Buddha or an arhat to this age. The sovereign and his subjects who rejoice at my exile are truly the most shameless and pitiable of all. Those slanderous priests who have been bewailing the exposure of their errors may be overjoyed for the moment, but eventually they will suffer no less than myself and my followers. Their joy is like Yasuhira's when he killed his younger brother and Kuro Hogan.[11] The demon who will destroy the ruling clan has already entered the country. This is the meaning of the passage from the Lotus Sutra that reads, "Evil demons will take possession of others."[12]

The persecutions Nichiren has faced are the result of karma formed in previous lifetimes. The "Never Disparaging" chapter reads, "when his offenses had been wiped out,"[13] indicating that Bodhisattva Never Disparaging[14] was vilified and beaten by countless slanderers of the correct teaching because of his past karma. How much more true this is of Nichiren, who in this life was born poor and lowly to a chandala[15] family. In my heart I cherish some faith in the Lotus Sutra, but my body, while outwardly human, is fundamentally that of an animal. It was conceived of the two fluids, one white and one red, of a father and mother who subsisted on fish and fowl. My spirit dwells in this body as the moon is reflected in muddy water, or as gold is wrapped in a filthy bag. Since my heart believes in the Lotus Sutra, I do not fear even Brahma or Shakra,[16] but my body is still that of an animal. With such disparity between my body and my mind, no wonder the foolish despise me. Without doubt, when compared to my body, my mind shines like the moon or like gold. Who knows what slander I may have committed in the past? I may possess the soul of the monk Superior Intent[17] or the spirit of Mahadeva.[18] Perhaps I am descended from those who contemptuously persecuted Bodhisattva Never Disparaging, or am among those who forgot the seeds of enlightenment sown in their lives.[19] I may even be related to the five thousand arrogant people,[20] or belong to the third group [who failed to take faith in the Lotus Sutra] in the days of the Buddha Great

Universal Wisdom Excellence.[21] It is impossible to fathom one's karma.

Iron, when heated in the flames and pounded, becomes a fine sword. Worthies and sages are tested by abuse. My present exile is not because of any secular crime. It is solely so that I may expiate in this lifetime my past grave offenses and be freed in the next from the three evil paths.

The Parinirvana Sutra states: "Those who enter the monastic order, don clerical garments, and make a show of studying my teachings will exist in ages to come. Being lazy and remiss, they will slander the correct and equal sutras. You should be aware that all these people are followers of the non-Buddhist doctrines of today." Those who read this passage should reflect deeply on their own practice. The Buddha is saying that those of our contemporary priests who wear clerical garments, but are idle and negligent, were disciples of the six non-Buddhist teachers[22] in his day.

The followers of Honen,[23] who call themselves the Nembutsu school, not only turn people away from the Lotus Sutra, telling them to "discard, close, ignore, and abandon"[24] it, but also advocate chanting only the name of the

Buddha Amida,[25] a Buddha described in the provisional teachings. The followers of Dainichi,[26] known as the Zen school, claim that the Buddha's true teachings have been transmitted apart from the sutras. They ridicule the Lotus Sutra as nothing more than a finger pointing at the moon or a meaningless string of words. Those priests must both have been followers of the six non-Buddhist teachers, who only now have entered the stream of Buddhism.

According to the Nirvana Sutra, the Buddha emitted a radiant light that illuminated the 136 hells underground[27] and revealed that not a single offender remained there. This was because they had all achieved Buddhahood through the "Life Span" chapter of the Lotus Sutra. What a pity, however, that the icchantikas,[28] or persons of incorrigible disbelief, who had slandered the correct teaching, were found to have been detained there by the wardens of hell.[29] They proliferated until they became the people of Japan today.

Since Nichiren himself committed slander in the past, he became a Nembutsu priest in this lifetime, and for several years he also laughed at those who practiced the Lotus Sutra, saying that "not a single person has ever attained Buddhahood"[30] through that sutra, or that "not even one person in a thousand"[31] can be saved by it. Awakening from my intoxicated state of slander, I felt like a drunken son who, on becoming sober, laments at having delighted in striking his parents. He regrets it bitterly, but to no avail. His offense is extremely difficult to erase. Even more so are the past slanders of the correct teaching that stain the depths of one's heart. A sutra states that both the crow's blackness and the heron's whiteness are actually the deep stains of their past karma. The non-Buddhists failed to recognize this and claimed it was the work of nature. Today, when I expose people's slanders in an effort to save them, they deny it with every excuse possible and argue back with Honen's words about barring the gates to the Lotus Sutra. From Nembutsu believers this is hardly surprising, but even priests of the Tendai[32] and True Word[33] schools actively support them.

    On the sixteenth and seventeenth days of the first month of this year, hundreds of priests and lay believers from the Nembutsu and other schools here in the province of Sado came to debate

> with me. A leader of the Nembutsu school, Insho-bo, said: "The Honorable Honen did not instruct us to abandon the Lotus Sutra. He simply wrote that all people should chant the Nembutsu, and that its great blessings assure their rebirth in the Pure Land. Even the priests of Mount Hiei and Onjo-ji temple who have been exiled to this island praise him, saying how excellent his teaching is. How dare you try to refute it?" The local priests are even more ignorant than the Nembutsu priests in Kamakura. They are absolutely pitiful. (WND-1, 302–04)

LECTURE

For what purpose were we born? We were born to become happy and to help others do the same. Crucial to this goal is winning over our weaknesses. We practice Nichiren Buddhism so that we can triumph over ignorance, over our karma, over obstacles and devilish functions, and over the three powerful enemies.[34] Buddhism teaches that we each inherently possess the wisdom and power to win in all areas of our lives. It is a philosophy for victory. We must engage in "Buddhist study for winning" to make this hope-filled philosophy the source of successive victories in our lives.

I recall my mentor, second Soka Gakkai president Josei Toda, encouraging a young woman whose father had died when she was very young. Then she lost her mother, who had been her sole support. While struggling to make ends meet, she battled ill health. When she came to President Toda for guidance, he gazed at her kindly and said with strict compassion: "I wonder how seriously you're really grappling with your problems. Practicing Buddhism is all about grappling with problems. Struggling with problems and solving them is what faith is all about." These words get right at the heart of Nichiren Buddhism.

In a similar vein, he once said to me: "Dai, life means suffering. Only when you suffer can you understand faith and become a great individual" (A *Youthful Diary*, p.276). That was just before I plunged into the historic Osaka Campaign of 1956.[35]

As practitioners of Nichiren Buddhism, when we have problems, worries or sufferings, we see them as opportunities to challenge karma arising from the four universal sufferings—birth, aging, sickness and death. If we merely let ourselves be overwhelmed or just weep and lament over our situation, we cannot break through our karma, which exists precisely so that we can overcome it. From the standpoint of Buddhism, karma is an expedient means for us to prove the greatness of the Mystic Law.

The young woman who received encouragement from President Toda lifted herself out of her sorrow and self-pity. She realized that we only lose our way when we forget our commitment to our mission for kosen-rufu. Eventually going on to become a young women's division leader and then a women's division leader, she strove as a disciple with a deep sense of gratitude until the very last moment of her life. Her noble victory continues to inspire many to this day.

During his harsh exile on Sado Island, Nichiren taught his disciples the essence of faith for realizing absolute victory. At the outset of "Letter from Sado," therefore, with the wish that his disciples might triumph over all obstacles, he stresses the importance of practicing faith with a selfless spirit and the heart of a lion king. He communicates the boundless joy of dedicating oneself to the Law.

In the section we are studying this time, Nichiren describes the lionhearted actions he took to defeat evil rulers and erroneous priests. At the same time, he uses himself as an example to drive home to his disciples the key to faith for changing one's karma.

The main theme of this section is that we should follow in the unerring footsteps of the Daishonin and, by practicing with the same dignified and undaunted spirit as he, win an unsurpassed victory for Buddhism and for our own lives.

The Fulfillment of the Prophecies in "On Establishing the Correct Teaching"

Twenty-six years have passed since the battle of Hoji, and fighting has already broken out twice, on the eleventh and the seventeenth days of the second month of this year. Neither non-Buddhists nor the enemies of Buddhism can destroy the correct teaching of the Thus Come One, but the Buddha's disciples definitely can. As a sutra says, only worms born of the lion's body feed on the lion. A person of great fortune will never be ruined by enemies, but may be ruined by those who are close. The current battle is what the Medicine Master Sutra means by "the calamity of revolt within one's own domain." The Benevolent Kings Sutra states, "Once the sages have departed, then the seven disasters are certain to arise." The Golden Light Sutra states, "The thirty-three heavenly gods become furious because the king permits evil to run rampant and fails to subdue it." (WND-1, 302)

The battle of Hoji refers to a conflict in 1247 (the first year of the Hoji era) in which the regent Hojo Tokiyori destroyed the Miura clan, whose members commanded broad influence within the government. The defeat of its great rival enabled the Hojo clan to establish dictatorial rule. But in the twenty-sixth year after this event, an internal power struggle erupted within the Hojo clan. This was the February Disturbance of 1272[36] [which occurred the month before "Letter from Sado" was written]. Here, Nichiren Daishonin states that this latest outbreak of fighting represents the calamity of internal strife, or revolt within one's own domain, described in the Medicine Master Sutra, affirming that the predictions he made about this in his treatise "On Establishing the Correct Teaching for the Peace of the Land" had come to pass.

The fundamental cause of the three calamities and seven disasters, which include internal strife, rests with a country losing sight of the correct teaching. When erroneous priests appear and distort the teaching, Buddhism is destroyed from within. Nichiren declares that evil priests who slander the Law are an influence that destroys Buddhism, likening them to "worms born of the lion's body."

Confused values stemming from erroneous ideas and beliefs activate and strengthen the workings of the three or four evil paths[37] in people's lives. Consequently, ruled by anger, greed, foolishness and jealousy, people persecute and try to drive from society those of wisdom who spread the correct teaching. That is the reality of the Latter Day of the Law. When wise individuals are ousted through the collusion of evil rulers and errant priests, a brutish and animalistic spirit pervades society. As a result, internal strife occurs and the people suffer.

Unless we view things with the eye of the Buddha and the eye of the Law, we cannot truly apprehend the deep-seated reasons for persecutions directed against the correct teaching or the fundamental cause for upheavals and disturbances in society. Practicing Buddhism means fighting to achieve victory. Therefore, we have to stand up with the heart of a lion king and win.

A Sage Understands the True Nature of Social Phenomena

Although I, Nichiren, am not a sage, I am equal to one, for I uphold the Lotus Sutra exactly as it teaches. Furthermore, since I have long understood the ways of the world, the prophecies I have made in this life have all come true. Therefore, you must never doubt what I have told you concerning future existences. (WND-1, 302)

Whether someone is a sage cannot be judged by outward appearances or social standing. The key standard is a person's conduct and actions. One who practices the Lotus Sutra exactly as the Buddha teaches is a true sage.

It is indeed the case that "all phenomena are manifestations of the Buddhist Law" ("On the Eighteen Perfections," WND-2, 906). A sage who thoroughly grasps the teachings of Buddhism also possesses a deep understanding of the ways of society. Further, with the ability to keenly discern the true nature of social phenomena, a person will have a clear and accurate vision of the future.

Nichiren Daishonin's resounding declaration in "Letter from Sado" that his prophecies have been fulfilled must have been an immense source of encouragement for his followers valiantly pursuing their Buddhist practice amid harassment and persecution.

In another writing, Nichiren states, "It would seem that, when one who is able to show clearly visible proof in the present expounds the Lotus Sutra, there also will be persons who will believe" ("Letter to Horen," WND-1, 512). As these words indicate, kosen-rufu greatly advances when there is "clearly visible proof."

In this particular section of "Letter from Sado," Nichiren writes: "The prophecies I have made in this life have all come true. Therefore, you must never doubt what I have told you concerning future existences." The Daishonin was truly a sage who understood the three existences—past, present and future. The accuracy of his predictions must have greatly strengthened his followers' conviction in faith.

SGI members have also placed utmost importance on "clearly visible proof" in accord with Nichiren's teachings, and have shown countless examples of splendid actual proof of victory in society. That is why we have won such trust around the world.

Remonstrating for the Sake of People's Happiness

On the twelfth day of the ninth month of last year [1271], when I was arrested [on the occasion of the Tatsunokuchi Persecution], I called out in a loud voice, "I, Nichiren, am the pillar, sun, moon, mirror, and eyes of the ruling clan of Kanto. If the country abandons me, the seven disasters will occur without fail." Did not this prophecy come true just 60 days and then 150 days later? And those battles were only the first signs. What lamenting there will be when the full effect appears! (WND-1, 302–03)

The statement "I, Nichiren, am the pillar, sun, moon, mirror, and eyes of the ruling clan of Kanto" has profound significance. "Ruling clan" specifically indicates the Hojo clan, but it can also be taken to mean the leading military government figures and, in a still broader sense, the nation of Japan as a whole. "Pillar" signifies the virtue of sovereign; "sun, moon, mirror, and eyes" signifies the virtue of teacher; and "father and mother," mentioned in the subsequent section, signifies the virtue of parent. Nichiren Daishonin thus indicates that he is the Buddha of the Latter Day of the Law who possesses the three virtues—sovereign, teacher and parent[38]—of a Buddha.

Echoing the earlier cited passage from the Benevolent Kings Sutra, "Once the sages have departed, then the seven disasters are certain to arise," he expresses the conviction, "If the country abandons me, the seven disasters will occur without fail" (WND-1, 302). He then points out that the events that had transpired so far were only the first signs and urges people to awaken to the truth before the full effect—the true retribution—appeared. Internal strife, or civil war, had to be prevented at all costs. He therefore, with a selfless commitment, persists in his remonstrations, calling on the rulers and people of Japan to open their eyes for the sake of peace before it is too late.

Repaying the Boundless Debt Owed to the Mentor

Ignorant people wonder why Nichiren is persecuted by the rulers if he is truly a wise man. Yet it is all just as I expected. King Ajatashatru tormented his father and mother, for which he was hailed by the six royal ministers. When Devadatta killed an arhat and caused the Buddha to bleed, Kokalika and others were delighted. (WND-1, 303)

Next, Nichiren Daishonin refers to the common criticism people made that, if he were truly a wise person, why then had he been persecuted by the authorities and exiled? This criticism is founded on two assumptions: that a wise person would foresee the threat of persecution and avert it, and that a person of genuine wisdom would surely be respected by society. Nichiren, however, dismisses such views as the thinking of ignorant people.

"It is all just as I expected," he says, indicating that he had known from the outset he would be persecuted. Buddhas invariably encounter great obstacles and opposition. This is an unchanging principle of Buddhism.

When the votary of the Lotus Sutra is persecuted, the life condition of the votary's followers is plainly revealed. Do they show themselves to be wise or foolish? Are they disciples who—with gratitude for their teacher who has borne the brunt of persecution—are resolved to struggle alongside the teacher? Or do they side with those doing the persecution, aiding and abetting their evil?

Commenting on this reference to persecution by the authorities in "Letter from Sado," Mr. Toda said: "I have experienced persecution by the authorities once and, if I have the good fortune, I'd like to encounter such persecution again ... I am fully prepared for something like that. I couldn't be the leader of our movement if I wasn't."[39]

When I was arrested and jailed on trumped-up charges at the time of the Osaka Incident,[40] Mr. Toda, though extremely ill and frail, went to the Osaka District Prosecutor's office to lodge a protest with the chief public prosecutor. "Tell the prosecutor that if his aim is to crush the Soka Gakkai, he should arrest me!" he declared. And on another occasion, he demanded to know, "How long do you intend to keep my innocent disciple locked up?"

He was a truly wonderful mentor. It is the way of a disciple to repay the boundless debt owed to one's mentor. For sixty-two years, I have sincerely dedicated myself to correctly following the path of a disciple. I have not the slightest regret.

Working To Establish the Correct Teaching for the Peace of the Land

Nichiren is father and mother to the ruling house and is like a Buddha or an arhat to this age. The sovereign and his subjects who rejoice at my exile are truly the most shameless and pitiable of all. Those slanderous priests who have been bewailing the exposure of their errors may be overjoyed for the moment, but eventually they will suffer no less than myself and my followers. Their joy is like Yasuhira's when he killed his younger brother and Kuro Hogan. The demon who will destroy the ruling clan has already entered the country. This is the meaning of the passage from the Lotus Sutra that

reads, "Evil demons will take possession of others." (WND-1, 303)

"Nichiren is father and mother to the ruling house"—what a magnificent declaration! Nichiren Daishonin was not in the least afraid of the powerful. Rather, he boldly proclaims himself to be the father and mother of the Hojo clan that had tried to execute him and had now sentenced him to exile. This was the immense life condition of the Buddha of the Latter Day of the Law.

As to the fate of the sovereign and subjects who persecuted him and rejoiced over his misfortunes, Nichiren asserts that they are bound to experience great suffering. This principle is the same in any age.

The first three Soka Gakkai presidents struggled on through great persecution and won. I hope you will never forget this solemn and noble history.

Nichiren further declares, "The demon who will destroy the ruling clan has already entered the country." Rejoicing at a person of justice being tormented is a hallmark of a society in which people have been possessed by evil demons. This means the land is filled with powerful devilish functions that skew people's faculties of judgment.

Nothing is more fearful than misguided ideas and philosophies. By working to establish the correct teaching for the peace of the land, we can transform society for the better. This is the spirit of Nichiren Buddhism.

***

The Great Struggle To Transform the Karma of Humankind

The persecutions Nichiren has faced are the result of karma formed in previous lifetimes. The "Never Disparaging" chapter reads, "when his offenses had been wiped out" indicating that Bodhisattva Never Disparaging was vilified and beaten by countless slanderers of the correct teaching because of his past karma. How much more true this is of Nichiren, who in this life was born poor and lowly to a chandala family. In my heart I cherish some faith in the Lotus Sutra, but my body, while outwardly human, is fundamentally that of an animal. It was conceived of the two fluids, one white and one red, of a father and mother who subsisted on fish and fowl. My spirit dwells in this body as the moon is reflected in muddy water, or as gold is wrapped in a filthy bag. Since my heart believes in the Lotus Sutra, I do not fear even Brahma or Shakra, but my body is still that of an animal. With such disparity between my body and my mind, no wonder the foolish despise me. Without doubt, when compared to my body, my mind shines like the moon or like gold. Who knows what slander I may have committed in the past? I may possess the soul of the monk Superior Intent or the spirit of Mahadeva. Perhaps I am descended from those who contemptuously persecuted Bodhisattva Never Disparaging, or am among those who forgot the seeds of enlightenment sown in their lives. I may even be related to the five thousand arrogant people, or belong to the third group [who failed to take faith in the Lotus Sutra] in the days of the Buddha Great Universal Wisdom Excellence. It is impossible to fathom one's karma. (WND-1, 303)

"Letter from Sado" is about the shared struggle of mentor and disciple. It is not only a record of Nichiren Daishonin's spirited efforts as a lion king but also calls on his disciples to follow his example.

Earlier, he described how, as the votary of the Lotus Sutra, he forged ahead despite momentous obstacles, and how, because of his fearless remonstrations, the true base natures of the evil rulers and priests of erroneous teachings persecuting him was revealed. He goes on to describe his dauntless spiritual struggle toward attaining Buddhahood.

Attaining Buddhahood means transforming one's karma. By challenging persecution or other difficult obstacles, we can overcome our karma from previous existences. To persevere with the selfless dedication to Buddhist practice is itself the path to eternal happiness. Great hardships lead directly to changing our karma. That is why we must always remember to have a fighting spirit. Overcoming karma is in fact no simple matter. Hence, Nichiren teaches the importance of being steadfast in our Buddhist practice. Above all, he urges that we be resolved to battle our karma to the very end.

Through his statement "The persecutions Nichiren has faced are the result of karma formed in previous lifetimes," he explains that, regardless of the social dynamics that may have created an oppressive environment, his being subject to persecution was actually due to offenses committed in past existences. This accords with the teachings of the Lotus Sutra, he says, citing specifically the principle of karma being eradicated through hardships—as expressed in the passage "when his offenses had been wiped out," which refers to the struggles of Bodhisattva Never Disparaging.

Bodhisattva Never Disparaging bowed in reverence to the Buddha nature inherent in people's lives and faithfully practiced the principles expounded in the Lotus Sutra, a teaching of universal enlightenment. As a result, he was cursed and abused, as well as beaten with sticks and pelted with tiles and stones (see LSOC, 309); but such persecution was in fact retribution for his own past offenses. The Lotus Sutra goes on to explain that by persisting in his practice of revering people even amid persecution, he could expiate those offenses and ultimately attain Buddhahood.

In the same way, through battling the "three obstacles and four devils"[41] and the "three powerful enemies," we, too, can erase our karma accumulated from past existences and establish a state of absolute and eternal happiness. That is the benefit of attaining Buddhahood.

Next, writing, "Nichiren ... in this life was born poor and lowly to a chandala family," he touches on his own origins. Nichiren Buddhism is an ally of the people and a genuinely humane teaching. For practitioners of this teaching, starting out "poor and lowly" is a source of great pride. The Soka Gakkai is forever committed to standing on the side of the people. This is a commitment that will never change.

Returning to the text, the Daishonin emphasizes that his own body is "fundamentally that of an animal." Nevertheless, he infers that, owing to his unwavering faith in the Lotus Sutra, his mind shines with a luminous nobility and is filled with an inner dignity and confidence that make him unafraid of anything. And he further acknowledges that, given the huge disparity between the animal tendencies of his body and the loftiness of his mind, it is perhaps only natural that he should be scorned and reviled. Moreover, deeply pondering his own life, he suggests the likelihood that he possesses within him the same kind of ignorance exhibited by those in the past who persecuted Buddhist practitioners or who themselves abandoned the path of Buddhism. Nichiren makes several profound observations in this regard.

"It is impossible to fathom one's karma," he says, implying that he must have committed unimaginably grave offenses in past lifetimes. Nichiren was uncompromising with himself. He gazed unflinchingly at the true reality of his life. And, through his rigorous spiritual struggle, he opened the universal path by which all people, all humanity, can change their karma.

Nichiren provided the means for all human beings in the Latter Day of the Law to block off the road to the hell of incessant suffering. The countless dramas of our SGI members successfully transforming their lives offer brilliant actual proof of people freeing themselves of the chains of karma through faith in Nichiren Buddhism. Without doubt, future history will record that this great philosophy combined with the dedicated efforts of a remarkable community of ordinary people served as a powerful positive impetus for changing the karma, or destiny, of humankind.

Cultivating One's Life Is the Supreme Benefit

Iron, when heated in the flames and pounded, becomes a fine sword. Worthies and sages are tested by abuse. My present exile is not because of any secular crime. It is solely so that I may expiate in this

lifetime my past grave offenses and be freed in the next from the three evil paths. (WND-1, 303)

Here Nichiren Daishonin underscores the importance of practicing Buddhism to transform our karma.

Developing inner strength and fortitude is the supreme benefit of practicing Nichiren Buddhism. A thoroughly forged life ensures our eternal happiness. The Daishonin says that his present ordeal "is not because of any secular crime," even going so far as to assert that he was exiled solely so that he could change his karma in this lifetime.

We practice Buddhism to forge and transform our lives. Indeed, as the Russian author Mikhail Sholokhov states, each of us is "the blacksmith of our own happiness."[42] My disciples, become as strong as steel, as strong as finely tempered swords! Stand up as true worthies and sages!

Nichiren vigorously encourages his embattled followers as if shaking them by the shoulders: "You have to change your karma! The power to do so exists within you! Don't run away from hardships! True victory means winning over your own weaknesses! Great suffering produces great character! Become an enduring victor!"

A Land Pervaded With Slander

The Parinirvana Sutra states: "Those who enter the monastic order, don clerical garments, and make a show of studying my teachings will exist in ages to come. Being lazy and remiss, they will slander the correct and equal sutras. You should be aware that all these people are followers of the non-Buddhist doctrines of today." Those who read this passage should reflect deeply on their own practice. The Buddha is saying that those of our contemporary priests who wear clerical garments, but are idle and negligent, were disciples of the six non-Buddhist teachers in his day.

The followers of Honen, who call themselves the Nembutsu school, not only turn people away from the Lotus Sutra, telling them to "discard, close, ignore, and abandon" it, but also advocate chanting only the name of the Buddha Amida, a Buddha described in the provisional teachings. The followers of Dainichi, known as the Zen school, claim that the Buddha's true teachings have been transmitted apart from the sutras. They ridicule the Lotus Sutra as nothing more than a finger pointing at the moon or a meaningless string of words. Those priests must both have been followers of the six non-Buddhist teachers, who only now have entered the stream of Buddhism.

According to the Nirvana Sutra, the Buddha emitted a radiant light that illuminated the 136 hells underground and revealed that not a single offender remained there. This was because they had all achieved Buddhahood through the "Life Span" chapter of the Lotus Sutra. What a pity, however, that the icchantikas, or persons of incorrigible disbelief, who had slandered the correct teaching, were found to have been detained there by the wardens of hell. They proliferated until they became the people of Japan today. (WND-1, 303–04)

Here, Nichiren Daishonin shifts his focus to the karmic retribution that will await those persecuting him and his followers—in other words, the priests who expound erroneous teachings and the people throughout the land whose minds have been poisoned by those teachings. To borrow the words of "The Life Span of the Thus Come One," the 16th chapter of the Lotus Sutra, "The poison has penetrated deeply and their minds no longer function as before" (LSOC, 269).

According to the Parinirvana Sutra, corrupt priests who are lazy and remiss, and who slander the correct teaching of the Lotus Sutra are the spiritual descendants of those who upheld non-Buddhist doctrines and criticized Shakyamuni's teachings during his lifetime. Nichiren then goes on to refute the positions of various Buddhist priests of his own time who denigrate the Lotus Sutra. What they all have in common is the self-righteous attitude to groundlessly malign this supreme teaching, turning people away from it in favor of their own doctrines. The Daishonin asserts that these priests must be "followers of the six non-Buddhist teachers" of Shakyamuni's day.

Discussing this passage from the Parinirvana Sutra, Mr. Toda declared: "The evil priests who harassed Nichiren will now likely appear in the various Buddhist schools of the present age and also within Nichiren Shoshu." In view of the disturbing actions of Nikken Abe[43] and his cohorts in recent years, showing themselves to be enemies of kosen-rufu, Mr. Toda's words indeed proved to be prescient.

Nichiren then points out that the people throughout Japan who have vilified and criticized him are no different from the *icchantikas,* or people of incorrigible disbelief, who could not attain enlightenment even after having heard Shakyamuni preach the "Life Span" chapter of the Lotus Sutra. In this section, the Daishonin clarifies the true nature of the enemies of the Lotus Sutra whom he has battled. "Six non-Buddhist teachers" and icchantikas epitomize the negative tendency to disbelieve and slander the correct teaching.

What lies at the root of this tendency? It is the deluded state of mind unable to comprehend the Lotus Sutra's spirit of respect and reverence for all. In modern terms, it means disregard for the sanctity of life, for human equality and the infinite potential of each person.

Nichiren keenly observed that the erroneous priests of his day and their followers, despite lacking true insight into their own lives, rejected the correct teaching that would have enabled them to develop such insight and denigrated anyone who practiced it. His observation could equally well describe the tendency of many in Japan today who disdain religion and belittle philosophy.

The eminent Buddhist scholar Hajime Nakamura has noted: "It is very difficult to say whether or not the Japanese were devoted to Buddhism from the bottom of their hearts and recognized its intrinsic value. Often they simply followed it, even travestying the teaching or character of Buddha, as in such common sayings: 'Not knowing is the state of Buddhahood' (Ignorance is bliss), or 'Even the face of a Buddha changes (shows anger) after the third time' (There are limits to one's endurance). A Buddha is represented as something extremely close and familiar to [human beings] ... Buddhist terminology is quite commonly parodied in vernacular expressions of everyday language."[44]

Many Japanese show little interest in earnestly seeking out the principles of Buddhism, which teaches the ultimate essence of life. Rather, they have disdain for it, and they ridicule it. Amid this spiritual climate in Japan, which reflects a pervasive lack of firm convictions, we of the Soka Gakkai have continued our tenacious efforts to reach out to others in dialogue, working tirelessly to elevate people's state of life.

Buddhism Exists for People's Happiness

Since Nichiren himself committed slander in the past, he became a Nembutsu priest in this lifetime, and for several years he also laughed at those who practiced the Lotus Sutra, saying that "not a single person has ever attained Buddhahood" through that sutra, or that "not even one person in a thousand" can be saved by it. Awakening from my intoxicated state of slander, I felt like a drunken son who, on becoming sober, laments at having delighted in striking his parents. He regrets it bitterly, but to no avail. His offense is extremely difficult to erase. Even more so are the past slanders of the correct teaching that stain the depths of one's heart. A sutra states that both the crow's blackness and the heron's whiteness are actually the deep stains of their past karma. The non-Buddhists failed to recognize this and claimed it was the work of nature. Today, when I expose people's slanders in an effort to save them they deny it with every excuse possible and argue back with Honen's words about

barring the gates to the Lotus Sutra. From Nembutsu believers this is hardly surprising, but even priests of the Tendai and True Word schools actively support them.

On the sixteenth and seventeenth days of the first month of this year, hundreds of priests and lay believers from the Nembutsu and other schools here in the province of Sado came to debate with me. A leader of the Nembutsu school, Insho-bo, said: "The Honorable Honen did not instruct us to abandon the Lotus Sutra. He simply wrote that all people should chant the Nembutsu, and that its great blessings assure their rebirth in the Pure Land. Even the priests of Mount Hiei and Onjo-ji temple who have been exiled to this island praise him, saying how excellent his teaching is. How dare you try to refute it?" The local priests are even more ignorant than the Nembutsu priests in Kamakura. They are absolutely pitiful. (WND-1, 304)

Nichiren Daishonin notes that the people of his day were confused, failing to realize the shallowness of the all-too-pervasive Nembutsu teaching, which allowed forces hostile to the Lotus Sutra and its practitioners to fill the land. But an even greater problem than this stemmed from those who claimed to practice the Lotus Sutra yet did nothing to oppose its enemies. Fine temples, solemn traditions and formalities, and high social standing in society are all rendered meaningless once the spirit to vigorously defend the correct teaching is lost. In that event, authoritarianism sets in and corruption and decline ensue, leaving only a hollow shell of the original intention of the teachings.

Buddhism exists for the sake of people's happiness. Erroneous teachings and interpretations, however, can plunge people into suffering and misery. To turn a blind eye to such misleading ideas and forget the desire to guide all people to enlightenment is to become an enemy of the people. This cannot be condoned. Nichiren's practice of *shakubuku*—of refuting error and revealing the truth—is a struggle to restore the authentic spirit of Buddhism, reviving the true compassionate spirit of Shakyamuni Buddha and elevating the life condition of all people.

As the German poet Heinrich Heine wrote: "The greater the person, the better the target for arrows of ridicule he will make. It is difficult to send arrows at those of puny stature."[45]

Through the example of his own life, undaunted by all persecution and criticism, the Daishonin taught the ultimate way for changing our karma and attaining Buddhahood. He aspires for his disciples to stand up and realize victory based on faith "like Nichiren" (WND-1, 302) and with the "same mind as Nichiren" ("The True Aspect of All Phenomena," WND-1, 385). We of the SGI are carrying on this brilliant tradition of mentor and disciple.

Now, in the twenty-first century, the Soka Gakkai shines brightly as the pillar of Japan, the eyes of the world and the great ship of humankind.[46]

As long as the mentor-disciple spirit of Nichiren Buddhism that has been solidified in the present age through the selfless struggles of the first three presidents—Mr. Makiguchi, Mr. Toda and me—is maintained, the Soka Gakkai will flourish. I would especially like the members of the youth division, the successors of our movement, to deeply engrave in their hearts this formula for victory in our movement for kosen-rufu.

This lecture was originally published in the February 2009 issue of the Daibyakurenge, *the Soka Gakkai's monthly study journal.*

NOTES

[1] It was actually twenty-five years since the battle of Hoji occurred, but when counted in the customary Japanese way it corresponds to the twenty-sixth year.

[2] The fighting actually took place on the eleventh and fifteenth of February 1272. For further details, see footnote 36.

[3] Worms born of the lion's body: A metaphor for those who, despite being followers of Buddhism, destroy its teachings, just as worms born from the carcass of the lion devour the lion. The intention of this metaphor is to underscore that it is members of the Buddhist Order, rather than non-Buddhists, who are capable of destroying Buddhism.

[4] Three calamities and seven disasters: The three calamities are warfare, pestilence and famine. The seven disasters are said to be caused by slander of the correct teaching. The Medicine Master Sutra defines the seven disasters as: (1) pestilence; (2) foreign invasion; (3) internal strife; (4) extraordinary changes in the heavens; (5) solar and lunar eclipses; (6) unseasonable storms; and (7) drought.

[5] Thirty-three heavenly gods: Also, thirty-three gods. The gods said to live on a plateau at the top of Mount Sumeru. Shakra rules from his palace in the center, and the other thirty-two gods live on four peaks, eight gods to a peak, at each of the plateau's four corners.

[6] It is unclear exactly what incident the Daishonin is referring to as having taken place sixty days after the Tatsunokuchi

Persecution on September 12, 1271. It may have been some specific incident of rebellion. Some believe it may refer to the arrival of another Mongol emissary in November 1271. The event that happened one hundred fifty days later is the February Disturbance of 1272.

[7] King Ajatashatru: A king of Magadha in India in the time of Shakyamuni. Incited by Devadatta, he gained the throne by killing his father, King Bimbisara, a follower of Shakyamuni. He also made attempts on the lives of the Buddha and his disciples by releasing a drunken elephant upon them, again at Devadatta's urging.

[8] Devadatta: A cousin of Shakyamuni who first followed him but later out of arrogance became his enemy and committed various actions of extreme evil, such as attempting to kill the Buddha. As a result of his offenses, he is said to have fallen into hell alive.

[9] Arhat: One who has attained the highest stage of Hinayana enlightenment. Arhat means "one worthy of respect."

[10] Kokalika: A member of the Shakya tribe of ancient India and an enemy of Shakyamuni Buddha. He became a disciple of Shakyamuni but, falling under

Devadatta's influence, slandered the Buddha's disciples Shariputra and Maudgalyayana.

[11] Yasuhira refers to Fujiwara Yasuhira (1155–89), the son of Fujiwara Hidehira, lord of the province of Mutsu in northeastern Japan. Yasuhira killed his brother and seized power for himself. Minamoto no Yoritomo, the Kamakura shogun, ordered him to kill Kuro Hogan Yoshitsune, Yoritomo's brother, which he did to prove his loyalty. Later, however, Yoritomo had him executed to consolidate his own power in the northern part of Japan.

[12] This line appears in "Encouraging Devotion," the 13th chapter of the Lotus Sutra.

[13] "When his offenses had been wiped out": This line from "Bodhisattva Never Disparaging," the 20th chapter of the Lotus Sutra, means that Bodhisattva Never Disparaging expiated his past offense of slandering the Law by being subjected to persecutions on account of the Law and that he thereby attained Buddhahood.

[14] Bodhisattva Never Disparaging: A bodhisattva described in "Bodhisattva

Never Disparaging," the 20th chapter of the Lotus Sutra. Never Disparaging, Shakyamuni in a previous existence, lived at the end of the Middle Day of the Law after the death of Buddha Awesome Sound King. He venerated all people, saying repeatedly: "I have profound reverence for you, I would never dare treat you with disparagement or arrogance. Why? Because you will all practice the bodhisattva way and will then be able to attain Buddhahood" (LSOC, 308). Though attacked by arrogant people, he persevered in his practice and, as a result, attained Buddhahood.

[15] *Chandala:* A class of untouchables, below the lowest of the four castes in the ancient Indian caste system. People in this class, who carried out tasks associated with death and the killing of living things, were subject to extreme discrimination. The Daishonin declared himself to be a member of the chandala class because he was born the son of a fisherman. He taught that even someone from the lowest rung of society could attain supreme enlightenment.

[16] Brahma and Shakra are the two principal tutelary—or protector—gods of Buddhism.

[17] Superior Intent: A monk who lived in the latter age after the passing of the Buddha Lion Sound King. According to the Non-substantiality of All Phenomena Sutra, he slandered the monk Root of Joy who taught the correct doctrine and therefore fell into hell.

[18] Mahadeva: A monk who lived about one hundred years after Shakyamuni and provoked the first division within the Buddhist Order. Before joining the Order, he killed his father, his mother and an arhat. Later, he advanced his own arbitrary views regarding Buddhism, and controversy over them precipitated a schism in the Order.

[19] "Those who forgot the seeds of enlightenment" are individuals who, because of the slanders they have committed, do not remember that they received the seeds of Buddhahood from Shakyamuni Buddha numberless major world system dust particle kalpas ago.

[20] According to "Expedient Means," the 16th chapter of the Lotus Sutra, five thousand people—monks, nuns, laymen

and laywomen—left the assembly as Shakyamuni began to preach about "the replacement of the three vehicles with the one vehicle," because they supposed they had attained what they had not attained.

[21] The "Parable of the Phantom City," the seventh chapter of the Lotus Sutra, explains the story of the Buddha Great Universal Wisdom Excellence and his sixteen sons. Major world system dust particle kalpas ago, this Buddha preached the Lotus Sutra to his sons, who then in turn preached the sutra to the people. Among the people, the third group comprises those who heard the Lotus Sutra at that time but did not take faith in it and could not attain enlightenment, even when the sixteenth son appeared in India as Shakyamuni Buddha and preached it to them again.

[22] Six non-Buddhist teachers: A term of general reference to thinkers who had risen to prominence in Shakyamuni's day.

[23] Honen (1133–1212): Founder of the Pure Land (Nembutsu) school of Buddhism in Japan. He advocated the exclusive practice of Nembutsu—the chanting of Amida Buddha's name. In his

work *The Nembutsu Chosen above All*, Honen urges that people discard all sutras, including the Lotus Sutra, other than the three basic sutras of the Pure Land teaching.

[24] Honen does not use these words in this particular form. Nichiren Daishonin took these words from *The Nembutsu Chosen above All* and placed them together.

[25] Amida is a Buddha described in the Pure Land sutras as dwelling in the Pure Land of Perfect Bliss in the west. He is revered by the followers of the Pure Land school.

[26] Dainichi (n.d.): A Japanese priest who was among the first to spread the Zen teachings in Japan during the twelfth century.

[27] The Great Teacher T'ien-t'ai delineates 136 kinds of hell—eight hot hells, each with sixteen subsidiary hells. The last and worst of the eight hot hells is the hell of incessant suffering.

[28] Icchantikas: Persons of incorrigible disbelief who have no aspiration for enlightenment and thus no prospect of attaining Buddhahood.

[29] Wardens of hell: Demons in Buddhist mythology who torment transgressors who have fallen into hell.

[30] Tao-ch'o (562–645), *Collected Essays on the World of Peace and Delight.*

[31] Shan-tao (613–81), *Praising Rebirth in the Pure Land.*

[32] Tendai school: The Japanese counterpart of the Chinese T'ien-t'ai school of Buddhism, founded in the early ninth century by the Japanese priest Dengyo (767–822). Because of a tolerant attitude toward the erroneous teachings of other schools, including True Word, Pure Land and Zen, by Nichiren's time it had lost the stance of strictly basing itself on the Lotus Sutra.

[33] True Word school: A Japanese Buddhist school established by Kobo (774–835), also known as Kukai, that follows the esoteric doctrines and practices found in the Mahavairochana and Diamond Crown sutras.

[34] Three powerful enemies: Three types of arrogant people who persecute those who propagate the Lotus Sutra in the evil age after Shakyamuni Buddha's death: arrogant lay people, arrogant priests and arrogant false sages.

[35] Osaka Campaign: In May 1956, the Soka Gakkai members in the Kansai region of Japan—rallying around a young Daisaku Ikeda who had been dispatched by second president Josei Toda to support them—introduced 11,111 households to the practice of Nichiren Buddhism. In elections held two months later, the Soka Gakkai-backed candidate in Kansai won a seat in the Upper House, an accomplishment that was thought all but impossible at the time.

[36] February Disturbance of 1272: A revolt that took place within the ruling Hojo clan. It resulted in fighting in Kyoto and Kamakura. In February 1272, Hojo Tokisuke, an influential commissioner in Kyoto hatched rebellions to overthrow his younger half brother, the regent Hojo Tokimune, in an attempt to seize power. Tokisuke's co-conspirators in Kamakura were killed by government forces on February 11, while Tokisuke himself was attacked and killed in Kyoto on the February 15. The reference to February 17 in "Letter from Sado" either was based on inaccurate information or else was a mistake entered when the original document was copied.

[37] The three evils paths are the worlds of hell, hunger and animality, the lowest of the ten states of life known as the Ten Worlds. "Four evil paths" refers to the three evil paths plus the world of anger. Considered the lowest four of the Ten Worlds, they are called evil because they are characterized by suffering.

[38] Three virtues: The virtue of sovereign is the power to protect all living beings, the virtue of teacher is the wisdom to instruct and lead them to enlightenment, and the virtue of parent is the compassion to nurture and support them.

[39] Translated from Japanese. Josei Toda, *Toda Josei zenshu* (Collected Writings of Josei Toda) (Tokyo: Seikyo Shimbunsha, 1986), vol.6, p.555.

[40] Osaka Incident: An occasion in 1957 when Daisaku Ikeda, then Soka Gakkai youth division chief of staff, was arrested and wrongfully charged with election law violations in an Upper House by-election in Osaka. At the end of the court case, which dragged on for almost five years, he was exonerated of all charges.

[41] Three obstacles and four devils: Various obstacles and hindrances to the practice

of Buddhism. The three obstacles are: (1) the obstacle of earthly desires; (2) the obstacle of karma; and (3) the obstacle of retribution. The four devils are: (1) the hindrance of the five components; (2) the hindrance of earthly desires; (3) the hindrance of death; and (4) the hindrance of the devil king.

[42] From the December 16, 2008, *Seikyo Shimbun*, the Soka Gakkai's daily newspaper, p.3.

[43] Nikken Abe: The sixty-seventh chief priest of Taiseki-ji, the head temple of Nichiren Shoshu, who distorted the teachings of Nichiren Daishonin. Among other offenses, he plotted to destroy the Soka Gakkai, eventually excommunicating the members of the SGI. In an attempt to justify this arbitrary action toward the SGI, the priesthood propounded the erroneous doctrine of absolute faith in and strict obedience to the high priest. See www.sokaspirit.org for more information.

[44] Hajime Nakamura, *Ways of Thinking of Eastern Peoples: India, China, Tibet, Japan*, edited by Philip P. Wiener (Honolulu: East-West Center Press, 1969), p.528.

[45] Translated from German. Heinrich Heine, "Die romantische schule" (The Romantic School), in *Sämtliche werke* (Collected Works), edited by Hans Kaufmann (Munich: Kindler Verlag, 1964), vol.9, p.149.

[46] In "The Opening of the Eyes," the Daishonin declares: "I will be the pillar of Japan. I will be the eyes of Japan. I will be the great ship of Japan. This is my vow, and I will never forsake it!" (WND-1, 280–81).

CHAPTER 3

"LETTER FROM SADO"—PART 3 OF 3

DEDICATING OUR LIVES TO THE GREAT PATH OF MENTOR AND DISCIPLE

Passage for Study in This Lecture

How terrible are the slanders Nichiren has committed in his past and present existences! Since you have been born into this evil country and become the disciples of such a man, there is no telling what will happen to you. The Parinirvana Sutra[1] states: "Good man, because people committed countless offenses and accumulated much evil karma in the past, they must expect to suffer retribution for everything they have done. They may be despised, cursed with an ugly appearance, be poorly clad and poorly fed, seek wealth in vain, be born to an impoverished and lowly family or one with erroneous views, or be persecuted by their sovereign." It continues: "They may be subjected to various other sufferings and retributions. It is due to the blessings obtained by protecting the Law that they can diminish in this lifetime their suffering and retribution." Were it not for Nichiren, these passages from the sutra would virtually make the Buddha a liar. The sutra says, first, "They may be despised"; second, "They may be cursed with an ugly appearance"; third, "They may be poorly clad"; fourth, "They may be poorly fed"; fifth, "They may seek wealth in vain"; sixth, "They may be born to an impoverished and lowly family"; seventh, "They may be born to a family with erroneous views"; and eighth, "They may be persecuted by their sovereign."[2] These eight phrases apply only to me, Nichiren.

One who climbs a high mountain must eventually descend. One who slights another will in turn be despised. One who deprecates those of handsome appearance will be born ugly. One who robs another of food and clothing is sure to fall into the world of hungry spirits. One who mocks a person who observes the precepts and is worthy of respect will be born to an impoverished and lowly family. One who slanders a family that embraces the correct teaching will be born to a family that holds erroneous views. One who laughs at those who cherish the precepts faithfully will be born a commoner and meet with persecution from one's sovereign. This is the general law of cause and effect.

My sufferings, however, are not ascribable to this causal law. In the past I despised the votaries of the Lotus Sutra. I also ridiculed the sutra itself, sometimes with exaggerated praise and other times with contempt—that sutra as magnificent as two moons shining side by side, two stars conjoined, one Mount Hua[3] placed atop another, or two jewels combined. This is why I have experienced the aforementioned eight kinds of sufferings. Usually these sufferings appear one at a time, on into the boundless future, but Nichiren has denounced the enemies of the Lotus Sutra so severely that all eight have descended at once.

This is like the case of a peasant heavily in debt to the steward of his village and to other authorities. As long as he remains in his village or district, rather than mercilessly hounding him, they are likely to defer his debts from one year to the next. But when he tries to leave, they rush over and demand that he repay everything at once. This is what the sutra[4] means when it states, "It is due to the blessings obtained by protecting the Law."

The Lotus Sutra says: "There will be many ignorant people who will curse and speak ill of us and will attack us with swords and staves, with rocks and tiles ... they will address the rulers, high ministers, Brahmans, and householders, [as well as the other monks, slandering and speaking evil of us] ... again and again we will be banished."[5] If the offenders are not tormented by the wardens of hell,[6] they will never be able to [pay for their offenses and] escape from hell. Were it not for the rulers and ministers who now persecute me, I would be unable to expiate my past sins of slandering the correct teaching.

Nichiren is like Bodhisattva Never Disparaging of old, and the people of this day are like the four categories of Buddhists[7] who disparaged and cursed him. Though the people are different, the cause is the same. Though different people kill their parents, they all fall into the same hell of incessant suffering. Since Nichiren is making the same cause as Never Disparaging, how could it be that he would not become a Buddha equal to Shakyamuni? Moreover, those who now slander him are like Bhadrapala[8] and the others [who cursed Never Disparaging]. They will be tortured in the Avichi hell[9] for a thousand kalpas. I therefore pity them deeply and wonder what can be done for them. Those who belittled and cursed Never Disparaging acted that way at first, but later they took faith in his teachings and willingly became his followers. The greater part of the fault of their slander was thus expiated, but even the small part that remained caused them to suffer as terribly as one who had killed one's parents a thousand times. The people of this age refuse to repent at all; therefore, as the "Simile and Parable" chapter states, they must suffer in hell for a countless number of kalpas; they may even suffer there for a duration of major world system dust particle kalpas or of numberless major world system dust particle kalpas.[10]

Aside from these people, there are also those who appeared to believe in me, but began doubting when they saw me persecuted. They not only have forsaken the Lotus Sutra, but also actually think themselves wise enough to instruct me. The pitiful thing is that these perverse people must suffer in the Avichi hell even longer than the Nembutsu believers.

An asura[11] contended that the Buddha taught only eighteen elements,[12] but that he himself expounded nineteen. The non-Buddhist teachers claimed that the Buddha offered only one way to enlightenment, but that they had ninety-five.[13] In the same way, the renegade disciples say, "Though the priest Nichiren is our teacher, he is too forceful. We will spread the Lotus Sutra in a more peaceful way." In so asserting, they are being as ridiculous as fireflies laughing at the sun and moon, an anthill belittling Mount Hua, wells and brooks despising the river and the ocean, or a magpie mocking a phoenix. Nammyoho-renge-kyo.

Nichiren

The twentieth day of the third month in the ninth year of Bun'ei (1272), cyclical sign *mizunoe-saru*

To Nichiren's disciples and lay supporters

There is very little writing paper here in the province of Sado, and to write to you individually would take too long. Nevertheless, if even one person fails to hear from me, it will cause resentment. Therefore, I want people with seeking minds to meet and read this letter together for encouragement. When great trouble occurs in the world, minor troubles become insignificant. I do not know how accurate the reports reaching me are, but there must surely be intense grieving over those killed in the recent battles. What has become of the lay priests Izawa and Sakabe? Send me news of Kawanobe, Yamashiro, Tokugyoji,[14] and the others. Also, please be kind enough to send me *The Essentials of Government in the Chen-kuan Era*,[15] the collection of tales from the non-Buddhist classics, and the record of the teachings transmitted within the eight schools.[16] Without these, I cannot even write letters. (WND-1, 304–06)

LECTURE

Whenever I read "Letter from Sado," I vividly recall an episode from my youth. It was during the period when the business operations of my mentor, Josei Toda, were in dire financial straits. He had just stepped down as Soka Gakkai general director in order to protect the organization and was struggling to break through these difficulties.

I remember him one day reading a portion of "Letter from Sado." It was the part where Nichiren Daishonin explains that the various hardships he is undergoing—such as being cursed and spoken ill of, and lacking food and clothing—are exactly as described in the sutras. Mr. Toda remarked: "To think that the Daishonin endured such circumstances. And now, I am experiencing the same. In my case, no matter how much money I make, I can't seem to turn a profit!" As he uttered these words, he was smiling. Even with enormous troubles, he could smile like that! The image of his serene composure amid adversity is forever engraved in my mind.

I remember another occasion when Mr. Toda returned from a visit he had made to the Finance Ministry concerning his business woes. Sleet fell on that frigid day, and he was shivering. "The world is really a cold place," he laughed, adding: "Daisaku, I haven't been defeated. My businesses have failed, that's all. The true struggle lies ahead." Though it appeared he'd been wiped out financially, he had not been defeated in the slightest in terms of life and faith. After all, he had a genuine disciple, and the real test was still to come. His dauntless spirit fueled my resolve and fighting spirit. I vowed I wouldn't allow anyone to defame or harm my mentor.

Nichiren's writings can rouse an indomitable fighting spirit in the hearts of those buffeted by the bitter winds of suffering and adversity. When his invincible spirit pulses in our lives, nothing can intimidate us.

As long as we make a point of reading his writings and internalizing their lessons, no karma can defeat us. And as long as we dedicate ourselves to the way of mentor and disciple, no obstacles or devilish functions can hinder us. Please be confident that by living based on Nichiren's writings and in accord with the path of a disciple, you can break through any obstacle or limitation.

In this installment, I will focus on Nichiren's towering life state as a person of incomparable courage—a lion king—who made it possible for all people to transform their karma.

A Teaching of Empowerment

How terrible are the slanders Nichiren has committed in his past and present existences! Since you have been born into this evil country and become the disciples of such a man, there is no telling what will happen to you. (WND-1, 304)

For me, there has been no greater pride than meeting my mentor in life and devoting myself to kosen-rufu as his disciple.

Nichiren Buddhism is a teaching of empowerment that shows people how to become lion kings.

In "Letter from Sado," Nichiren Daishonin outlines the importance of walking the great path of mentor and disciple throughout one's life. His message is that, just as he has forged ahead in every struggle with the heart of a lion king, his disciples should do likewise, for through such efforts, they will definitely attain Buddhahood. His concern for the well-being of his disciples pervades this writing from beginning to end. He seeks to convey to them that it is precisely in the midst of tremendous hardships that they can fundamentally transform their karma and secure the way to enlightenment. And he calls on them to follow his example of personally engaging in that crucial struggle.

As I noted in the last installment, in order to explain the principle of changing karma, the Daishonin first refers to the practice of Bodhisattva Never Disparaging.[17] He then speaks about his own travails, saying that the life-threatening persecution of being exiled to Sado was due to "karma formed in previous lifetimes."[18] And, while acknowledging that it is "impossible to fathom one's karma" (WND-1, 303), he squarely considers what negative causes he has most likely made in past lifetimes.

In the section we are discussing this time, Nichiren even says that he has doubtless committed slander of the Law not only in past existences but also while studying Buddhism in his present life. But his exclamation "How terrible are the slanders..." can also be taken to indicate the reality of the established Buddhist schools in Japan in his day, which denigrated and devalued the correct teaching of Buddhism. What was truly frightening, in other words, was that slander of the Law had become so pervasive throughout the entire land that even someone who sincerely sought to study Buddhism would unwittingly end up committing grave error.

Nichiren further states, "Since you have ... become the disciples of such a man, there is no telling what will happen to you" (WND-1, 304). Here he confirms the deep bonds that unite him and his disciples. His real intent, I feel, is to communicate the joy of working together for kosen-rufu. He consistently emphasized how noble and honorable it is to battle hardships and undergo persecution as his disciples.

The Eight Kinds of Retribution

The Parinirvana Sutra states: "Good man, because people committed countless offenses and accumulated much evil karma in the past, they must expect to suffer retribution for everything they have done. They may be despised, cursed with an ugly appearance, be poorly clad and poorly fed, seek wealth in vain, be born to an impoverished and lowly family or one with erroneous views, or be persecuted by their sovereign." It continues: "They may be subjected to various other sufferings and retributions. It is due to the blessings obtained by protecting the Law that they

can diminish in this lifetime their suffering and retribution." Were it not for Nichiren, these passages from the sutra would virtually make the Buddha a liar. The sutra says, first, "They may be despised"; second, "They may be cursed with an ugly appearance"; third, "They may be poorly clad"; fourth, "They may be poorly fed"; fifth, "They may seek wealth in vain"; sixth, "They may be born to an impoverished and lowly family"; seventh, "They may be born to a family with erroneous views"; and eighth, "They may be persecuted by their sovereign." These eight phrases apply only to me, Nichiren. (WND-1, 304–05)

In the previous installment, I discussed a passage Nichiren Daishonin quoted from the Parinirvana Sutra. That particular passage stated that priests who slander the correct teaching in the evil age after the Buddha's passing were disciples of the non-Buddhist teachers in Shakyamuni's lifetime (see WND-1, 303).

The Parinirvana Sutra passage cited in this present section immediately follows the former. It describes the benefit of upholding the correct teaching in an age of crisis when such erroneous priests are rampant, and the correct teaching is in danger of being lost. This is a reference to the principle of "lessening one's karmic retribution."[19] Nichiren points to eight examples of retribution said to result from past offenses or evil karma, clarifying that such painful suffering and negative effects can be diminished in this lifetime due to "the blessings obtained by protecting the Law." He asserts that he personally embodied all eight of these forms of retribution, thus corroborating the truth of the Buddha's words. In terms of Nichiren's life, we can interpret these eight forms as follows:

1. "They may be despised": Nichiren was slandered and maligned throughout the land because he propagated the correct teaching.
2. "They may be cursed with an ugly appearance": This could be taken as a reference to the vile reputation he had acquired as an exile.
3. "They may be poorly clad": He lacked adequate clothing to withstand the bitter cold on Sado Island.
4. "They may be poorly fed": His food supplies on Sado were so meager that he was even prepared for starvation.
5. "They may seek wealth in vain": He lived in great privation without proper shelter or other basic necessities.
6. "They may be born to an impoverished and lowly family": He described himself as being "born poor and lowly" (WND-1, 303).
7. "They may be born to a family with erroneous views": He was not born into a family that upheld the correct teaching.

8. "They may be persecuted by their sovereign": He suffered persecution at the hands of the ruling authorities, which included being exiled to Izu and to Sado.

He concludes by writing: "These eight phrases apply only to me, Nichiren." In his treatise "The Opening of the Eyes," he also enumerates these eight kinds of retribution described in the Parinirvana Sutra, commenting after each one, "That applies to me" (see WND-1, 281).

Although he found himself in such dire circumstances, the Daishonin was not one to lament his situation. He faced persecution with a smile. He was like a towering rock impervious to the crashing waves. If anything, this section from "Letter from Sado" conveys Nichiren's joy in embodying these sutra passages and his dauntless life state.

Buddhism Seeks To Free People From the Sufferings of Karma

One who climbs a high mountain must eventually descend. One who slights another will in turn be despised. One who deprecates those of handsome appearance will be born ugly. One who robs another of food and clothing is sure to fall into the world of hungry spirits. One who mocks a person who observes the precepts and is worthy of respect will be born to an

impoverished and lowly family. One who slanders a family that embraces the correct teaching will be born to a family that holds erroneous views. One who laughs at those who cherish the precepts faithfully will be born a commoner and meet with persecution from one's sovereign. This is the general law of cause and effect. (WND-1, 305)

"One who climbs a high mountain must eventually descend"—using reasoning that anyone can understand, Nichiren Daishonin outlines the conventional Buddhist principle of karmic retribution.

The word *karma* derives from the pre-Buddhist Indian word *karman,* meaning "action." In ancient India, liberation from the suffering of negative karma was thought to require special rites performed by priests on behalf of individuals who would then have to wait for the gods to grant salvation.

By contrast, Buddhism radically changed the concept of karma. It rejected the view that one's destiny is influenced by gods or transcendent beings. As an internally directed teaching—a philosophy that teaches that enlightenment comes from within—Buddhism holds that we create our own destiny. Our present self is the result of our past choices and actions. Our future self will be determined by what we do in the present—whether we accumulate "good karma" or "evil karma."

This was a point I discussed with British historian Arnold J. Toynbee in our dialogue. Dr. Toynbee asserted that we have the freedom to improve our destiny at any moment, right here and now. As he noted, Buddhism is a philosophy that places the utmost importance on our own actions and thinking.

The conventional Buddhist view of karmic retribution explains that present negative effects result from past negative causes, and present positive effects result from past positive causes. But this view does not in fact yield a principle for changing karma.

In "Letter from Sado," the Daishonin states that this view of karmic retribution is based on "the general law of cause and effect" (WND-1, 305)—implying that his teaching is not rooted in this general causality.

The Causality of the Mystic Law Is the Basis for Transforming Our Karma

My sufferings, however, are not ascribable to this causal law. In the past I despised the votaries of the Lotus Sutra. I also ridiculed the sutra itself, sometimes with exaggerated praise and other times with contempt—that sutra as magnificent as two moons shining side by side, two stars conjoined, one Mount Hua placed atop another, or two jewels combined. This is why I have experienced the

aforementioned eight kinds of sufferings. Usually these sufferings appear one at a time, on into the boundless future, but Nichiren has denounced the enemies of the Lotus Sutra so severely that all eight have descended at once. This is like the case of a peasant heavily in debt to the steward of his village and to other authorities. As long as he remains in his village or district, rather than mercilessly hounding him, they are likely to defer his debts from one year to the next. But when he tries to leave, they rush over and demand that he repay everything at once. This is what the sutra means when it states, "It is due to the blessings obtained by protecting the Law." (WND-1, 305)

Nichiren Daishonin here reveals a more fundamental causality of life. He explains that the reason he has undergone the eight kinds of retribution is not due to the law of karmic retribution, or the general law of cause and effect, as outlined above. Rather, he attributes it to past slander of the Law in the form of denigrating the votaries of the Lotus Sutra—the king of sutras, which is "as magnificent as two moons shining side by side, two stars conjoined, one Mount Hua placed atop another, or two jewels combined." It is because of this fundamental negative karma formed through having attacked those who uphold this supreme teaching that he has experienced the eight kinds of retribution. He indicates that at the heart of all negative causes that bring suffering to people is slander of the Law.

Therefore, by dedicating ourselves as votaries of the Lotus Sutra—battling the enemies of the sutra and propagating the Mystic Law—we can break free from our negative karma and accumulate fundamental positive karma in our lives.

What Nichiren is explaining here is the causality for attaining Buddhahood—eliminating fundamental evil and powerfully manifesting the world of Buddhahood, the ninth consciousness[20] existing at the deepest level of life. This is the causality of the Mystic Law implicit in the Lotus Sutra—namely, Nammyoho-renge-kyo.

Even if we are presently suffering some form of karmic retribution, by basing ourselves on this causality of the Mystic Law, we can instantly bring forth the vast life state of Buddhahood. In other words, we can only truly change our karma through the Mystic Law of the simultaneity of cause and effect,[21] which enables us to actualize an inner transformation based on the principle that the nine worlds and the world of Buddhahood are mutually inherent—that is, the nine worlds possess the potential for Buddhahood, while the world of Buddhahood retains the nine worlds.

By contrast, the general causality of the pre-Lotus Sutra teachings operates on the principle of the non-simultaneity of cause and effect.[22] Since eliminating countless negative offenses from past existences based on such sequential causality would take an inexorably long time, changing one's karma in this lifetime would effectively be impossible.

Highlighting the difference between these two types of causality, Nichiren says, "Usually these sufferings appear one at a time, on into the boundless future, but Nichiren has denounced the enemies of the Lotus Sutra so severely that all eight have descended at once." He clarifies the kind of Buddhist practice that allows us to make fundamental positive causes. This is none other than the practice of *shakubuku*—correcting false views and awakening others to the truth of Buddhism; specifically expressed here as "denouncing the enemies of the Lotus Sutra"—an action that embodies the causality of the Mystic Law and enables us to change our karma.

"Like Nichiren, for example" (WND-1, 302)—when we "summon up the courage of a lion king" ("On Persecutions Befalling the Sage," WND-1, 997), practice with the same spirit as the Daishonin and strive intrepidly to spread the correct teaching, a life state of Buddhahood identical to that manifested by Nichiren begins to well forth within us.

"It is due to the blessings obtained by protecting the Law"—this means we can transform our karma by becoming lion kings like Nichiren, earnestly safeguarding the Law by speaking out against those who attack the Lotus

Sutra. In other words, Nichiren assures us, through the practice of shakubuku, any painful karmic retribution will vanish "instantly" (see "Lessening One's Karmic Retribution," WND-1, 199). Moreover, we can establish the life state of Buddhahood.

For us, "the blessings obtained by protecting the Law" refers to the benefit we gain by struggling for the sake of kosen-rufu together with our mentor.

***

The Principle of the Oneness of Mentor and Disciple Found in the Lotus Sutra

The Lotus Sutra says: "There will be many ignorant people who will curse and speak ill of us and will attack us with swords and staves, with rocks and tiles ... they will address the rulers, high ministers, Brahmans, and householders, [as well as the other monks, slandering and speaking evil of us] ... again and again we will be banished." If the offenders are not tormented by the wardens of hell, they will never be able to [pay for their offenses and] escape from hell. Were it not for the rulers and ministers who now persecute me, I would be unable to expiate my past sins of slandering the correct teaching.

> **Nichiren is like Bodhisattva Never Disparaging of old, and the people of this day are like the four categories of Buddhists who disparaged and cursed him. Though the people are different, the cause is the same. Though different people kill their parents, they all fall into the same hell of incessant suffering. Since Nichiren is making the same cause as Never Disparaging, how could it be that he would not become a Buddha equal to Shakyamuni? (WND-1, 305)**

Here, Nichiren Daishonin again highlights the nature of the enemies of the Lotus Sutra that practitioners should be prepared to face. These are none other than the three powerful enemies[23] described in "Encouraging Devotion," the 13th chapter of the Lotus Sutra.

The sutra passage "there will be many ignorant people who will curse and speak ill of us and will attack us with swords and staves, with rocks and tiles" describes arrogant lay people who shower the votaries of the Lotus Sutra with slander and abuse and seek to do them harm. "They will address the rulers, high ministers, Brahmans, and householders" refers to spurious accusations by arrogant false sages. And "again and again we will be banished"[24] describes the situation where priests of erroneous teachings and evil rulers conspire together to oust and banish the votaries of the Lotus Sutra.

The appearance of the three powerful enemies constitutes proof that the votaries of the Lotus Sutra are living the teachings of the sutra. It is just such persecution or opposition that enables these votaries to change their karma and attain Buddhahood. As Nichiren says, "Were it not for the rulers and ministers who now persecute me, I would be unable to expiate my past sins of slandering the correct teaching" (WND-1, 305). He further indicates that making continued efforts to spread the Law based on the conviction that persecution or opposition directly enables votaries to change their karma accords with the principle by which Bodhisattva Never Disparaging attained Buddhahood, as described in "The Bodhisattva Never Disparaging," the sutra's 20th chapter.

Never Disparaging respected and venerated all people and as a result was persecuted by the four categories of Buddhists, or four kinds of believers—monks, nuns, laymen and laywomen. Through encountering unceasing harassment, however, Never Disparaging expiated his negative karma from past existences. The Lotus Sutra describes the benefit he received "when his offenses had been wiped out."[25] Namely, he purified his six faculties or sense organs[26] and attained the Buddha way, while in a future lifetime he was reborn as Shakyamuni Buddha.

In light of this, he writes, "Nichiren is like Bodhisattva Never Disparaging of old." Those who practice the Lotus Sutra may differ with the age, but the fundamental cause for attaining Buddhahood is still the same. The basic formula remains. Accordingly, if we make the same kind of causes Bodhisattva Never Disparaging did through his Buddhist practice, then we can also become Buddhas without fail.

"How could it be that he [Nichiren] would not become a Buddha equal to Shakyamuni?"—Nichiren is saying this for the benefit of his disciples. It indicates the principle of the oneness of mentor and disciple. In other words, by following his example of triumphing over hardships and steadfastly carrying out the practice of shakubuku, his disciples, too, can definitely attain Buddhahood.

Of course, our ordinary lives may seem quite different from the life of a great predecessor like the Daishonin. That only stands to reason, because we are different individuals, with our own circumstances, personalities, abilities and so on. Nonetheless, if we make the same kind of causes—pursue the same practice and actions—as the courageous votaries of the Lotus Sutra who have gone before us, then we can achieve the same effects or results. This is a view of causality based on the path of mentor and disciple.

While disciples may feel unequal to the mentor in terms of wisdom or compassion, so long as they maintain the same commitment, ideals and dedicated efforts as the mentor, they can definitely attain the mentor's same expansive life state.

This is the path to attaining Buddhahood based on the spirit of the oneness of mentor and disciple found in the Lotus Sutra.

The Strict Law of Causality

Moreover, those who now slander him are like Bhadrapala and the others [who cursed Never Disparaging]. They will be tortured in the Avichi hell for a thousand kalpas. I therefore pity them deeply and wonder what can be done for them. Those who belittled and cursed Never Disparaging acted that way at first, but later they took faith in his teachings and willingly became his followers. The greater part of the fault of their slander was thus expiated, but even the small part that remained caused them to suffer as terribly as one who had killed one's parents a thousand times. The people of this age refuse to repent at all; therefore, as the "Simile and Parable" chapter states, they must suffer in hell for a countless number of kalpas; they may even suffer there for a duration of major world system dust particle kalpas or of numberless major world system dust particle kalpas. (WND-1, 305–06)

Regarding those who persecuted Bodhisattva Never Disparaging, as a result of their actions, they were destined to not encounter a Buddha for two hundred million kalpas and to suffer terrible agonies for one thousand kalpas in the Avichi hell, or hell of incessant suffering.[27] Nichiren Daishonin says he pities those who in the present age are making similar causes by persecuting him but that nothing can be done for them. No one can manipulate the law of cause and effect; it is strict and uncompromising.

Nichiren goes on to note that even people who had attacked Never Disparaging could eventually, through the connection they had formed with the bodhisattva, encounter his teaching again and, like Bhadrapala and others, become his disciples when he was reborn as Shakyamuni Buddha. But Nichiren points out that those slandering him in his current lifetime have no intention to reform or change their erroneous views. He laments that as a result, they will be consigned to endless suffering for innumerable kalpas.

***

The Fearful Nature of the Devil King of the Sixth Heaven

Aside from these people, there are also those who appeared to believe in me, but began doubting when they saw me persecuted. They not only have forsaken the Lotus Sutra, but also actually think themselves wise enough to instruct me. The pitiful thing is that these perverse

people must suffer in the Avichi hell even longer than the Nembutsu believers. (WND-1, 306)

Nichiren Daishonin explains that arrogant disciples pose the greatest problem. For the offense of erstwhile followers who do not merely abandon their faith but, out of an inflated opinion of themselves, denigrate their teacher and fellow practitioners is far more serious than that of those who reject and slander the correct teaching from the outset. Their retribution will also be more severe.

Moreover, disciples who have allowed their lives to be consumed by fundamental darkness and ignorance will seek to sway others, potentially causing many to stop practicing. Such is the fearful nature of the devil king of the sixth heaven.[28] In "The Workings of Brahma and Shakra," Nichiren remarks, "Those possessed by a great devil will, once they succeed in persuading a believer to recant, use that person as a means for making many others abandon their faith" (WND-1, 800). Even though such individuals had the fortune to encounter and take faith in the Mystic Law, they ultimately allowed their lives to be controlled by the devil king of the sixth heaven. The fundamental reason can be traced to arrogance, the essence of which is jealousy and contempt for the mentor. The Daishonin's description of such individuals as perverse people who "actually think themselves wise enough to instruct [him]" stands as an eternal admonition to his followers.

The Buddhist principle of cause and effect operates across eternity. Those who live in accord with the causality of the Mystic Law will prosper forever. Their good fortune will flow on to their loved ones and descendants for infinite future generations of the Latter Day of the Law. On the other hand, Nichiren declares that those followers who forget the way of mentor and disciple and betray their faith and fellow practitioners "must suffer in the Avichi hell even longer than the Nembutsu believers."

The Daishonin awakened to the Law that makes it possible for all people to achieve enlightenment. In terms of the fundamental path of attaining Buddhahood, the teaching of Nichiren Daishonin, the Buddha of the Latter Day, is absolute. As a teacher, he dedicated himself to fostering and training disciples, and therefore his instruction was often very strict. Some, however, failed to understand his heart and turned against him. Yet no matter how those perverse individuals might have maligned his name, Nichiren remained unperturbed.

***

A Promise of Victory to Disciples

An asura contended that the Buddha taught only eighteen elements, but that he

himself expounded nineteen. The non-Buddhist teachers claimed that the Buddha offered only one way to enlightenment, but that they had ninety-five. In the same way, the renegade disciples say, "Though the priest Nichiren is our teacher, he is too forceful. We will spread the Lotus Sutra in a more peaceful way." In so asserting, they are being as ridiculous as fireflies laughing at the sun and moon, an anthill belittling Mount Hua, wells and brooks despising the river and the ocean, or a magpie mocking a phoenix. Nam-myoho-renge-kyo.

Nichiren

The twentieth day of the third month in the ninth year of Bun'ei (1272), cyclical sign *mizunoesaru*
To Nichiren's disciples and lay supporters (WND-1, 306)

Nichiren Daishonin closes the main body of the text of "Letter from Sado" with a passage expressing the towering conviction of a lion king.

Here, he points out that the arrogant will try to add their personal, arbitrary views to the Buddha's teaching. For instance, when Shakyamuni taught the existence of eighteen elements, an *asura* bragged of knowing nineteen elements; and when the Buddha taught that there was only one ultimate way to enlightenment, the non-Buddhists claimed that they knew of ninety-five ultimate ways.

Among Nichiren's disciples were similarly arrogant and ignorant people who looked down on him and said disparagingly: "Though the priest Nichiren is our teacher, he is too forceful. We will spread the Lotus Sutra in a more peaceful way." While it might appear at first that they maintained faith in the Lotus Sutra, they had in fact lost sight of the sutra's essence. Consequently, they could not appreciate the true greatness of their teacher, Nichiren Daishonin, in propagating the Lotus Sutra in the Latter Day.

From the viewpoint of Buddhism, the Sado Exile and other persecutions were ultimately the result of the devil king of the sixth heaven having entered the lives of the ruler and other powerful figures in order to drive a wedge between Nichiren and his followers. When the bonds uniting mentor and disciple are healthy and strong, the power and influence of the Mystic Law increases, the momentum for the eternal perpetuation of the correct teaching strengthens and spreads, and the great path leading to happiness and peace for all humanity—the fundamental goal of Buddhism—opens wide. The devil king, therefore, seeks to prevent this at any cost.

In that sense, the disciples who criticized Nichiren while avoiding hardship themselves had, despite their seeming reasonableness, been utterly defeated by the devil king. They had surrendered the all-important spirit of mentor and disciple to the devilish nature, to their inner fundamental darkness.

I can vividly picture the Daishonin proclaiming, "They are being as ridiculous as fireflies laughing at the sun and moon, an anthill belittling Mount Hua, wells and brooks despising the river and the ocean, or a magpie mocking a phoenix."

The first three Soka Gakkai presidents have forged ahead in their efforts for kosen-rufu with this same conviction.

"Letter from Sado" reveals Nichiren's towering state of mind while undergoing life-threatening persecution; it is the mentor's declaration of victory. At the same time, it is both a call to and promise of victory, addressed to his courageous disciples struggling alongside him to surmount great challenges.

The Victory of Disciples Is the Victory of Soka

There is very little writing paper here in the province of Sado, and to write to you individually would take too long. Nevertheless, if even one person fails to hear from me, it will cause resentment. Therefore, I want people with seeking minds to meet and read this letter together for encouragement. When great trouble occurs in the world, minor troubles become insignificant. I do not know how

accurate the reports reaching me are, but there must surely be intense grieving over those killed in the recent battles. What has become of the lay priests Izawa and Sakabe? Send me news of Kawanobe, Yamashiro, Tokugyo-ji, and the others. Also, please be kind enough to send me *The Essentials of Government in the Chenkuan Era,* the collection of tales from the non-Buddhist classics, and the record of the teachings transmitted within the eight schools. Without these, I cannot even write letters. (WND-1, 306)

This section constitutes a postscript. It shows Nichiren Daishonin's concern and profound compassion for each of his followers. He inquires after the welfare of specific individuals and asks to be sent various texts to use as references for his writing. At his remote place of exile on Sado, Nichiren continued his tireless spiritual struggle motivated by his immense compassion for all humanity.

I have always felt that it is incredibly fortunate for a person to have a mentor. I have been committed to repaying even the smallest kindness that my mentor has shown to me by devoting myself wholeheartedly to kosen-rufu.

At the end of April 1951, immediately before my mentor, Josei Toda, was inaugurated as second Soka Gakkai president, I reread "Letter from Sado" as a testament to the victory of mentor and disciple. In my diary that month, I specifically wrote down the following passages:

April 27

When an evil ruler in consort with priests of erroneous teachings tries to destroy the correct teaching and do away with a man of wisdom, those with the heart of a lion king are sure to attain Buddhahood. Like Nichiren, for example. (WND-1, 302)

April 28

In the same way, the renegade disciples say, "Though the priest Nichiren is our teacher, he is too forceful. We will spread the Lotus Sutra in a more peaceful way." In so asserting, they are being as ridiculous as fireflies laughing at the sun and moon, an anthill belittling Mount Hua, wells and brooks despising the river and the ocean, or a magpie mocking a phoenix. (WND-1, 306)[29]

For me, "Letter from Sado" is a writing of the victory of mentor and disciple, which President Toda and I studied and used as inspiration in overcoming adversity. I vowed that in order to actualize his vision, I would first do my best and take full responsibility.

Toward that end, I resolved to develop my district. I started by visiting members at their homes, holding discussion meetings and stirring a great groundswell of propagation. This is because the future victory of kosen-rufu lies in expanding the unparalleled realm of mentor and disciple of Soka outward from our own districts.

To engage in one-to-one dialogue to convey the greatness of Nichiren Buddhism, to courageously share the noble path of mentor and disciple with others—this is what it means in modern terms to put into practice the spirit of "Letter from Sado."

This lecture was originally published in the March 2009 issue of the Daibyakurenge, *the Soka Gakkai's monthly study journal.*

NOTES

[1] Parinirvana Sutra: Also known as the Mahaparinirvana Sutra. A Chinese version of the Nirvana Sutra in six volumes, translated by Fa-hsien and Buddhabhadra around 417.

[2] Together these eight constitute what are known as the eight kinds of suffering, or the eight kinds of retributions. They refer to hardships that one must undergo as retribution for countless past offenses.

[3] Mount Hua: A high mountain in China's Shaanxi Province. One of the five sacred mountains of China.

[4] Nichiren, here, refers to the Parinirvana Sutra.

[5] From "Encouraging Devotion," the 13th chapter of the Lotus Sutra (LSOC, 232). This chapter actually refers only to "swords and staves." "Rocks and tiles" is added from "The Bodhisattva Never Disparaging," the 20th chapter.

[6] Wardens of hell: Demons in Buddhist mythology who torment transgressors who have fallen into hell. They work for King Yama, the king of hell who is said to judge and determine the rewards and punishments of the dead.

[7] Four categories of Buddhists: Monks, nuns, laymen and laywomen.

[8] Bhadrapala: A bodhisattva who was a disciple of Shakyamuni Buddha. In "The Bodhisattva Never Disparaging," the 20th chapter of the Lotus Sutra, it is revealed that in the past, he was one of the Buddhist practitioners among the four kinds of believers who slandered Bodhisattva Never Disparaging. For that offense, he fell into the Avichi hell for the period of a thousand kalpas. Later, through the benefit of the reverse relationship he had formed in the past, he was reborn in the time of

Shakyamuni—who had been Never Disparaging in a former existence—and became his disciple.

[9] Avichi hell: Also, hell of incessant suffering. The most terrible of the eight hot hells. The Sanskrit word *avichi* was rendered into Chinese as "incessant," indicating that in this hell pain and suffering continue without interruption.

[10] "Major world system dust particle kalpas" and "numberless major world system dust particle kalpas": Immensely long periods of time.

[11] *Asura:* A type of demon in Indian mythology, contentious and belligerent by nature, who continually fights with the gods, especially Shakra.

[12] Eighteen elements: The comprehensive concept of the three interrelated categories: the six sense organs (eyes, ears, nose, tongue, body and mind); the six objects they perceive; and the six consciousnesses, or the sense organs' functions of perceiving the six objects.

[13] Based on a passage in *The Treatise on the Great Perfection of Wisdom.* The "ninety-five" ways may be ascribable to the fact that there were ninety-five

non-Buddhist schools during Shakyamuni's day.

[14] Kawanobe, Yamashiro and Tokugyo-ji were followers of Nichiren, said to have been imprisoned in a dungeon following the Tatsunokuchi Persecution.

[15] *The Essentials of Government in the Chen-kuan Era:* A work edited by Wu Ching, a historian of the T'ang dynasty (618–907) in China. It was widely studied by government officials in Japan during Nichiren's day.

[16] Eight schools: The eight major schools of Buddhism in Japan before the Kamakura period (1185–1333): the Dharma Analysis Treasury, Establishment of Truth, Precepts, Dharma Characteristics, Three Treatises, Flower Garland, Tendai and True Word schools. The first six schools flourished in the Nara period (710–94), while the Tendai and True Word schools rose to prominence during the Heian period (794–1185).

[17] Bodhisattva Never Disparaging: A bodhisattva described in the 20th chapter of the Lotus Sutra. This bodhisattva—Shakyamuni in a previous lifetime—would bow to everyone he

met and say: "I have profound reverence for you, I would never dare treat you with disparagement or arrogance. Why? Because you will all practice the bodhisattva way and will then be able to attain Buddhahood" (LSOC, 308). He was attacked, however, by arrogant people, who beat him with sticks and staves and threw stones at him. The sutra explains that Never Disparaging's practice of bowing to others' Buddha nature became the cause for him to attain Buddhahood.

[18] Karma formed in previous lifetimes: Although this can refer to either good or evil karma, it is usually used to refer to evil karma. See WND-1, 303.

[19] Lessening karmic retribution: The principle that one can experience the effects of bad karma from the past to a lesser degree through Buddhist faith and practice.

[20] Ninth consciousness: Also called amala-consciousness. The ninth consciousness is the Buddha nature, or the fundamental purifying force, that is free from all karmic impediments.

[21] Simultaneity of cause and effect: The principle that both cause and effect exist

together simultaneously in a single moment of life.

[22] Non-simultaneity of cause and effect: The view that there is a gap in time between cause and effect. In Buddhist practice based on teachings other than the Lotus Sutra, it is only possible to gain the effect of enlightenment after an extremely long period of time spent accumulating good causes in order to cancel out previous evil causes.

[23] Three powerful enemies: Three types of arrogant people who persecute those who propagate the Lotus Sutra in the evil age after Shakyamuni Buddha's death, described in a twenty-line verse section of "Encouraging Devotion," the 13th chapter of the Lotus Sutra. The Great Teacher Miao-lo (711–82) of China summarizes them as arrogant lay people, arrogant priests and arrogant false sages.

[24] "Again and again we will be banished" (LSOC, 234): A passage in "Encouraging Devotion," the 13th chapter of the Lotus Sutra. It explains that when votaries of the Lotus Sutra expound the correct teaching in the Latter Day of the Law, they will be repeatedly driven away. In keeping with the predictions in

this passage, Nichiren was exiled to Izu and to Sado.

[25] See LSOC, 312. This line from "The Bodhisattva Never Disparaging," the 20th chapter of the Lotus Sutra, indicates that the bodhisattva was able to expiate his offenses of slandering the Law in the past as a result of being persecuted by others.

[26] Purification of the six sense organs: Also, purification of the six senses. This refers to the six sense organs of eyes, ears, nose, tongue, body and mind becoming pure, making it possible to apprehend all things correctly. "Benefits of the Teacher of the Law," the 19th chapter of the Lotus Sutra, explains that those who uphold and practice the sutra acquire eight hundred benefits of the eyes, nose and body, and twelve hundred benefits of the ears, tongue and mind, and that through these benefits the six sense organs become refined and pure.

[27] In the Lotus Sutra, Shakyamuni says: "The Bodhisattva Never Disparaging who lived at that time—could he be unknown to you? In fact he was none other than I myself! ... The four kinds of believers,

the monks, nuns, laymen, and laywomen, because anger arose in their minds and they treated me with disparagement and contempt, were for two hundred million kalpas never able to encounter a Buddha, to hear the Law, or to see the community of monks. For a thousand kalpas they underwent great suffering in the Avichi hell. After they had finished paying for their offenses, they once more encountered the bodhisattva Never Disparaging [Shakyamuni], who instructed them in supreme perfect enlightenment" (LSOC, 310–11).

[28] Devil king of the sixth heaven: Also, devil king or heavenly devil. The king of devils, who dwells in the highest or the sixth heaven of the world of desire. He is also named Freely Enjoying Things Conjured by Others, the king who makes free use of the fruits of others' efforts for his own pleasure. Served by innumerable minions, he obstructs Buddhist practice and delights in sapping the life force of other beings. The devil king is a personification of the negative tendency to force others to one's will at any cost.

[29] Daisaku Ikeda, *A Youthful Diary: One Man's Journey From the Beginning of Faith to Worldwide Leadership for Peace* (Santa Monica, California: World Tribune Press, 2006), p.109.

CHAPTER 4

"LETTER TO THE BROTHERS"—PART 1 OF 3

OVERCOME ALL OBSTACLES THROUGH STEADFAST FAITH!

Passage for Study in This Lecture

The Lotus Sutra is the heart of the eighty thousand teachings[1] and the core of the twelve divisions of the scriptures.[2] The Buddhas throughout the three existences attain enlightenment because they take this sutra as their teacher. The Buddhas of the ten directions[3] guide living beings with the teaching of the one vehicle as their eyes. (WND-1, 493)

***

Moreover, it is extremely difficult to meet a person who expounds this sutra exactly as the sutra directs. It is even more difficult than for a one-eyed turtle to find a piece of floating sandalwood,[4] or for someone to hang Mount Sumeru from the sky with the fiber from a lotus stem.[5] (WND-1, 495)

***

Since this is so, believers in the Lotus Sutra should fear those who attempt to obstruct their practice more than they fear bandits, burglars, night raiders, tigers, wolves, or lions—even more than invasion now by the Mongols. This world is the domain of the devil king of the sixth heaven.[6] All of its people have been under the rule of this devil king since time without beginning. Not only has he built the prison of the twenty-five realms of existence[7] within the six paths[8] and confined all humankind within it, but also he has made wives and children into shackles, and parents and sovereigns into nets that block off the skies. To deceive the true mind of the Buddha nature, he causes the people to drink the wine of greed, anger, and foolishness, and feeds them nothing but dishes of evil that leave them prostrate on the ground of the three evil paths.[9] When he happens on persons who have turned their hearts to goodness, he acts to obstruct them. He is determined to make believers in the Lotus Sutra fall into evil, but if he is unsuccessful, he tries to deceive them gradually by luring them toward the Flower Garland Sutra,[10] which resembles the Lotus Sutra.

This was done by Tu-shun, Chih-yen, Fa-tsang, and Ch'engkuan.[11] Then Chiahsiang and Seng-ch'üan[12] were the evil companions who craftily deceived believers in the Lotus Sutra into falling back to the Wisdom sutras. Similarly, Hsüan-tsang and Tz'u-en[13] led them toward the Profound Secrets Sutra, while Shan-wu-wei, Chin-kang-chih, Pu-k'ung,[14] Kobo, Jikaku, and Chisho[15] deceived them into following the Mahavairochana Sutra. Bodhidharma and Hui-k'o[16] caused them to stray into the Zen school, while Shan-tao and Honen[17] tricked them into believing the Meditation Sutra. In each case, the devil king of the sixth heaven possessed these men of wisdom in order to deceive good people. This is what the Lotus Sutra means when it says in its fifth volume, "Evil demons will take possession of others."[18]

The great demon of fundamental darkness[19] can even enter the bodies of bodhisattvas who have reached near-perfect enlightenment[20] and prevent them from attaining the Lotus Sutra's blessing of perfect

> enlightenment.[21] How easily can he then obstruct those in any lower stage of practice! The devil king of the sixth heaven takes possession of the bodies of wives and children, and causes them to lead their husbands or parents astray. He also possesses the sovereign in order to threaten the votary of the Lotus Sutra, or possesses fathers and mothers, and makes them reproach their filially devoted children. (WND-1, 495–96)

LECTURE

"The great undertaking of kosen-rufu is a struggle against devilish functions. We cannot afford to cower at their onslaughts. If we allow them to defeat us, humanity will be forever enveloped in darkness." This was the powerful declaration of my mentor, second Soka Gakkai president Josei Toda—words that carry an important message for posterity.

Mr. Toda never retreated a single step in battling malicious or destructive forces that sought to block the flow of kosen-rufu; he fought on, determined to put a stop to them. The happiness of all humanity was his goal. Because he wished to rid the world of suffering and misery, he strove tirelessly to vanquish all negative forces that inflicted pain and torment on people. To the very end of his life, he led the way as supreme commander of kosen-rufu.

In particular, 1957, the year before Mr. Toda's death—a year that saw many of his aspirations for our movement reach their culmination—the Soka Gakkai was fiercely buffeted by a host of obstacles, which Buddhist scriptures refer to as the "three obstacles and four devils."[22] In addition to harassment and persecution in the form of the Yubari Coal Miners Union Incident[23] and the Osaka Incident,[24] illness struck Mr. Toda, the organization's president, more severely than ever before.

But President Toda always discerned the true nature of things and events from the perspective of the Buddha and the Law. On one occasion, he said: "We are about to realize the goal of a 750,000-household membership, so it is only natural that devilish functions will vie with one another to obstruct our progress. The devil of illness now plaguing me, however, only qualifies as a minor demon. If I let such insignificant devils defeat me, I can never accomplish kosen-rufu." Undaunted, Mr. Toda faced the onslaughts of devilish functions. He also once said: "My being sick like this is a major instance of lessening karmic retribution.[25] I am convinced that because of this illness, the immense difficulties that the Soka Gakkai would otherwise have to face are being reduced."

True to his powerful conviction, Mr. Toda overcame his health threat. To celebrate his recovery, he held a special dinner on his fifty-eighth birthday, on February 11, 1958. Having won a victory over the devil of illness, Mr. Toda handed the baton of kosen-rufu to his youthful successors on March 16. And then, having fulfilled his noble mission in this world, he passed away with complete peace of mind on April 2.

This year [2009] marks the fifty-first anniversary of my mentor's death, a day when I, as his loyal disciple, made a vow to dedicate my life to repaying my profound debt of gratitude to him.

The Five Eternal Guidelines of the Soka Gakkai

In December 1957, while President Toda was battling illness, the Soka Gakkai finally reached a membership of 750,000 households—a goal he had pledged to achieve during his lifetime. At the headquarters leaders meeting that month announcing the fulfillment of his vow, Mr. Toda presented his beloved fellow members with what later came to be known as the three eternal guidelines of the Soka Gakkai:

(1)   Faith for a harmonious family
(2)   Faith for each person to become happy
(3)   Faith for surmounting obstacles

Each of these short guidelines encapsulates an important purpose of faith and the essential spirit with which we should pursue our Buddhist practice.

My mentor entrusted me with realizing all of his plans and visions. So, after becoming third Soka Gakkai president (in May 1960), I decided to reaffirm these three guidelines in the New Year's speeches I gave in both 1961 and 1962. I knew that if we lost sight of the fundamental purpose of Buddhist practice Mr. Toda had taught us, we would risk being defeated by devilish functions, resulting in apathy, stagnation and, ultimately, the disintegration of our faith.

In 2003, after the start of the new century, I again reconfirmed the essence of President Toda's guidelines and added two new ones:

(4) Faith for health and long life
(5) Faith for absolute victory

Together, they form five eternal guidelines—guidelines that express the cherished hope and conviction of President Toda as well as my own. Comprising the vital ingredients for attaining Buddhahood in this lifetime, these guidelines are infused with our prayer that members everywhere will, undefeated by any obstacle, dedicate their lives to kosen-rufu and achieve a state of absolute happiness.

"Letter to the Brothers" is a writing that my mentor and I studied together as a crucial text for learning the correct attitude in faith. In it, Nichiren Daishonin teaches his followers to triumph boldly over all devilish functions—whether they appear as the three obstacles and four devils, or as the workings of the devil king of the sixth heaven—and attain Buddhahood. He urges them to do so by striving in faith with the same commitment as his and uniting solidly with their fellow believers. This writing could indeed be called the basis or source of the five eternal guidelines of the Soka Gakkai.

Unless we win in the struggle against devilish functions, we cannot achieve true harmony, happiness, health and longevity, or victory—goals that form the heart of the five guidelines.

In this and the next two installments, let us study "Letter to the Brothers" and learn the formula for total victory that Nichiren outlines for his followers in this writing.

Great Obstacles Are the Direct Path To Transforming Our Karma and Attaining Buddhahood

The Lotus Sutra is the heart of the eighty thousand teachings and the core of the twelve divisions of the scriptures. The Buddhas throughout the three existences attain enlightenment because they take this sutra as their teacher. The Buddhas of the ten directions guide living beings with the teaching of the one vehicle as their eyes. (WND-1, 493)

I shall begin by explaining a few points concerning the recipients of this letter and the situation they were facing.

The letter is addressed to the brothers Ikegami—Munenaka and Munenaga. It is not clear when they took faith in Nichiren Daishonin's teachings, but they are generally thought to have been among his earliest followers. The brothers belonged to the Ikegami clan, a prominent samurai family that served as a leading construction contractor for government building projects.[26] Their father, Ikegami Yasumitsu[27] [an ardent supporter of Ryokan,[28] chief priest of Gokuraku-ji, a temple of the True Word Precepts school], opposed their faith and had disowned Munenaka, the older brother.

Disownment in feudal society was a severe sanction. It not only meant loss of the right of succession but also being deprived of both economic foundation and social standing. Moreover, in this particular case, since only the elder brother had been disowned, there was now a chance for Munenaga to become his father's heir, if only he would be willing to give up his faith. This was a cunning tactic by the father to weaken his younger son's resolve.

Nichiren wrote this letter in response to the news of Munenaka's disownment. Throughout its pages, he teaches the Ikegami brothers that the obstacles confronting them are the inevitable consequence of their steadfast faith in the Lotus Sutra, and that the path to attaining Buddhahood ultimately lies in battling devilish functions in accord with the sutra.

Hence, in the opening paragraph, Nichiren emphasizes the superiority of the Lotus Sutra to all other teachings of the Buddha. The Lotus Sutra, he explains, is the heart of the vast body of sutras known as the "eighty thousand teachings," and the core of the Buddha's teachings referred to generally as the "twelve divisions of the scriptures." He also says that not only have all Buddhas throughout time and space attained enlightenment themselves by taking this sutra as their teacher but that they also guide living beings toward that goal by expounding the teaching of the Lotus Sutra.

We can surmise it is because of the gravity of the brothers' situation that Nichiren begins by outlining the fundamental significance of faith in this way. He teaches that to deeply recognize the supreme value of upholding the Lotus Sutra results in a conviction and joy that produces the strength to overcome any hardship.

He then discusses from various perspectives the serious consequences of abandoning faith in the Lotus Sutra. Forsaking this teaching constitutes such a grave offense because "the Lotus Sutra is the eye of all the Buddhas. It is the original teacher of Shakyamuni Buddha himself, the lord of teachings" (WND-1, 494). In other words, to discard one's faith is to discard the ultimate teaching.

On a deeper level, abandoning the Lotus Sutra amounts to rejecting the fundamental principles the sutra embodies, such as universal enlightenment, respect for all people and harmonious coexistence. Doing so, therefore, causes the three poisons—greed, anger and foolishness[29]—which prompt people to act in opposition to the ultimate Law—to intensify in people's lives until eventually darkness dominates and they are destined to wander through the evil paths of existence.

The Daishonin seeks to strongly impress upon the Ikegami brothers an understanding of the Lotus Sutra's paramount importance, explaining that to discard one word or even one brushstroke (see WND-1, 494) would constitute a serious offense. In this caution, we can sense his immense compassion to do everything in his power to dissuade the two brothers from abandoning their faith at this challenging crossroads in their lives.

***

It Is Difficult To Encounter a True Teacher

Moreover, it is extremely difficult to meet a person who expounds this sutra exactly as the sutra directs. It is even more difficult than for a one-eyed turtle to find a piece of floating sandalwood, or for someone to hang Mount Sumeru from the sky with the fiber from a lotus stem. (WND-1, 495)

Having discussed the significance of the teaching of the Lotus Sutra, or the Mystic Law, Nichiren Daishonin next focuses on the importance of the people who expound and practice the Lotus Sutra.

Ultimately, not even the most exalted teaching can amount to anything unless someone puts it into practice. This is as indicated by Nichiren's pronouncement, "The Law does not spread by itself: because people propagate it, both people and the Law are respectworthy" (GZ, 856).[30]

It is exceedingly rare to encounter a person who expounds the Lotus Sutra exactly as the sutra directs. Nichiren explains that meeting so rare a teacher is even more difficult than such singular or impossible feats as a one-eyed turtle finding a piece of floating sandalwood or someone hanging Mount Sumeru from the sky with the fiber from a lotus stem.

The person or teacher mentioned here is the votary of the Lotus Sutra, a reference specifically to Nichiren. It is something truly extraordinary to have encountered the Daishonin in this saha world[31] during this evil age of the Latter Day, which is defiled by the five impurities.[32]

Likewise, it is equally difficult for those living in the world after the Daishonin's passing to meet an authentic leader of Buddhism who propagates the Mystic Law, the essence of the Lotus Sutra, exactly as he teaches. For me, there is no greater joy than having been born in this world and becoming the disciple of President Toda, a great teacher of kosen-rufu. When we first met, I instinctively knew I could trust him. He is the reason I decided to practice Nichiren Buddhism.

In an exchange of letters with the well-known Japanese novelist and poet Yasushi Inoue, I wrote: "I first learned about Buddhism from Josei Toda. Faith did not come first; my encounter with him did."[33] Mr. Inoue responded as follows to a letter in which I described meeting my mentor and the decisive impact it had on my life:

> I was very moved by [your letter] ... Not often are human beings granted the opportunity to encounter a person of such scope as Mr. Toda was, to find a person whose ideas coincide with one's own, to show devotion to such a person, thus to plot one's life path, and then always to love and respect that person.[34]

The mentor-disciple relationship is a precious treasure in life. From the standpoint of Buddhism, it is a supremely noble bond. Had it not been for the mentor, Tsunesaburo Makiguchi, and his disciple, Josei Toda—the first and second presidents of the Soka Gakkai—the revival of Nichiren Buddhism in the modern age would never have taken place.

This is because the Law only comes to life in the lives of those who practice it, and its real worth only manifests through their behavior and actions. Unless there are people who correctly uphold the Buddha's teaching, who practice true to its spirit, nothing of value will be created through that teaching.

Having a teacher in faith is vital to practicing Buddhism correctly. And it is by disciples acting with the same spirit as their mentor that the Law is transmitted. The mentor-disciple relationship is a cornerstone of Nichiren Buddhism.

Our Soka network has now spread throughout the world. Transcending differences of language and ethnicity, millions of members today are making dedicated efforts to expound the sutra exactly as the sutra directs. To embrace and carry on the noble heritage of mentor and disciple and advance together with the SGI is to lead a truly sublime and meaningful existence. All who do so would surely earn Nichiren's highest praise.

***

Beware of Negative Influences

Since this is so, believers in the Lotus Sutra should fear those who attempt to obstruct their practice more than they fear bandits, burglars, night raiders, tigers, wolves, or lions—even more than invasion now by the Mongols. (WND-1, 495)

Who is it that we, as practitioners of the Lotus Sutra, should really fear? Nichiren Daishonin says that rather than fearing bandits, thieves or wild animals, we should fear those who attempt to obstruct our practice. To whom, then, does this specifically refer?

In the paragraphs immediately preceding this passage, the Daishonin cites the examples of respected Chinese T'ang dynasty Buddhist teachers, such as Tz'u-en and Shan-wu-wei, who held fast to the Buddha's provisional teachings rather than embracing the Lotus Sutra. He notes that each of these learned men had at some point recognized the Lotus Sutra's superiority but in the end had forgone upholding faith in this sutra. The root cause behind their rejection, he asserts, is their having been led astray by "someone who was an evil influence" (WND-1, 495)—meaning an "evil friend" or "evil teacher."

"Those who attempt to obstruct one's practice" are known as "negative influences." What makes them so frightening is that they can corrupt people's minds and destroy their faith. If practitioners of the Lotus Sutra allow themselves to be swayed by negative influences, to be deceived by evil teachers, thereby losing their commitment to the correct path of faith, they cannot attain the Buddha way.

Conversely, if practitioners remain steadfast in their commitment, they can eventually, through the power of faith, surmount even the greatest difficulties. It is really true, as Nichiren often says, that the heart is most important. To forge the inner strength to withstand negative influences, we must have the wisdom to discern that they are devilish functions and courageously battle them.

Faith Is a Struggle Against the Workings of the Devil King

This world is the domain of the devil king of the sixth heaven. All of its people have been under the rule of this devil king since time without beginning. Not only has he built the prison of the twenty-five realms of existence within the six paths and confined all humankind within it, but also he has made wives and children into shackles, and parents and sovereigns into nets that block off the skies. To deceive the true mind of the Buddha nature, he causes the people to drink the wine of greed, anger, and foolishness, and feeds them nothing but dishes of evil that leave them prostrate on the ground of the three evil paths. When he happens on persons who have turned their hearts to goodness, he acts to obstruct them. (WND-1, 495–96)

"This world is the domain of the devil king of the sixth heaven. All of its people have been under the rule of this devil king since time without beginning." This is an important passage expressing Nichiren Daishonin's keen insight into the true nature of devilish functions. I have read this passage countless times since I started practicing Nichiren Buddhism, engraving it deeply in my heart.

In this and the following passages, Nichiren indicates that the workings of the devil king of the sixth heaven are the evil influences that we should fear most as practitioners. First, he declares that "this world"—meaning the saha world in which we live—is the "domain" of the devil king of the sixth heaven. This is because the devil king—reigning as he does over the threefold world[35] from the summit of the world of desire[36]—has ruled people's lives since time without beginning.

The devil king represents negative forces that manipulate at will the lives of others, that obstruct good and that cause people to fall into evil paths. Devilish functions deprive believers of the Lotus Sutra of the benefit of their Buddhist practice and cut off the flow of wisdom in their lives. They destroy the roots of goodness people have cultivated, causing them to transmigrate through the six paths of the threefold world. The forces of the devil king also devise various schemes to hinder the progress of the Buddha's forces. The Daishonin lists three specific examples of the insidious workings of the devil king: (1) making wives and children into shackles; (2) making parents and sovereigns into nets that block off the skies; and (3) causing people to drink the wine of greed, anger and foolishness to cloud the true mind of their Buddha nature. These three types of hindrances correspond to the three obstacles—karma, retribution and earthly desires.

In the many momentous persecutions that beset him, Nichiren was actually fighting the negative forces personified by the devil king of the sixth heaven.

In another writing, he says, "The devil king of the sixth heaven has roused the ten kinds of troops[37] and, in the midst of the sea of the sufferings of birth and death, is at war with the votary of the Lotus Sutra to stop him from taking possession of and to wrest away from him this impure land where both ordinary people and sages dwell" ("The Great Battle," WND-2, 465).

The devil king, commanding his ten armies, wages battle to prevent the votary of the Lotus Sutra from gaining influence in the saha world. And if the votary should succeed in spite of all of these attacks, the devil king will still make every effort to wrest back control. Fully aware of this, Nichiren declares: "It has been twenty or more years now since I found myself in that situation and began the great battle. Not once have I thought of retreat" ("The Great Battle," WND-2, 465). In other words, his life was a continuous struggle against the forces of the devil king. Kosen-rufu will forever entail an unremitting struggle between Buddhahood and the negative functions inherent in life.

The SGI is the organization that has inherited the true spirit of Nichiren Daishonin. As a result, the more dynamically our noble Soka movement has grown, the more intense have been the onslaughts of the devil king and other negative forces.

President Toda instructed: "Fight fearlessly against devilish functions! Don't let them cause mischief! Don't ever give in to them!"

He, together with his mentor, first Soka Gakkai president Tsunesaburo Makiguchi—both great leaders of kosen-rufu who had an utterly selfless commitment to spreading the Mystic Law—bore the full brunt of all persecution. They fought the devilish nature of authority and staunchly protected their fellow members and the Soka Gakkai organization. As the third president, I have striven with exactly the same spirit.

The first three Soka Gakkai presidents dauntlessly battled the three obstacles and four devils and the three powerful enemies[38] and triumphed over them.

***

Recognizing Negative Influences

He is determined to make believers in the Lotus Sutra fall into evil, but if he is unsuccessful, he tries to deceive them gradually by luring them toward the Flower

Garland Sutra, which resembles the Lotus Sutra.

This was done by Tu-shun, Chih-yen, Fa-tsang, and Ch'eng-kuan. Then Chiahsiang and Seng-ch'üan were the evil companions who craftily deceived believers in the Lotus Sutra into falling back to the Wisdom sutras. Similarly, Hsüan-tsang and Tz'u-en led them toward the Profound Secrets Sutra, while Shan-wu-wei, Chin-kang-chih, Pu-k'ung, Kobo, Jikaku, and Chisho deceived them into following the Mahavairochana Sutra. Bodhidharma and Hui-k'o caused them to stray into the Zen school, while Shan-tao and Honen tricked them into believing the Meditation Sutra. In each case, the devil king of the sixth heaven possessed these men of wisdom in order to deceive good people. This is what the Lotus Sutra means when it says in its fifth volume, "Evil demons will take possession of others." (WND-1, 496)

The devil king of the sixth heaven resorts to any and all means to prevent those who believe in the Lotus Sutra from attaining Buddhahood. As a simple illustration of this, Nichiren Daishonin cites the actions of priests of various Buddhist schools, asserting that they seek to gradually deceive believers by luring them away from the Lotus Sutra with something that "resembles" it.

He writes, "In each case, the devil king of the sixth heaven possessed these men of wisdom in order to deceive good people." As examples of such "men of wisdom," Nichiren lists many high-ranking priests revered within the different Buddhist schools of his day. Because they lead sincere practitioners astray, he says, they represent "evil companions" or "evil teachers" and epitomize those ruled by the workings of the devil king. This is what is meant by the passage in "Encouraging Devotion," the 13th chapter of the Lotus Sutra, "Evil demons will take possession of others" (LSOC, 233).

Since these are eminent priests respected in society, people fail to discern their true nature. On the contrary, they esteem these misguided individuals and prize their teachings, allowing "poison to penetrate deeply into their lives"[39] without realizing it and ultimately losing their "true minds."[40] This causes them to turn away from the Lotus Sutra and even denigrate it. This is the frightening outcome of a society in which people have succumbed to negative influences. People's normal sensibilities at some point become numbed, and the very fabric of society starts to decay. Yet, people cannot understand the cause for this.

The votary of the Lotus Sutra endeavors to teach people the truth about the poison that has deeply penetrated their lives, but those he seeks to teach, being deluded, perceive him as a villain. Nevertheless, using the power of words and reasoning based on the Lotus Sutra, he strives to reveal the ugly face of slander of the Law and expose for all to see the true nature of erroneous teachers and other negative influences. This is the struggle described in the twenty-line verse section of the "Encouraging Devotion" chapter.[41]

In this passage from "Letter to the Brothers," the Daishonin unhesitatingly names the founders and eminent priests of the various prominent schools of his day, openly denouncing them as the main culprits undermining people's faith in the Lotus Sutra. He did not fear criticism or abuse. We even find him proclaiming in other writings: "Let others hate [me] if they will" (see "The Unity of Husband and Wife," WND-1, 464), and "Let them say what they will" ("The Embankments of Faith," WND-1, 626). His unshakable commitment and resolve show him to be a true votary of the Lotus Sutra. Because without this resolute spirit, one cannot battle the negative forces inherent in life personified by the devil king of the sixth heaven.

President Toda, too, took an uncompromising stance toward evil priests and other negative influences—people whose lives were ruled by the workings of the devil king of the sixth heaven. And those committing the gravest offense were the corrupt and degenerate members of the Nichiren Shoshu priesthood—the very ones who were supposed to be upholding Nichiren's teaching. He never minced words with such priests, letting them know in no uncertain terms just what he thought of them. He castigated them for having turned their backs on Nichiren's teaching during World War II and for insulting and deserting President Makiguchi at the crucial moment.

The behavior of those who would undermine and destroy the correct teaching can never be condoned. This spirit is an essential aspect of Nichiren Buddhism.

Defeating Fundamental Darkness Through the Power of Faith

The great demon of fundamental darkness can even enter the bodies of bodhisattvas who have reached near-perfect enlightenment and prevent them from attaining the Lotus Sutra's blessing of perfect enlightenment. How easily can he then obstruct those in any lower stage of practice! (WND-1, 496)

Up to this point, Nichiren Daishonin has clarified that the "evil friends" or negative influences that obstruct people's faith in the Lotus Sutra are personified by "men of wisdom possessed by evil demons" and that these influences are actually the workings of the devil king of the sixth heaven.

But if they are people of wisdom, how then can the devil king of the sixth heaven take possession of them? The reason is that they are not defeated from without but from within; they are defeated by the devilish nature known as fundamental darkness innate in life. In another writing, Nichiren states, "Fundamental darkness manifests itself as the devil king of the sixth heaven" ("The Treatment of Illness," WND-1, 1113).

All people have fundamental darkness in their lives. The Daishonin says that it also exists in the lives of Buddhas. Therefore, even in the case of bodhisattvas at the stage of near-perfect enlightenment, the fundamental darkness in their lives can activate the function of the devil king and prevent them from reaching the stage of perfect enlightenment, or Buddhahood. If this is so for bodhisattvas at this stage, then it must hold true all the more for us ordinary people.

The devil king of the sixth heaven is the fundamental negative impulse that resides in the depths of people's lives. This devilish nature or negativity gives rise to the desire to control others or even take others' lives and causes destruction and war. To conquer this devilish nature, we need to bring forth our inherent Dharma nature, or fundamental nature of enlightenment,[42] which exists along with our fundamental darkness. Toward that end, it is vital that we continue striving in faith, practicing Nichiren Buddhism ourselves and sharing it with others.

In one of his lectures, President Toda commented on the devil king of the sixth heaven being inscribed on the Gohonzon: "The devil king of the sixth heaven is depicted on the Gohonzon. So when we pray to the Gohonzon, the devil king obeys the Gohonzon. The devil king will issue orders keeping the leaders of his devilish forces in check. The original enlightened potential of the devil king is manifested through the Gohonzon. Indeed, all entities depicted on the Gohonzon display their innate dignified attributes when illuminated by Nam-myoho-renge-kyo."

Continuing, he went so far as to say, "The devil king of the sixth heaven then changes for the first time into an entity that helps and benefits others." These remarks embody a profound principle that is at the heart of Nichiren Buddhism.

In *The Record of the Orally Transmitted Teachings,* Nichiren states, "The single word 'belief' is the sharp sword with which one confronts and overcomes fundamental darkness or ignorance" (pp.119–20). As these words indicate, the sharp sword of faith allows us to defeat fundamental darkness. This means persevering and challenging ourselves in faith throughout our lives. It means seeing devils for what they are and constantly bringing forth the fundamental nature of enlightenment from within. Through faith that grows stronger day by day and month after month (see "On Persecutions Befalling the Sage," WND-1, 997), we can, at a fundamental level, win over the workings of our darkness or ignorance.

This is also why it is important to have a mentor in faith to give us correct direction. President Toda often told me: "If you are a true disciple of mine, then you must carry on in my footsteps to the end without fearing hardship. You must never be defeated." Day after day, I have fought on, just as my mentor instructed, and I have overcome all devilish functions.

The mentor-disciple spirit is a powerful driving force for defeating any form of devilish function. By contrast, those who lose sight of this spirit and forget their debt of gratitude to their mentor will become increasingly consumed by fundamental darkness until they eventually turn into subjects or followers of the devil king.

To remain fearless no matter what happens, to refuse to succumb to darkness or negativity—this is the spirit of faith needed to battle devilish functions. With this spirit, we can definitely prevail. This is the secret to a victorious life.

Overcoming the Three Obstacles and Four Devils in Order To Attain Buddhahood

The devil king of the sixth heaven takes possession of the bodies of wives and children, and causes them to lead their husbands or parents astray. He also possesses the sovereign in order to threaten the votary of the Lotus Sutra, or possesses fathers and mothers, and makes

them reproach their filially devoted children. (WND-1, 496)

Nichiren Daishonin states that workings of the devil king also manifest as opposition from parents, from partners and children, and even from the secular authorities, in order to obstruct the practice of those who uphold the Lotus Sutra. No doubt the lines "The devil king ... possesses fathers and mothers, and makes them reproach their filially devoted children" (WND-1, 496) struck a powerful chord with the Ikegami brothers. This was because their predicament was brought about in large part by the scheming of the priest Ryokan of Gokuraku-ji, a temple in Kamakura, and other negative influences. In addition, Nichiren says that their father, Yasumitsu, had succumbed to the influence of the devil king of the sixth heaven, who was attacking them in a bid to obstruct their faith. Therefore, the Daishonin tells the brothers that they must discern the true nature of these devilish forces and must on no account acquiesce to them.

In "Letter to the Brothers" and many other writings, Nichiren offers unstinting guidance and encouragement to disciples being pressured to choose between faith and filial devotion. True filial devotion is to attain Buddhahood by following the supreme Buddhist teaching and to guide one's parents to eternal happiness.

The Ikegami brothers carried through with faith exactly as the Daishonin taught and splendidly triumphed over the obstacles confronting them.

Today, as the world grapples with an unprecedented economic crisis, obstacles of all kinds appear. Therefore, it is crucial that we win in our hearts, chanting Nam-myoho-renge-kyo through everything. When we make "faith for overcoming hardships" the foundation of our lives, we can definitely transform the negative into something positive in accord with the principle of "changing poison into medicine." We can also definitely transform our karma, attain Buddhahood in this lifetime and open the path of kosen-rufu ever wider.

Let's mark the eightieth anniversary of the Soka Gakkai's founding with each person showing actual proof of great victory.

This lecture was originally published in the April 2009 issue of the Daibyakurenge, *the Soka Gakkai's monthly study journal.*

NOTES

[1] Eighty thousand teachings: Also, the "eighty thousand sacred teachings" and the "eighty-four thousand teachings." The entire body of teachings expounded by Shakyamuni Buddha during his lifetime. The figure is frequently given as eighty-four thousand. These figures are

not intended to be literal but are simply used to indicate a large number.

[2] Twelve divisions of the scriptures: A classification of Shakyamuni Buddha's teachings according to their content and style of presentation. This is often used in the same sense as "the eighty thousand teachings," indicating the entire body of the Buddha's teachings.

[3] Ten directions: The entire universe, all physical space. Specifically, the ten directions are the eight directions of the compass, plus up and down. Buddhist scriptures refer to the existence of Buddha lands in all directions throughout the universe, each with its own Buddha. The expression *the Buddhas of the ten directions* in the sutras indicates these Buddhas.

[4] A metaphor that appears in "Former Affairs of King Wonderful Adornment," the 27th chapter of the Lotus Sutra, indicating that it is as rare for a person to encounter the Buddha and his teachings as it is for a one-eyed turtle to find a floating sandalwood log with a hollow just the right size to hold him.

[5] A metaphor for an impossible action. In Indian cosmology, Mount Sumeru is a

towering peak that stands at the center of the world.

[6] Devil king of the sixth heaven: Also, "devil king" or "heavenly devil." The king of devils, who dwells in the highest or the sixth heaven of the world of desire. He is also named Freely Enjoying Things Conjured by Others, the king who makes free use of the fruits of others' efforts for his own pleasure. Served by innumerable minions, he obstructs Buddhist practice and delights in sapping the life force of other beings. The devil king is a manifestation of the fundamental darkness or ignorance inherent in life.

[7] Twenty-five realms of existence: Subdivisions of the threefold world in which living beings repeat the cycle of birth and death—fourteen realms in the world of desire, seven in the world of form and four in the world of formlessness. All twenty-five fall into the category of the "six paths," or lower worlds.

[8] Six paths: Hell and the realms of hungry spirits, animals, *asuras,* human beings and heavenly beings. "Path" here means the path a life follows in the process of transmigration; it also indicates a realm

or state of existence. The six paths were viewed traditionally as realms within which unenlightened beings repeatedly transmigrate. When regarded as conditions of life, they indicate states of delusion or suffering.

[9] Three evil paths: The lowest three of the six paths. They are hell and the realms of hungry spirits and animals.

[10] Flower Garland Sutra: Also known as the Avatamsaka Sutra. The basic text of the Flower Garland school of Buddhism. According to this sutra, Shakyamuni expounded the teaching it contains immediately after he attained enlightenment under the bodhi tree in the kingdom of Magadha, India.

[11] Tu-shun (557–640), Chih-yen (602–68), Fa-tsang (643–712) and Ch'eng-kuan (738–839) were, respectively, the founder and successive patriarchs of the Flower Garland (Hua-yen) school in China.

[12] Chia-hsiang (549–623) is sometimes regarded as the founder of the Three Treatises (San-lun) school in China, while Seng-ch'üan (n.d.) was an early practitioner of the same school.

[13]   Hsüan-tsang (602–64) and Tz'u-en (632–82) are regarded as the founders of the Dharma Characteristics (Fa-hsiang) school in China.

[14]   Shan-wu-wei (637–735), Chin-kang-chih (671–741) and Pu-k'ung (705–74) were priests who disseminated Esoteric Buddhism in China and were venerated by the True Word school in Japan.

[15]   Kobo (774–835) was the founder of the True Word school in Japan. Jikaku (794–864) and Chisho (814–91) were priests of the Tendai school in Japan.

[16]   Bodhidharma (n.d.) and Hui-k'o (487–593) were, respectively, the founder and second patriarch of the Zen (Ch'an) school in China.

[17]   Shan-tao (613–81) and Honen (1133–1212) were, respectively, the third patriarch of the Pure Land (Ching-t'u) school in China and the founder of the Pure Land school in Japan.

[18]   LSOC, 233.

[19]   Fundamental darkness: Also, fundamental ignorance or primal ignorance. The most deeply rooted illusion inherent in life, said to give rise to all other illusions. Fundamental darkness means the inability to see or recognize the truth,

particularly the true nature of one's own life. Nichiren Daishonin interprets fundamental darkness as ignorance of the ultimate Law, or ignorance of the fact that one's life is essentially a manifestation of the Law, which he identifies as Nam-myoho-renge-kyo.

[20] Near-perfect enlightenment: The fifty-first of the fifty-two stages of bodhisattva practice. The stage nearly equal to the Buddha's perfect enlightenment, the last stage before a bodhisattva attains Buddhahood.

[21] Perfect enlightenment: The highest of the fifty-two stages of bodhisattva practice, or Buddhahood.

[22] Three obstacles and four devils: Various obstacles and hindrances to the practice of Buddhism. They are listed in the Nirvana Sutra and Nagarjuna's *Treatise on the Great Perfection of Wisdom*. The three obstacles are: (1) the obstacle of earthly desires; (2) the obstacle of karma; and (3) the obstacle of retribution. The four devils are: (1) the hindrance of the five components; (2) the hindrance of earthly desires; (3) the hindrance of death; and (4) the hindrance of the devil king.

[23]   Yubari Coal Miners Union Incident: A case of blatant religious discrimination and persecution in which miners in Yubari, Hokkaido, were threatened with losing their jobs because they belonged to the Soka Gakkai.

[24]   Osaka Incident: The occasion when SGI President Ikeda, then Soka Gakkai youth division chief of staff, was arrested and wrongfully charged with election law violations in a House of Councillor's by-election in Osaka in 1957. At the end of the court case, which dragged on for almost five years, he was exonerated of all charges.

[25]   Lessening karmic retribution: The principle that, through Buddhist faith and practice, one can reduce the effects of negative karma created in the past.

[26]   This is based on recent research. Previously, it was thought that members of the Ikegami clan occupied important positions in the Office of Construction and Repairs of the Kamakura military government, but this now appears not to have been the case.

[27]   Ikegami Yasumitsu: A loyal follower of Ryokan. Yasumitsu strenuously opposed the beliefs of his sons, Munenaka and

Munenaga. He disowned the elder Munenaka twice, in 1275 and again in 1277. In doing so, Yasumitsu was in effect trying to provoke a rift between the two sons, tempting the younger Munenaga to trade his beliefs for the right to inherit his father's estate. Supported by Nichiren's guidance and encouragement, however, Munenaga upheld his faith together with his brother, and in 1278, after twenty-two years of practice, their united efforts finally led their father to accept faith in Nichiren's teachings.

[28] Ryokan (1217–1303): Also known as Ninsho. A priest of the True Word Precepts school in Japan. In 1267, with the patronage of the Hojo clan, Ryokan became chief priest of Gokuraku-ji, a temple of the True Word Precepts school in Kamakura. Hostile to Nichiren, he used his connections with powerful figures to harass Nichiren and his followers and was behind numerous persecutions that befell them.

[29] Three poisons—greed, anger and foolishness: The fundamental evils inherent in life that give rise to human suffering. In Nagarjuna's *Treatise on the*

Great Perfection of Wisdom, the three poisons are regarded as the source of all illusions and earthly desires. The three poisons are so called because they pollute people's lives and work to prevent them from turning their hearts and minds to goodness.

[30] From *"Hyaku rokka sho"* (The One Hundred and Six Comparisons); not included in WND, vols.1 and 2.

[31] Saha world: Our present world, which is filled with suffering. Often translated as the world of endurance. In Sanskrit, *saha* means "the earth"; it derives from a root meaning "to bear" or "to endure." In this context, the saha world indicates a world in which people must endure suffering. It is also defined as an impure land, a land defiled by earthly desires and illusions, in contrast with a pure land.

[32] Five impurities: Also, "five defilements." Impurity of the age, of desire, of living beings, of thought (or view) and of life span. This term appears in "Expedient Means," the second chapter of the Lotus Sutra. (1) Impurity of the age includes repeated disruptions of the social or natural environment. (2) Impurity of

desire is the tendency to be ruled by the five delusive inclinations, such as greed, anger, foolishness, arrogance and doubt. (3) Impurity of living beings is the physical and spiritual decline of human beings. (4) Impurity of thought, or view, is the prevalence of wrong views such as the "five false views." (5) Impurity of life span is the shortening of the life spans of living beings.

[33] See Daisaku Ikeda and Yasushi Inoue, *Letters of Four Seasons,* translated by Richard L. Gage (Tokyo: Kodansha International, 1980), p.35.

[34] Ibid., 44.

[35] Threefold world: The world of unenlightened beings who transmigrate within the six paths (from hell through the realm of heavenly beings). The threefold world consists of, in ascending order, the world of desire, the world of form and the world of formlessness. (1) The world of desire comprises the four evil paths (hell and the realms of hungry spirits, animals and *asuras*), the four continents surrounding Mount Sumeru (that contain the realm of human beings) and the first six divisions of heaven (the lowest part of the realm

of heavenly beings). The beings in this world are ruled by various physical cravings. (2) The world of form consists of the four meditation heavens, which are further divided into eighteen heavens (sixteen or seventeen according to other explanations). The beings here are free from desires, cravings and appetites, but still have physical form and thus are subject to certain material restrictions. (3) The world of formlessness comprises the four realms of Boundless Empty Space, Boundless Consciousness, Nothingness and Neither Thought Nor No Thought. Here beings are free from desires and from physical form with its material restrictions.

[36] Summit of the world of desire: The devil king of the sixth heaven is said to dwell in the highest or the sixth heaven of the world of desire, the lowest division of the threefold world. See also footnote 35.

[37] Ten kinds of troops: Also, the ten kinds of troops of the devil king or the ten armies of the devil king. They represent ten kinds of hindrances. Nagarjuna's *Treatise on the Great Perfection of Wisdom* lists them as: (1) greed; (2) care and

worry; (3) hunger and thirst; (4) love of pleasure; (5) drowsiness and languor; (6) fear; (7) doubt and regret; (8) anger; (9) preoccupation with wealth and fame; and (10) arrogance and contempt for others.

[38] Three powerful enemies: Three types of arrogant people who persecute those who propagate the Lotus Sutra in the evil age after Shakyamuni Buddha's death, described in the twenty-line verse section of "Encouraging Devotion," the 13th chapter of the Lotus Sutra. The Great Teacher Miao-lo (711–82) of China summarizes them as arrogant lay people, arrogant priests and arrogant false sages.

[39] "The Life Span of the Thus Come One," the 16th chapter of Lotus Sutra, speaks of the poison penetrating deeply (see LSOC, 269), in the parable of the skilled physician and his sick children. One day, when the physician is away from home, his children mistakenly drink poison. As a result, they lose their true minds and cannot bring themselves to take the medicine that their father has prepared for them.

[40] Earlier in "Letter to the Brothers," Nichiren writes: "The Great Teacher T'ien-t'ai [of China] commented, 'If they encounter an evil friend, they will lose their true mind.' 'True mind' means the mind that believes in the Lotus Sutra, while 'lose' means to betray one's faith in the Lotus Sutra and transfer one's allegiance to other sutras" (WND-1, 495).

[41] Twenty-line verse section: The concluding verse section of "Encouraging Devotion," the 13th chapter of the Lotus Sutra, in which countless multitudes of bodhisattvas vow to Shakyamuni Buddha to propagate the sutra in the evil age after his passing. It is called the twenty-line verse section because the Chinese translation consists of twenty lines.

[42] Fundamental nature of enlightenment: The original nature of the Buddha's ultimate enlightenment with which life is originally endowed. Corresponds to the world of Buddhahood or the Buddha nature.

CHAPTER 5

"LETTER TO THE BROTHERS"—PART 2 OF 3

PURSUE THE GREAT PATH OF MENTOR AND DISCIPLE, REGARDING HARDSHIPS AS A BADGE OF HONOR

Passage for Study in This Lecture

We, who now believe in the correct teaching, in the past once committed the offense of persecuting its practitioners, and therefore are destined to fall into a terrible hell in the future. The blessings gained by practicing the correct teaching, however, are so great that by meeting minor sufferings in this life we can change the karma that destines us to suffer terribly in the future. As the sutra[1] says, one's past slander may cause one to suffer various retributions, such as being born into a poor family or a family with erroneous views or being persecuted by one's sovereign. A "family with erroneous views" means one that slanders the correct teaching, and "persecution by one's sovereign" means to live under the reign of an evil ruler. These are the two sufferings confronting you now...

Both of you have continued believing in the Lotus Sutra; thus you are now ridding yourselves of your grave offenses from the past. For example, the flaws in iron come to the surface when it is forged. Put into flames, a rock simply turns to ashes, but gold becomes pure gold. This trial, more than anything else, will prove your faith genuine, and the ten demon daughters[2] of the Lotus Sutra will surely protect you. The demon who appeared to test the boy Snow Mountains was actually Shakra. The dove saved by King Shibi was the heavenly king Vaishravana. It is even possible that the ten demon daughters have possessed your parents and are tormenting you in order to test your faith. Any weakness in faith will be a cause for regret. The cart that overturns on the road ahead is a warning to the one behind.

In an age like this no one can help but thirst for the way. You may hate this world, but you cannot escape it. The people of Japan are certain to meet with terrible misfortune in the immediate future. (WND-1, 497)

***

You must grit your teeth and never slacken in your faith. Be as fearless as Nichiren when he acted and spoke out before Hei no Saemon-no-jo. Although theirs was not the path to Buddhahood, the sons of Lord Wada and of the governor of Wakasa,[3] as well as the warriors under Masakado and Sadato,[4] fought to the death to preserve their honor. Death comes to all, even should nothing untoward ever happen. Therefore, you must never be cowardly, or you will become the object of ridicule. (WND-1, 498)

***

When the Thus Come One Shakyamuni was a prince, his father, King Shuddhodana,[5] could not bear losing his only heir and so would not allow him to renounce his royal station. The king kept two thousand soldiers posted at the palace's four gates to prevent him from leaving. Nevertheless, the prince eventually left the palace against his father's will. In all worldly affairs, it is the son's duty to obey his parents, yet on the path to Buddhahood, disobeying

> **one's parents ultimately constitutes filial piety.[6] (WND-1, 499)**

LECTURE

"In making the ascent from a low-lying mountain to a high mountain, you will inevitably have to pass through valleys in between," my mentor, second Soka Gakkai president Josei Toda, once said. He then explained:

> If attaining Buddhahood is compared to reaching the summit of the highest mountain, then the benefit you receive upon first taking faith corresponds merely to scaling a low-lying mountain. Attaining Buddhahood means scaling a far higher mountain. It is vital that you don't lose your way in the valleys you pass through on your journey. These are valleys where the "three obstacles and four devils"[7] vie with one another to attack. You mustn't become drunk on the benefit that you receive upon first taking faith. You mustn't become remiss in your daily Buddhist practice, but always remember that the purpose of faith is to climb out of these valleys.

This was President Toda's guidance to a group of members, most of whom were experiencing the first benefits of practicing Nichiren Buddhism. They had all joined the Soka Gakkai amid the continuing confusion and turmoil of the early postwar years. He was teaching them in a readily accessible way that the true benefit of faith is attaining an unshakable state of absolute happiness. He taught them that in order to reach the highest summit of Buddhahood, they must press onward through the valleys of training and development, which are all ultimately part of our Buddhist practice.

As we traverse these valleys on the way to ascending the highest summit, various obstacles will emerge to hinder our progress. Yet without passing through valleys and climbing steep inclines, we cannot reach the top. The appearance of the three obstacles and four devils shows that we are on the correct path of Buddhist practice.

With President Toda's encouragement and kind face engraved in their hearts, our pioneering members bravely challenged the onslaughts of the three obstacles and four devils and forged an inner state of indestructible happiness. Battling devilish functions is the direct path to attaining Buddhahood in this lifetime. This is a pivotal tenet of Nichiren Buddhism.

In "Letter to the Brothers," Nichiren Daishonin teaches the embattled Ikegami brothers, Munenaka and Munenaga, the essence of faith for defeating obstacles and devilish functions and ultimately attaining Buddhahood. He discusses from three perspectives the reason that Lotus Sutra practitioners encounter hardships and the significance of those hardships.

First, he explains that hardships arise due to the devil king of the sixth heaven[8] harassing practitioners by negatively influencing those around them—including people of wisdom, the ruler, and the practitioners' own parents, partners or children—to prevent them from obtaining enlightenment. I discussed this principle in the previous installment of this series.

Second, Nichiren explains that practitioners encounter hardships because of their own karma from past lifetimes. He clarifies, however, that hardships arising as a result of practicing the Lotus Sutra should in fact be considered a benefit in the form of "lessening one's karmic retribution."[9]

Third, he explains that hardships can also be seen as ordeals devised by the heavenly deities—the protective functions of the universe—to test the strength of a person's faith. As such, hardships represent opportunities to forge and develop one's life with a view toward attaining Buddhahood.

In this installment, I will focus on the second and third perspectives.

Hardships Are Proof of Lessening Karmic Retribution

We, who now believe in the correct teaching, in the past once committed the offense of persecuting its practitioners, and therefore are destined to fall into a terrible hell in the future. The blessings gained by

practicing the correct teaching, however, are so great that by meeting minor sufferings in this life we can change the karma that destines us to suffer terribly in the future. As the sutra says, one's past slander may cause one to suffer various retribution, such as being born into a poor family or a family with erroneous views or being persecuted by one's sovereign. A "family with erroneous views" means one that slanders the correct teaching, and "persecution by one's sovereign" means to live under the reign of an evil ruler. These are the two sufferings confronting you now. (WND-1, 497)

In this section, Nichiren Daishonin explains that although practitioners of the correct teaching of the Lotus Sutra may meet with great hardships as a result of their Buddhist practice, this is actually a benefit because it enables them to lessen their karmic retribution and fundamentally change their karma. For instance, he says, we may have persecuted Lotus Sutra practitioners in a past existence, an offense that would normally destine us "to fall into a terrible hell in the future," but because of the powerful benefit of our Buddhist practice in this lifetime, we can call forth the retribution of great suffering that awaits us in the future and instead experience it in the present in a lesser form.

Nichiren Buddhism—a teaching of changing karma—first recognizes that the cause of all negative karma can be traced to disbelief in and disrespect for the Mystic Law—which is termed "slander of the Law." This clarification of fundamental evil also illuminates that which constitutes fundamental good. If we are to change our karma, a clear understanding of the basic causality of good and evil in life is vital.

One form that this fundamental evil of slander takes is people denigrating the Lotus Sutra, a teaching of universal enlightenment, because they cannot believe that everyone possesses the Buddha nature.[10] Another manifestation of slander is people maligning and attacking the sutra's votary, who is dedicated to helping others reveal their Buddha nature. Fundamental good, therefore, is the exact opposite—namely, upholding and preserving the Lotus Sutra's teachings and fighting together with the votary of the Lotus Sutra against this most basic evil—that of denying people's Buddha nature.

Receiving the painful retributions we were destined to incur in the future in a lesser form in the present through the "blessings obtained by protecting the Law"[11] (WND-1, 497) is the heart of the Buddhist principle of "lessening one's karmic retribution." By experiencing hardships in the course of practicing the Mystic Law in this life, "the sufferings of hell will vanish instantly" ("Lessening One's Karmic Retribution," WND-1, 199), and then, completely freed from these grave offenses (see "The Opening of the Eyes,"

WND-1, 281), we can realize the sublime life state of Buddhahood. In other words, we can change the inner direction of our lives—moving from the negative cycle of transmigration in the evil paths to the positive cycle of transmigration in the realm of Buddhahood. This is Nichiren's teaching of changing karma.

Consequently, the hardships we experience in the course of our Buddhist practice as a result of the principle of lessening karmic retribution are the benefits or blessings of protecting the Law. They could also be called proof that we are changing karma.

In the above passage from "Letter to the Brothers," Nichiren singles out two of the eight kinds of retribution described in the Parinirvana Sutra as specific examples of "minor sufferings" encountered in this lifetime as a function of lessening karmic retribution. These are the sufferings arising from: (1) being born into a family with erroneous views and (2) falling victim to persecution by one's sovereign. He asserts that both of these reflect the situation faced by the Ikegami brothers.

Nichiren explains that a "family with erroneous views" means a family that slanders the correct teaching of the Lotus Sutra, while "persecution by one's sovereign" means living under the reign of an evil ruler. The latter specifically refers to being born in an age when the ruler and society as a whole persecute the votary of the Lotus Sutra. These circumstances created sufferings or hardships for the Ikegami brothers because of their earnest efforts to propagate the Mystic Law alongside the Daishonin. This fact also proved that the brothers were practicing with the same commitment as their teacher in faith.

***

The Process of Changing Karma Forges and Polishes Our Lives to the Highest Degree

Both of you have continued believing in the Lotus Sutra; thus you are now ridding yourselves of your grave offenses from the past. For example, the flaws in iron come to the surface when it is forged. Put into flames, a rock simply turns to ashes, but gold becomes pure gold. (WND-1, 497)

When iron is repeatedly heated and hammered, impurities that can give rise to brittleness are literally driven out and, as the forging process is continued, the iron becomes even stronger. In the same way, Nichiren Daishonin says, the Ikegami brothers are experiencing retribution in the form of hardships in this lifetime. That is, because of their strong faith, they are drawing forth retribution for past grave offenses and thereby expiating their negative karma.

As this passage indicates, when viewed in terms of the Buddhist principles of lessening karmic retribution and changing karma, hardships take on deeper meaning and come to signify opportunities for forging and developing our faith and our inner state of life.

Elsewhere, Nichiren writes, "Iron, when heated in the flames and pounded, becomes a fine sword" ("Letter from Sado," WND-1, 303). The process of confronting and challenging our karma enables us to polish and strengthen our faith. When we are tested by the fires of karma, we can show our true mettle. If we are irresolute, we will be like ash and crumble, but if we maintain a firm resolve, we will become pure gold, our lives growing ever more radiant.

The supreme purpose of Buddhism is to forge, polish and strengthen our lives. Without polishing and developing, people with ability and talent will not shine their brightest. Without training, people of genuine commitment will not be fostered. By striving wholeheartedly for kosen-rufu, we can transform our negative karma from past existences and bring our lives to shine with the brilliance of a gleaming, unbreakable sword.

Speaking of training and development, on the Soka path of mentor and disciple walked by our first and second presidents, Tsunesaburo Makiguchi and Josei Toda, and in turn by Mr. Toda and me, every day was one of forging and polishing our lives. Mr. Toda was nineteen when he met Mr. Makiguchi. In a diary entry the following year in April 1920, Mr. Toda wrote:

> I must forge myself so that I can take on the great mission of being an asset to my country and a leader of the world, and I must polish myself so that I can carry out that mission ... I will pay no attention to the criticism or derision of my contemporaries; all that matters is that I achieve my goal.[12]

At the time, the young Mr. Toda had just been hired as a temporary substitute teacher at the Nishimachi Elementary School (in present-day Taito Ward, Tokyo), where Mr. Makiguchi was the principal. Having encountered a great mentor in life, he deeply determined to "forge" himself—to polish his character and ability, and to develop himself mentally and physically—so that he could realize a great objective.

When I had my fateful first meeting with Mr. Toda, I, too, was nineteen, and I embarked on the great and noble path of striving with the same commitment as my mentor. Even facing the bitterest adversity, when Mr. Toda's businesses fell into dire financial straits, I gave my all to support and protect him, taking on the full brunt of all criticism from society.

The following entry in my diary from December 1950 expresses my feelings at that challenging time:

> Struggles and hardships!

In their midst, you will develop true humanity.
In their midst, you will forge an iron will.
In their midst, you will know real tears.
In their midst, know that there lies the human revolution.[13]

Many individuals who had been deeply indebted to President Toda abruptly turned on him. Betraying his kindness, they cursed and abused and deserted him. But I did not waver, not in the least. It was an honor to undergo hardships with my mentor. Forging one's life amid adversity is the path to victory. I prayed earnestly that President Toda could lead our movement for kosen-rufu as the Soka Gakkai's second president, and I fought a desperate, all-out struggle to make that happen.

Heavenly Deities Test One's Faith

This trial, more than anything else, will prove your faith genuine, and the ten demon daughters of the Lotus Sutra will surely protect you. The demon who appeared to test the boy Snow Mountains was actually Shakra. The dove saved by King Shibi was the heavenly king Vaishravana. It is even possible that the ten demon daughters have possessed your parents and are tormenting you in order to test your faith. (WND-1, 497)

Next, Nichiren Daishonin assures the Ikegami brothers that their demonstration of genuine faith guarantees the protection of the heavenly deities, who vowed in the Lotus Sutra to safeguard the sutra's practitioners. Having said this, he adds that the heavenly deities at times also seek to test the genuineness of people's faith. This, he says, is like what happened when the god Shakra took the form of a demon to test the seeking spirit of the boy Snow Mountains, or when the heavenly king Vaishravana took the form of a dove to test the compassion of King Shibi.

Based on this principle, Nichiren suggests that the brothers' present ordeal—that of the elder brother being disowned by their father because of his Buddhist practice—is likely an instance of the ten demon daughters influencing the brothers' parents to torment them in order to test their faith.

In other writings as well, Nichiren discusses this principle of heavenly deities creating obstacles to test the faith of practitioners. For example, at the time of the Atsuhara Persecution,[14] farmers who followed Nichiren were cruelly interrogated because of their faith by the powerful official Hei no Saemon.[15] But not one of them recanted his beliefs. Though persecuted by the authorities, they fearlessly continued chanting Nam-myoho-renge-kyo. As soon as the news reached him, Nichiren immediately wrote to Nikko Shonin and other close disciples in a letter titled "Reply to the Sages":

I am sure that the ten demon daughters must have taken possession of Hei no Saemon and induced him to test the faith of these votaries of the Lotus Sutra. It was similar to the way in which the boy Snow Mountains and King Shibi were tested. (WND-2, 831)

In the previous installment, we looked at persecution befalling Lotus Sutra practitioners from the perspective of it being a function of evil demons. Specifically, we saw how the workings of the devil king of the sixth heaven took possession of, or negatively influenced people of wisdom, the ruler and parents to harass practitioners.

Why on earth, then, would heavenly deities such as the ten demon daughters—rightly the protective forces of the universe—take possession of Hei no Saemon and thereby try to test the faith of the farmer followers of Atsuhara? In Buddhism, unremitting faith is the cause for attaining enlightenment, and obstacles are viewed as an inevitable consequence of upholding the correct teaching of the Lotus Sutra. The crux of the matter, therefore, is whether, when great hardships or persecutions arise, we are consumed by fear and abandon our faith or muster our courage and remain steadfast.

If our resolve is weak and we discard our faith, it means we have been defeated by the torments of the devil king of the sixth heaven. But if we win over such painful ordeals with firm resolve and maintain unwavering faith, then in hindsight, we may also say we have passed a test by the heavenly deities. In other words, everything depends on our own heart or resolve. The protection of the heavenly deities is in essence nothing more than the power of our own faith.

President Toda declared:

> The Daishonin writes that he regards Hei no Saemon—an archenemy of Buddhism who has unceasingly harassed him—as a good friend or positive influence for his own Buddhist practice.[16] Never fear enemies! Their onslaughts are all just swirling dark winds that help us perfect ourselves and attain Buddhahood.

This is the lionhearted essence of Nichiren Buddhism. It is crucial that we have a fearless spirit, a fearless resolve.

In his writings, Nichiren frequently cites the line from the Great Teacher Miao-lo[17] of China, "The stronger one's faith, the greater the protection of the gods."[18] The heavenly deities will unfailingly protect Lotus Sutra practitioners whose faith is genuine.

In "Reply to the Sages," which I quoted earlier, Nichiren further explains that the Buddhas Shakyamuni and Many Treasures, as well as the Buddhas of the ten directions and the heavenly deities, made a solemn vow at the assembly where the Lotus Sutra was preached, promising to guard and protect the sutra's votaries (see

WND-2, 831). He also says that based on the principle of "changing poison into medicine,"[19] reward and punishment will be forthcoming where they are deserved.

Truly the heart is what matters most. Our own faith ultimately determines our future victory.

The German poet and novelist Hermann Hesse wrote to the effect that only those who have the courage to fulfill their destinies can be called heroes.[20] Those confident that everything begins with their own inner transformation are people of true courage and heroism and can forge lasting happiness for themselves.

***

Maintaining Steadfast Faith at a Crucial Moment

Any weakness in faith will be a cause for regret. The cart that overturns on the road ahead is a warning to the one behind.

In an age like this no one can help but thirst for the way. You may hate this world, but you cannot escape it. The people of Japan are certain to meet with terrible misfortune in the immediate future. (WND-1, 497)

"Any weakness in faith will be a cause for regret"—we can read these words as an admonition for all who practice Nichiren Buddhism.

Ultimately, everything hinges on whether we can realize how fortunate we are to have encountered "a person who expounds this sutra exactly as the sutra directs" (WND-1, 495), and to strive with this teacher to propagate the Mystic Law. If our faith or resolve is weak at a crucial time, we'll be left with eternal regret.

When we encounter obstacles in the course of our Buddhist practice, we, in fact, find ourselves at a momentous crossroads, a vital juncture that will decide whether we open the gateway to attaining Buddhahood forever through strong faith or close off the path to happiness by forsaking our faith.

Whenever great obstacles confront us, let's challenge them intrepidly, bearing in mind this passage from Nichiren Daishonin's treatise "The Opening of the Eyes": "Although I and my disciples may encounter various difficulties, if we do not harbor doubts in our hearts, we will as a matter of course attain Buddhahood. Do not have doubts simply because heaven does not lend you protection. Do not be discouraged because you do not enjoy an easy and secure existence in this life. This is what I have taught my disciples morning and evening, and yet they begin to harbor doubts and abandon their faith. Foolish men are likely to forget the promises they have made when the crucial moment comes" (WND-1, 283).

Putting the spirit of this passage into action is the eternal lifeline of the SGI. If we keep advancing with these words as our point of reference, our faith will shine with indestructible brilliance.

Based on the spirit of this passage, any time we face hardships is a crucial moment. It is, therefore, essential that we have the dauntless faith to enable us to fight back bravely at such times—for instance, when the three obstacles and four devils strike, when we are challenging ourselves to change our karma or when we are engaged in a win-or-lose struggle for kosen-rufu. We should realize that every day we can learn this spirit of faith from Nichiren's example. We must never be foolish people who cave in at a crucial moment.

If our faith is weak or shallow, or if we are foolish, we will end up drifting along aimlessly like floating weeds, lacking fundamental purpose. Human beings are animals that seek meaning in life. Through this earnest pursuit, it is possible to give infinitely profound meaning to our existence. SGI members can limitlessly deepen their faith and the meaning of their lives, for they are all experts in the art of living and the art of happiness.

In this passage from "Letter to the Brothers," Nichiren further states, "In an age like this no one can help but thirst for the way." These words reflect society at that time, where people were filled with anxiety and uncertainty toward the future. There were repeated famines, epidemics and natural disasters. Certainly such an age would spur thinking people to seek the Buddha way. The more confused and disordered a society becomes, the more people will seek a profound philosophy on which to base their lives. Nichiren Buddhism is truly the Buddhism of the Sun with the power to illuminate the darkness of the evil age of the Latter Day of the Law.

But Japan, far from according Nichiren the respect he deserved, attacked and persecuted him. As a result, his predictions of internal strife and foreign invasion came to pass. The country was plunged into a dire predicament it was helpless to remedy. The inescapable suffering and misery that faced the entire land was a manifestation of what Buddhism terms "general punishment"—punishment that falls upon the people as a whole for slander of the Law. In "Letter to the Brothers," Nichiren declares that this state of affairs was self-evident given the recent events that had taken place—namely, internal strife in the form of the February Disturbance[21] (in 1272) and the Mongol invasion[22] (in 1274).

Especially after the first Mongol invasion, great anxiety spread throughout Japan as the entire country engaged in preparations for a surely imminent second invasion. A passage in "Letter to the Brothers" vividly captures the fear that gripped those who went off to confront the Mongol forces: "They had to leave behind their aged parents, small children, young wives, and cherished homes to go out and defend a sea to no avail. If they see clouds on the horizon, they imagine them to be the enemy's banners. If they see fishing boats, they think them Mongol warships and are paralyzed with fear" (WND-1, 497–98).

The sufferings of war are the same in any age. They are marked by painful partings from family and loved ones, and living with the constant knowledge that death may come at any moment. The ordinary people always suffer the most in war. Therefore, war must be prevented at all costs. This is the eternal cry of Buddhists.

Nichiren says of the mood prevalent among people in society, "Though still alive, they feel as if they were in the world of asuras"[23] (WND-1, 498). In one respect, his struggle was to transform such a society into one in which all people could enjoy peace and happiness.

At any rate, the responsibility for the situation causing the people immense suffering lay with the country's ruler, who had sided with unscrupulous and ill-intentioned individuals to persecute Nichiren, a person of the greatest good. Nichiren keenly observes that ultimately the Ikegami brothers were being treated harshly by their father because the ruler had been led astray by evil priests and had become an enemy of the Lotus Sutra (see WND-1, 498).

Buddhism is about winning. Nichiren writes: "You must ... see for yourselves the blessings of the Lotus Sutra. I, Nichiren, will also emphatically call on the heavenly gods" (WND-1, 498). He powerfully urges the two brothers to join him in showing everyone the truth of the great teaching they uphold through their united prayers and solidarity as mentor and disciple.

Nichiren consistently teaches these cherished disciples to boldly confront devilish functions—negative forces—and to always take the offensive in this struggle. If one is passive or fearful, such negative forces will only grow stronger. He instructs them, "You must never be cowardly" (WND-1, 498). Mr. Toda once also said quite sternly: "What can the fainthearted who shun difficulties possibly accomplish? I'm sure none of my disciples fit that description." He also declared: "The Soka Gakkai is an organization of lions, a gathering of lions. We have no use for cowards!"

***

"You Must Grit Your Teeth and Never Slacken in Your Faith"

You must grit your teeth and never slacken in your faith. Be as fearless as Nichiren when he acted and spoke out before Hei no Saemon-no-jo. Although theirs was not the path to Buddhahood, the sons of Lord Wada and of the governor of Wakasa, as well as the warriors under Masakado and Sadato, fought to the death to preserve their honor. Death comes to

all, even should nothing untoward ever happen. Therefore, you must never be cowardly, or you will become the object of ridicule. (WND-1, 498)

Nichiren Daishonin repeatedly encourages the Ikegami brothers, who were experiencing adversity because of their faith, by writing to them such passages as: "You must neither show nor feel any fear"; and "Never slacken in your faith" (WND-1, 498).

The purpose of our faith is to establish a serene state of happiness that nothing can destroy. Through his encouragement, therefore, Nichiren no doubt was urging the brothers to view their present struggles as opportunities to strengthen their character in order to remain undaunted amid any hardship.

Nichiren Buddhism is a teaching of mentor and disciple. If the mentor is a lion king, the disciples must also be lion kings. The mentor thus calls on his disciples to learn from and follow his example. As indicated by the statement, "Be as fearless as Nichiren when he acted and spoke out before Hei no Saemon-no-jo," Nichiren instructs the brothers to persevere in faith and fight with the same resolute spirit he has shown in his struggles.

Here, mention of Nichiren's conduct toward Hei no Saemon refers to the two occasions when he remonstrated with this powerful figure—at the time of the Tatsunokuchi Persecution in September 1271 and again after being pardoned from exile to Sado in April 1274. At the time of his arrest, Nichiren declared with towering conviction to Hei no Saemon: "Nichiren is the pillar and beam of Japan. Doing away with me is toppling the pillar of Japan!" ("The Selection of the Time," WND-1, 579). And after returning to Kamakura from Sado, he bluntly told Hei no Saemon. "Even if it seems that, because I was born in the ruler's domain, I follow him in my actions, I will never follow him in my heart" (WND-1, 579). He is referring specifically to the authoritarian regime of the Kamakura military government: while he might be physically forced to submit to its dictates, his spirit can never be forced to do so.

These were defiant statements, free of the slightest fear or servility. Similarly, disciples who embrace Nichiren's spirit and model their own actions on his example also have nothing to fear. By following Nichiren's lead and joining in his struggle, they can bring forth infinite strength and potential.

Incidentally, the latter quote from Nichiren's writing "The Selection of the Time" was included in the *Birthright of Man,* a collection of inspiring quotes on human rights compiled by UNESCO, the United Nations Educational, Scientific and Cultural Organization.[24]

Returning to "Letter to the Brothers," Nichiren also writes, "Death comes to all, even should nothing untoward ever happen." This quote has left a deep impression on me in the course of my more than half century of Buddhist practice.

As human beings, we will all have to die sometime. No one can escape this reality. The important thing is how we use this unique and precious existence. In a letter addressed to his youthful disciple Nanjo Tokimitsu,[25] Nichiren writes: "Since death is the same in either case, you should be willing to offer your life for the Lotus Sutra. Think of this offering as a drop of dew rejoining the ocean, or a speck of dust returning to the earth" ("The Dragon Gate," WND-1, 1003).

In a similar vein, Mr. Toda said: "Death is momentary, but life is eternal. The members of the Soka Gakkai have now raised the great banner of kosen-rufu. This is truly the time of kosen-rufu. We must be courageous."[26]

With these words, Mr. Toda rose up alone, shouldering the banner of the propagation of the Mystic Law and accomplished a Soka Gakkai membership of 750,000 households.

He also once said to us youth division members: "When you [die and] take your seat alongside Shakyamuni's disciples at Eagle Peak,[27] if everyone there ridicules you, saying, 'The youth of the Latter Day are a cowardly lot,' then you will be unworthy of the title of Bodhisattvas of the Earth."[28]

These strict words of encouragement were in keeping with Nichiren's injunction, "You must

never be cowardly, or you will become the object of ridicule."
The Meaning of True Filial Devotion

When the Thus Come One Shakyamuni was a prince, his father, King Shuddhodana, could not bear losing his only heir and so would not allow him to renounce his royal station. The king kept two thousand soldiers posted at the palace's four gates to prevent him from leaving. Nevertheless, the prince eventually left the palace against his father's will. In all worldly affairs, it is the son's duty to obey his parents, yet on the path to Buddhahood, disobeying one's parents ultimately constitutes filial piety. (WND-1, 499)

After explaining, in light of various Buddhist teachings, the importance of maintaining unwavering faith, Nichiren Daishonin offers further encouragement to drive home his point, citing several historical anecdotes. He does this because he is especially worried about the faith of the younger brother, Munenaga.

Nichiren always poured his whole life into encouraging his followers, not stopping until he was sure they understood his message from the depths of their lives and were ready to rise up and take action themselves. Being absolutely determined that they not be defeated by devilish functions and wishing to ensure that they stood up as genuine disciples, Nichiren guided and instructed them with wisdom and compassion—sometimes gently and patiently, sometimes strictly and directly.

A teacher or mentor in the realm of Buddhism is one who has battled and triumphed over devilish functions. Disciples, meanwhile, learn the essentials of faith from the mentor so that they can begin to do the same. Buddhism as a teaching of the oneness of mentor and disciple is only complete when disciples respond to the mentor's teaching and spur themselves to take action.

Wanting to see the Ikegami brothers win over the obstacle confronting them, Nichiren relates at length various pertinent historical anecdotes and tales. First, he cites the story of Po I and Shu Ch'i,[29] who since ancient times have been held up in the East as exemplars of filial virtue (see WND-1, 498–99). Next, referring to how both Shakyamuni and the Great Teacher T'ien-t'ai[30] faced obstruction from their parents, as well, he underscores the Buddhist teaching that one must not give in to the wishes of a parent aimed at hindering one's practice (see WND-1, 499). Further, citing stories relating to the Japanese imperial princes Nintoku and Uji,[31] the brothers Pure Storehouse and Pure Eye[32] who appear in the Lotus Sutra, and a hermit and his assistant[33] in ancient India, Nichiren repeatedly emphasizes the need for the Ikegami brothers to unite in spirit (see WND-1, 499–500).

Of these many examples, the story of Shakyamuni leaving home to pursue a religious life against the wishes of his father, King Shuddhodana, carries an especially important message for the Ikegami brothers who, agonizingly, had to choose between faith or filial duty.

Faith and filial devotion are normally not in opposition, so there's no need to choose one at the expense of the other. In fact, Nichiren Buddhism teaches the importance of filial devotion—being a good son or daughter to one's parents—and also clarifies what filial devotion really means.

Nichiren writes, "In all worldly affairs, it is the son's duty to obey his parents, yet on the path to Buddhahood, disobeying one's parents ultimately constitutes filial piety" (WND-1, 499). In this context, our attaining Buddhahood becomes the supreme expression of filial devotion. He further states, "Not only will they [those who hear the Lotus Sutra] themselves attain Buddhahood, but also their fathers and mothers will attain Buddhahood in their present forms" ("What It Means to Hear the Buddha Vehicle for the First Time," WND-2, 744).

Some of our members are also striving earnestly in their Buddhist practice and activities for kosen-rufu without the support or understanding of their parents. But there is no need to fret, to be impatient or to try to force Buddhism on them. As long as just one person in a family is practicing sincerely, then the whole family is assured of enjoying lasting success and prosperity through that one person's pervasive influence.

In an essay titled "Precepts for Youth," President Toda wrote: "Our struggle is one that requires that we develop compassion for all living beings. Many youth seem not to love even their parents. How, then, can they possibly hope to love others? The effort to overcome the coldness and indifference in our own lives and attain the same state of compassion as the Buddha is the essence of human revolution."[34]

Unless we have the spirit to treasure our own parents, we can neither achieve our human revolution nor transform society. I fully share these sentiments of my mentor.

As he recounts the different anecdotes, Nichiren pauses to praise the Ikegami brothers for uniting despite their father's attempts to divide them, saying, "Could there ever be a more wonderful story than your own?" (WND-1, 499). In other words, he is saying that their story will live on with unrivaled brilliance into the future.

Similarly, the lives of all those who stood up resolutely as Nichiren's disciples and enacted powerful dramas of faith in which they triumphed over devilish functions are also "wonderful stories" that will endure into future generations. Indeed, the experience of the Ikegami brothers who, through unity and perseverance in faith, not only overcame two instances of disownment but could eventually even lead their father to faith in Nichiren Buddhism has been a source of immeasurable hope for people of later times. Likewise, no one can imagine what an immense source of inspiration the diverse experiences in faith of our members today will be for those of future generations. Each person leaving behind stories of victory—this is the purpose of the path of mentor and disciple.

We cannot defeat devilish functions if we allow ourselves to be ruled by ego. The way to build a solid and unshakable self is to stand up with the same spirit and commitment as the teacher or leader of kosen-rufu. Those who can find this supreme path of happiness within the depths of their lives will never be defeated.

Walt Whitman writes in his "Song of the Open Road":

Henceforth I ask not good-fortune,
I myself am good-fortune,...

The earth, that is sufficient,
I do not want the constellations any
nearer,[35]

There is no need to try and capture distant stars from the sky, for the source of all victory lies within.

Mr. Toda once said to me: "Daisaku, don't be deterred by insults and criticisms that resound like the din of yapping dogs. Don't let yourself be swayed by anything so trivial. Walk the path of heroes. Walk the path of the great. What we're undergoing now is but a tiny fraction of the obstacles encountered by the Daishonin, whose teachings we uphold."

I have striven for more than sixty years with this determination. Great hardships are the badge of honor of those who walk the noble path of mentor and disciple. It is now my hope that many youthful successors will continue along this great path of Soka.

This lecture was originally published in the May 2009 issue of the Daibyakurenge, *the Soka Gakkai's monthly study journal.*

NOTES

[1] Nichiren Daishonin, here, is referring to a Chinese version of the Nirvana Sutra, translated by Fa-hsien and Buddhabhadra around 417. It describes eight kinds of suffering: (1) to be despised, (2) to be cursed with an ugly appearance, (3) to be poorly clad, (4) to be poorly fed, (5) to seek wealth in vain, (6) to be born to an impoverished and lowly family, (7) to be

born to a family with erroneous views and (8) to be persecuted by the sovereign.

[2] Ten demon daughters: Ten female protective deities who appear in the Lotus Sutra in "Dharani," the sutra's 26th chapter. They vow to guard and protect the sutra's votaries, saying that they will inflict punishment on any who trouble the sutra's practitioners.

[3] Lord Wada is Wada Yoshimori (1147–1213), a military official of the Kamakura regime, who was tricked into fighting against the Hojo clan and whose entire family was wiped out. The governor of Wakasa is Miura Yasumura (d. 1247), who was related to the Hojo by marriage, but was accused of treason; he and his entire family lost their lives in battle.

[4] Masakado is Taira no Masakado (d. 940), a warrior who wielded power in eastern Japan, and Sadato is Abe no Sadato (1019–62), the head of a powerful family in northeastern Japan. They both were killed in a battle with the imperial forces.

[5] King Shuddhodana: A king of Kapilavastu in northern India. Shuddhodana originally opposed his son Shakyamuni's desire to renounce the secular world and lead a religious life, but when Shakyamuni

returned to his home Kapilavastu after his awakening, Shuddhodana converted to his teachings.

[6] This passage is followed by the explanation: "[A sutra] explains the essence of filial piety: 'By renouncing one's obligations and entering the Buddhist life one can truly repay those obligations in full.' That is, in order to enter the true way, one leaves one's home against one's parents' wishes and attains Buddhahood. Then one can truly repay one's debt of gratitude to them" (WND-1, 499).

[7] Three obstacles and four devils: Various obstacles and hindrances to the practice of Buddhism. The three obstacles are (1) the obstacle of earthly desires, (2) the obstacle of karma and (3) the obstacle of retribution. The four devils are (1) the hindrance of the five components, (2) the hindrance of earthly desires, (3) the hindrance of death and (4) the hindrance of the devil king.

[8] Devil king of the sixth heaven: Also, "devil king" or "heavenly devil." The king of devils, who dwells in the highest or the sixth heaven of the world of desire, who makes free use of the fruits of others' efforts for his own pleasure. Served by

innumerable minions, he obstructs Buddhist practice and delights in sapping the life force of other beings. The devil king is a personification of the negative tendency to force others to one's will at any cost.

[9] Lessening one's karmic retribution: This term, which literally means, "transforming the heavy and receiving it lightly," appears in the Nirvana Sutra. "Heavy" indicates negative karma accumulated over countless past lifetimes. As a benefit of protecting the correct teaching of Buddhism, we can experience relatively light karmic retribution in this lifetime, thereby expiating heavy karma that ordinarily would adversely affect us not only in this lifetime but over many lifetimes to come.

[10] Buddha nature: The internal cause or potential for attaining Buddhahood.

[11] In "Letter to the Brothers," Nichiren cites the Parinirvana Sutra, "It is due to the blessings obtained by protecting the Law that they can diminish in this lifetime their suffering and retribution" (WND-1, 497).

[12] Josei Toda, *Wakaki hi no shuki gokuchu-ki* (The Diaries of My Youth and My

Imprisonment) (Tokyo: Seiga Shobo, 1970), p.86.

[13] Daisaku Ikeda, *A Youthful Diary: One Man's Journey From the Beginning of Faith to Worldwide Leadership for Peace* (Santa Monica, California: World Tribune Press, 2006), p.67.

[14] Atsuhara Persecution: A series of threats and acts of violence against followers of Nichiren in Atsuhara Village, in Fuji District of Suruga Province, Japan, starting around 1275 and continuing until around 1283. In 1279, twenty farmers, all believers, were arrested on false charges. They were interrogated by Hei no Saemon, who demanded that they renounce their faith. Not one of them yielded, however, and Hei no Saemon eventually had three of them executed.

[15] Hei no Saemon (d. 1293): Also known as Hei no Saemonno-jo Yoritsuna. A leading official in the Hojo regency, the de facto ruling body of Japan during the Kamakura period. He collaborated with Ryokan and other leading priests to persecute Nichiren and his followers.

[16] Nichiren writes: "For me, Nichiren, my best allies in attaining Buddhahood are Kagenobu, the priests Ryokan, Doryu,

and Doamidabutsu, and Hei no Saemon and the lord of Sagami. I am grateful when I think that without them I could not have proved myself to be the votary of the Lotus Sutra" ("The Actions of the Votary of the Lotus Sutra," WND-1, 770).

[17] The Great Teacher Miao-lo (711–82): Sixth patriarch of the T'ien-t'ai school in China.

[18] Miao-lo's *Annotations on "Great Concentration and Insight."*

[19] Changing poison into medicine: The principle that earthly desires and suffering can be transformed into benefit and enlightenment by virtue of the power of the Law.

[20] Translated from German. Hermann Hesse, "Eigensinn" (Self Will), in *Gesammelte werke* (Frankfurt am Main: Suhrkamp Taschenbuch Verlag, 1987), vol.10, p.457.

[21] February Disturbance: A revolt that took place within the ruling Hojo clan. It resulted in fighting in Kyoto and Kamakura. In the second month of 1272, Hojo Tokisuke revolted against his younger half brother, the regent Hojo Tokimune, in an attempt to seize power.

Tokisuke and others, including Nagoe Tokiakira and Nagoe Noritoki, were killed on suspicion of involvement.

[22] Mongol invasion: The Mongols had already attempted one invasion in 1274. The second Mongol invasion took place several years later in 1281.

[23] World of *asuras:* Also, realm of asuras, world of animosity or world of anger. The fourth of the Ten Worlds and one of the four evil paths. When viewed as a state of life, the world of asuras is a condition dominated by egoistic pride. Persons in this state are compelled by the need to be superior to others in all things, valuing themselves and devaluing others. Asuras, belligerent spirits or demons in Indian mythology, were regarded as typifying this condition of life.

[24] *Birthright of Man: A Selection of Texts,* edited by Jeanne Hersch (Paris: United Nations Educational, Scientific and Cultural Organization, 1969), p.127.

[25] Nanjo Tokimitsu (1259–1332): A staunch follower of Nichiren and the steward of Ueno Village in the Fuji District of Suruga Province (part of present-day Shizuoka Prefecture). During the

Atsuhara Persecution, he used his influence to protect his fellow practitioners, sheltering some in his home.

[26] Translated from Japanese: Josei Toda, *Toda Josei zenshu* (Collected Writings of Josei Toda) (Tokyo: Seikyo Shimbunsha, 1983), vol.3, p.72.

[27] Eagle Peak: The place where Shakyamuni preached the Lotus Sutra. It symbolizes the Buddha land or the eternal state of Buddhahood.

[28] Translated from Japanese: Josei Toda, *Toda Josei zenshu* (Collected Writings of Josei Toda) (Tokyo: Seikyo Shimbunsha, 1981), vol.1, p.59.

[29] Po I and Shu Ch'i: Brothers of ancient China known for their wisdom. Sons of the ruler Ku-chu. Their father had named the younger brother Shu Ch'i as his successor. But after Ku-chu died, Shu Ch'i refused to ascend the throne, not wanting to pass over his elder sibling.

[30] T'ien-t'ai (538–97): The founder of the T'ien-t'ai school in China. His lectures were compiled in such works as *The Profound Meaning of the Lotus Sutra*, *The Words and Phrases of the Lotus Sutra* and *Great Concentration and Insight*. He spread

the Lotus Sutra in China, and established the doctrine of "three thousand realms in a single moment of life." In "Letter to the Brothers," Nichiren refers to the time when T'ien-t'ai was engaging in meditation on the Lotus Sutra and devilish functions sought to obstruct him by appearing in the form of his deceased parents.

[31] Prince Nintoku and Prince Uji were the sons of Emperor Ojin (late fourth–early fifth century).

[32] Pure Storehouse and Pure Eye: The two sons of King Wonderful Adornment who appear in "Former Affairs of King Wonderful Adornment," the 27th chapter of the Lotus Sutra. Their father was a devout believer in non-Buddhist teachings, but they awakened him to the greatness of Buddhism by displaying supernatural powers.

[33] The hermit had ordered his assistant to stand guard so that he might awaken to the Law, but the latter failed in this task.

[34] *Toda Josei zenshu*, vol.1, p.60.

[35] Walt Whitman, "Song of the Open Road," *Leaves of Grass* (New York: Everyman's Library, 1968), p.125.

CHAPTER 6

"LETTER TO THE BROTHERS"—PART 3 OF 3

THE DISCIPLE'S VICTORY IS THE MENTOR'S GREATEST WISH AND JOY

> Passage for Study in This Lecture
>
> The Great Teacher T'ien-t'ai's[1] *Great Concentration and Insight*[2] is the essence of his lifetime teachings and the heart of the whole spectrum of the Buddha's sacred teachings...
>
> The doctrine of three thousand realms in a single moment of life[3] revealed in the fifth volume of *Great Concentration and Insight* is especially profound. If you propagate it, devils will arise without fail. If they did not, there would be no way of knowing that this is the correct teaching. One passage from the same volume reads: "As practice progresses and understanding grows, the three obstacles and four devils emerge

in confusing form, vying with one another to interfere ... One should be neither influenced nor frightened by them. If one falls under their influence, one will be led into the paths of evil. If one is frightened by them, one will be prevented from practicing the correct teaching." This statement not only applies to me, but also is a guide for my followers. Reverently make this teaching your own, and transmit it as an axiom of faith for future generations.

The three obstacles in this passage are the obstacle of earthly desires, the obstacle of karma, and the obstacle of retribution. The obstacle of earthly desires is the impediments to one's practice that arise from greed, anger, foolishness,[4] and the like; the obstacle of karma is the hindrances presented by one's wife or children; and the obstacle of retribution is the hindrances caused by one's sovereign or parents. Of the four devils, the workings of the devil king of the sixth heaven[5] are of this last kind.

In Japan today, many people claim they have mastered the practice of concentration and insight.[6] But is there anyone who has actually encountered the three obstacles and four devils? The statement "If one falls under their influence, one will be led into the paths of evil" indicates not only the three evil paths but also the worlds of human and heavenly beings, and in general, all of the nine worlds.[7] Therefore, with the exception of the Lotus Sutra, all of the sutras—those of the Flower Garland, Agama, Correct and Equal, and Wisdom periods, and the Nirvana and Mahavairochana sutras—will lead people toward the paths of evil. Also, with the exception of the Tendai school,[8] the adherents of the seven other schools[9] are in reality wardens of hell[10] who drive others toward the evil paths. Even in the Tendai school are found those who profess faith in the Lotus Sutra, yet actually lead others toward the pre-Lotus Sutra teachings. They, too, are wardens of hell who cause people to fall into the evil paths.

Now you two brothers are like the hermit and the man of integrity. If either of you gives up halfway, you will both fail to achieve Buddhahood...

You two wives should have no regrets even if your husbands do you harm because of your faith in this teaching. If both of you unite in encouraging your husbands' faith, you will follow the path of the dragon king's daughter[11] and become a model for women attaining Buddhahood in the evil latter age. Insofar as you can act this way, no matter what may happen, Nichiren will tell the two sages,[12] the two heavenly kings,[13] the ten demon daughters,[14] Shakyamuni, and Many Treasures[15] to make you Buddhas in every future existence. A passage in the Six Paramitas Sutra[16] says to become the master of your mind rather than let your mind master you.[17]

Whatever trouble occurs, regard it as no more than a dream, and think only of the Lotus Sutra. Nichiren's teaching was especially difficult to believe at first, but now that my prophecies[18] have been fulfilled, those who slandered without reason have come to repent. Even if in the future other men and women become my believers, they will not replace you in my heart...

This letter was written particularly for Hyoe no Sakan. It should also be read to his wife and to Tayu no Sakan's. (WND-1, 501–02)

LECTURE

Founding Soka Gakkai president Tsunesaburo Makiguchi once said: "Do we make our lives dwellings of the Buddha, which lead us to happiness, or do we instead make them abodes of devilish functions, which lead us to unhappiness? We have to choose either one or the other. Actively driving devilish functions out and defeating them will lead to happiness and kosen-rufu."

June 6 is President Makiguchi's birthday. [He was born in 1871.] Through his dauntless efforts to uphold Nichiren Buddhism, he taught us that the path of faith for attaining Buddhahood in this lifetime and realizing the goal of kosen-rufu entails an unceasing struggle against devilish functions.

There was a Soka Gakkai member, a young teacher, who received letters of encouragement and guidance from President Makiguchi on an almost monthly basis back in 1938. He was to recall many years later: "In nearly every third letter, Mr. Makiguchi would cite T'ien-t'ai's words, 'As practice progresses and understanding grows, the three obstacles and four devils[19] emerge in confusing form, vying with one another to interfere.'"[20] And he was not the only one to have this point impressed upon him. Mr. Makiguchi constantly emphasized to members the importance of practicing faith with the resolute spirit to battle and triumph over the three obstacles and four devils. This is because such faith is the very essence of Nichiren Buddhism. Inheriting the legacy of Mr. Makiguchi's valiant struggle against devilish functions, Soka Gakkai members have been practicing the correct teaching of Buddhism exactly as Nichiren Daishonin instructs.

Mr. Makiguchi's devoted disciple, second president Josei Toda, led the Soka Gakkai with the same unswerving commitment to battling devilish functions and speaking out for what is right. After his release from prison (in July 1945), Mr. Toda vowed to triumph over the oppressive forces of authority responsible for his mentor's death. He rose up as an indomitable champion of the Mystic Law and boldly carried the banner of kosen-rufu alone.

As Mr. Toda's disciple, I, in turn, did my utmost to support and assist him. Surmounting the storm of obstacles we battled together as mentor and disciple, Mr. Toda was finally inaugurated as the second Soka Gakkai president (in May 1951). He initiated an unprecedented religious revolution, a struggle to rid the world of misery and misfortune by dispelling the fundamental darkness[21]—the ultimate cause of all evil—in people's lives and thereby freeing them from suffering arising from poverty, hatred, violence and other negative circumstances. And he built a bastion committed to realizing Nichiren's principle of "establishing the correct teaching for the peace of the land."[22] This was achieved by calling forth a magnificent force of Bodhisattvas of the Earth[23] in the form of 750,000 Soka Gakkai households ready to bravely confront devilish functions and overcome the three powerful enemies[24] of Buddhism.

Also, as is evident in his 1957 Declaration for the Abolition of Nuclear Weapons,[25] Mr. Toda waged a lifelong, unremitting struggle against the evil and destructive impulses that reside in the human heart. In his final injunction to his disciples before his death, he urged them to fight against corruption and slander of the Law within the Nichiren Shoshu priesthood and to never let up in the struggle against any devilish functions that seek to destroy the inner realm of the human spirit.

Battling devilish functions is the core of the guidance given by the first three Soka Gakkai presidents throughout their struggles for kosen-rufu. This is in exact accord with Nichiren's teachings. If this spirit of faith to challenge devilish functions is maintained now and in the future, kosen-rufu will definitely be achieved. "Letter to the Brothers" sets forth the formula for this. In this installment, I will discuss the struggle against the three obstacles and four devils, the importance of unity of purpose, and faith based on the oneness of mentor and disciple.

"A Guide for My Followers" and "An Axiom of Faith for Future Generations"

The Great Teacher T'ien-t'ai's *Great Concentration and Insight* is the essence of his lifetime teachings and the heart of the whole spectrum of the Buddha's sacred teachings. (WND-1, 500)

The doctrine of three thousand realms in a single moment of life revealed in the fifth volume of *Great Concentration and Insight* is especially profound. If you propagate it, devils will arise without fail. If they did not, there would be no way of knowing that this is the correct teaching. One passage from the same volume reads: "As practice progresses and understanding grows, the three obstacles and four devils emerge in confusing form, vying with one another to interfere ... One should be neither influenced nor frightened by them. If one falls under their influence, one will be led into the paths of evil. If one is frightened by them, one will be prevented from practicing the correct teaching." This statement not only applies to me, but also is a guide for my followers. Reverently make this teaching your own, and transmit it as an axiom of faith for future generations. (WND-1, 501)

In this concluding section of "Letter to the Brothers," Nichiren Daishonin cites a passage from T'ient'ai's *Great Concentration and Insight* clarifying why the three obstacles and four devils appear. He uses this to drive home to the beleaguered Ikegami brothers[26] that they must on no account be defeated by such negative functions. He has already in the course of this letter explained in detail, from various perspectives, why difficulties befall practitioners of the Lotus Sutra, and he now reconfirms that faith in the Mystic Law is ultimately an unending struggle against the three obstacles and four devils.

Nichiren particularly turns his attention to volume five of T'ien-t'ai's *Great Concentration and Insight* and indicates that its profound doctrine of "three thousand realms in a single moment of life" reveals the heart of the Buddha's teachings. This doctrine expresses the essence of the Lotus Sutra's teaching of universal enlightenment as a guide for "observing the mind,"[27] the process for one's own inner transformation or enlightenment.

At the start of the "Correct Practice" chapter in volume five of *Great Concentration and Insight,* as he prepares to reveal this supreme doctrine, T'ien-t'ai first warns that Lotus Sutra practitioners must not abandon their practice out of fear of the three obstacles and four devils. As Nichiren keenly notes: "If you propagate it [this doctrine], devils will arise without fail. If they did not, there would be no way of knowing that this is the correct teaching." In other words, obstacles and devilish functions naturally arise to assail those who practice the correct teaching. Here, Nichiren teaches an important point for victory in our Buddhist practice—for only by recognizing this truth and courageously confronting and triumphing over such obstacles will it be possible for us to realize our own inner transformation.

The passage that Nichiren cites from *Great Concentration and Insight* begins, "As practice progresses and understanding grows," indicating a stage where practitioners have deepened their understanding of the Lotus Sutra and solidified their practice as a result. The three obstacles and four devils attack precisely because of the genuine efforts by practitioners to transform their lives at the fundamental level. In our own context today, it means such obstacles will appear when we exert ourselves wholeheartedly in the two ways of practice and study and move forward in our lives and in our efforts for kosen-rufu. Nichiren asserts that the three obstacles and four devils arise when we are on the verge of attaining Buddhahood.

Next, the passage states, "the three obstacles and four devils emerge in confusing form, vying with one another to interfere." These negative functions seek to catch Lotus Sutra practitioners off guard and, through various insidious means, to intimidate, tempt, discourage or exhaust them, or to lull them into complacency.

T'ien-t'ai outlines two key ingredients of the kind of faith needed to battle the three obstacles and four devils head-on: (1) not being influenced by them and (2) not being frightened by them. Those who let themselves be influenced by devilish functions will be drawn toward the evil paths of existence, while those who are intimidated by them will be prevented from practicing the correct teaching. In short, wisdom and courage are the foundation for victory in this struggle—the wisdom to see devilish functions for what they are and not be swayed by them and the courage to stand up to them without fear. Chanting Nam-myoho-renge-kyo is the source of the wisdom and courage needed to defeat such negative forces. The power of Nam-myoho-renge-kyo, the Mystic Law, can instantly transform innate darkness or ignorance into the fundamental nature of enlightenment,[28] enabling us to attain a state in which we can regard difficulties along the path of faith as peace and comfort (see OTT, 115).

In another writing, Nichiren cites the same passage from *Great Concentration and Insight* about the appearance of the three obstacles and four devils, but he includes the additional passage: "It will only be like a boar rubbing against the golden mountain;[29] like the various rivers flowing into the sea; like logs making a fire burn more briskly; or like the wind swelling the body of the kalakula insect"[30] ("The Actions of the Votary of the Lotus Sutra," WND-1, 770). Battling devilish functions polishes our faith. This is just like a golden mountain shining more brightly, like the ocean becoming fuller, like a fire blazing higher and like the *kalakula* growing larger. Strong faith in the Lotus Sutra can bring forth the wondrous benefit of the Mystic Law of "changing poison into medicine,"[31] thereby transforming misfortune into fortune.

Elsewhere, he says: "The votary of the Lotus Sutra is like the fire and the kalakula, while his persecutions are like the logs and the wind" ("The Difficulty of Sustaining Faith," WND-1, 471); and "The greater the hardships befalling him [the votary of the Lotus Sutra], the greater the delight he feels, because of his strong faith" ("A Ship to Cross the Sea of Suffering," WND-1, 33). Momentous obstacles strengthen the lives of genuine Lotus Sutra practitioners. By courageously confronting such challenges, they bring their Buddhahood to shine forth all the brighter.

In "Letter to the Brothers," we can see Nichiren teaching the Ikegami brothers the principle that "obstacles lead to enlightenment" and urging them to fight on to the end.

It is to the great fortune of his disciples that Nichiren Daishonin set an example by walking along this very path of battling and triumphing over devilish functions. He truly epitomizes the way of Buddhist practice. He calls on the Ikegami brothers to follow his lead and walk the same victorious path. Hence, referring to the passage from *Great Concentration and Insight* about the three obstacles and four devils, he declares, "This statement not only applies to me, but also is a guide for my followers." Confident that the Ikegami brothers' courageous Buddhist practice and ultimate victory will become an enduring model for future practitioners, he tells them, "Reverently make this teaching your own, and transmit it as an axiom of faith for future generations."

Let us, likewise, reverently embody and transmit the spirit of faith for battling devilish functions taught to us by Mr. Makiguchi and Mr. Toda, thereby creating causes in the present for the SGI's development into the eternal future.

***

Battling Devilish Functions Is the Essence of Genuine Faith

The three obstacles in this passage are the obstacle of earthly desires, the obstacle of karma, and the obstacle of retribution. The obstacle of earthly desires is the impediments to one's practice that arise from greed, anger, foolishness, and the like; the obstacle of karma is the hindrances presented by one's wife or children; and the obstacle of retribution is the hindrances caused by one's sovereign or parents. Of the four devils, the workings of the devil king of the sixth heaven are of this last kind.

In Japan today, many people claim they have mastered the practice of concentration and insight. But is there anyone who has actually encountered the

three obstacles and four devils? (WND-I, 501)

Next, for the Ikegami brothers' benefit, Nichiren Daishonin describes some specific forms in which the three obstacles and four devils manifest. He also alludes to the fact that he and his followers, in their committed struggle against devilish functions, are the only ones of their day truly practicing the correct teaching.

First, he discusses the "three obstacles," which function to obstruct Buddhist practice and undermine the good causes one has accumulated. The list of obstacles varies considerably depending on the sutra or treatise. The Nirvana Sutra and several other scriptures make mention of the three types of obstacles—the obstacles of earthly desires, karma and retribution.

(1) The obstacle of earthly desires refers to impediments to practice that arise from the three poisons—greed, anger and foolishness—and the like in one's own life. Earthly desires, or deluded impulses, can sap people's life force, deprive them of reason and even rob them of the energy to improve their lives.

(2) The obstacle of karma refers to hindrances that result from the influence of one's negative karma functioning to obstruct Buddhist practice. This might apply in the case where someone falls

away from the correct path of Buddhist practice because of his or her own mistaken actions or evil acts.

(3) The obstacle of retribution refers to obstacles deriving from the negative effects of grave offenses committed in past existences. A prime example of such retribution is being born in an evil age or in an environment hostile to or unsupportive of one's Buddhist practice.

In "Letter to the Brothers," Nichiren offers concrete examples of these three obstacles in a context that has relevance for the Ikegami brothers. He explains that the obstacle of karma corresponds to "hindrances presented by one's wife or children," while the obstacle of retribution corresponds to "hindrances caused by one's sovereign or parents." I wish to specifically clarify here that people who hinder one's Buddhist practice—such as spouses or children, authority figures or parents, as Nichiren indicates—are nothing more than "evil friends," or negative influences; they are not inherently evil in themselves. Ultimately, it is up to individual practitioners whether they remain steadfast or abandon their faith as a result of others' opposition. When we win over our own selves, we can see everyone as a "good friend," or a positive influence for our lives. To put an even finer point on this: By bringing about a change in the depths of our own lives, we can also change or exert a positive influence on the lives of others.

Next, Nichiren discusses the "four devils." The term *devil* or *devilish function* in Buddhism derives from the Sanskrit word *mara*, which was variously translated into Chinese as "murderer," "robber of life" or "destroyer." It refers to the negative workings within people's hearts that seek to destroy their spirit and even deprive them of life itself.

As in the case of obstacles, there are also various kinds of devils described in different sutras and treatises. The description of the four devils as the hindrances of earthly desires, the five components,[32] death and the devil king is contained in such works as Nagarjuna's *Treatise on the Great Concentration of Wisdom*.[33]

(1) The hindrance of the five components, which includes the hindrance of illness, refers to imbalances of the five components (e.g., one's mind and body) producing suffering and anguish that ultimately lead to destroying a person's faith.

(2) The hindrance of earthly desires refers to deluded impulses causing people to suffer spiritual torment and confusion and robbing them of wisdom.

(3) The hindrance of death means a practitioner being deprived of life—that

is, dying—and the person's death subsequently causing other practitioners to harbor doubts about faith.

(4) The hindrance of the devil king means the faith of practitioners being destroyed by the workings of the devil king, also known as "the heavenly devil Freely Enjoying Things Conjured by Others."

Here, of the four devils, Nichiren mentions just the hindrance of the devil king, most likely because he was focusing on the kind of hindrance the Ikegami brothers were facing.

So far in this letter, Nichiren has given guidance in various places concerning the need for resolute faith to confront the insidious workings of the devil king. In this closing section, he infers that only he and his followers can bring forth attacks from the three obstacles and four devils and triumph over them. This is implicit in his rhetorical question "Is there anyone who has actually encountered the three obstacles and four devils?" (WND-1, 501). He notes that there are many people who "claim they have mastered the practice of concentration and insight [taught by T'ien-t'ai as the correct practice for attaining enlightenment]." But, he asks, who is it that the three obstacles and four devils are attacking? The answer is self-evident: aside from Nichiren and his followers, there is no one.

Through our dedicated efforts for kosen-rufu as Soka Gakkai members united in the shared struggle of mentor and disciple, we have carried on Nichiren Daishonin's noble fighting spirit. As a result, in the present age, we have shown that we alone are the ones who have actually encountered the three obstacles and four devils.

In November 1942, at the height of World War II, the Soka Kyoiku Gakkai (Value-Creating Education Society, forerunner of the Soka Gakkai) held its fifth general meeting. In an address on that occasion, discussing this same passage from "Letter to the Brothers," Mr. Makiguchi declared:

> Who among the traditional believers of Nichiren Shoshu [the priesthood] have been assailed by the three obstacles and four devils? ... Aren't those who claim to guide others but fail to call forth obstacles no more than "wardens of hell who cause people to fall into the evil paths"? Experiencing attacks by devilish functions is what distinguishes "practitioners" from mere "believers"...
>
> People leading lives of minor good who practice faith only for their own benefit will certainly not encounter obstacles, but those leading lives of major good dedicated to altruistic bodhisattva practice will most definitely be assailed by devilish functions...
>
> Just like lotus flowers that bloom unsullied by the muddy water in which they grow, we (the members of the Soka Gakkai) boldly plunge into the midst of forces

hostile to the correct teaching—people of small and medium good who commit slander of the Law—and resolutely seek to redress their grave error and wrongdoing. It is only natural, therefore, that the three obstacles and four devils will furiously descend upon us. Indeed, their appearance earns us the name of "practitioners."[34]

We mustn't be fainthearted "believers" who only desire minor benefit for ourselves and are too fearful to battle devilish functions. Authentic practitioners throw themselves wholeheartedly into battling the three obstacles and four devils for the great benefits of attaining Buddhahood in this lifetime and advancing kosen-rufu for all people's happiness. All SGI members are noble "practitioners of the Lotus Sutra" of the modern day.

***

Battling Devilish Functions That Cause People To Fall Into the Evil Paths

The statement "If one falls under their influence, one will be led into the paths of evil" indicates not only the three evil paths but also the worlds of human and heavenly beings, and in general, all of the nine worlds. Therefore, with the exception of the Lotus Sutra, all of the sutras—those of the Flower Garland, Agama, Correct

and Equal, and Wisdom periods, and the Nirvana and Mahavairochana sutras—will lead people toward the paths of evil. Also, with the exception of the Tendai school, the adherents of the seven other schools are in reality wardens of hell who drive others toward the evil paths. Even in the Tendai school are found those who profess faith in the Lotus Sutra, yet actually lead others toward the pre-Lotus Sutra teachings. They, too, are wardens of hell who cause people to fall into the evil paths. (WND-1, 501)

Here, Nichiren Daishonin again cites the passage relating to the three obstacles and four devils from *Great Concentration and Insight,* "If one falls under their influence, one will be led into the paths of evil." By propagating erroneous teachings throughout the land, the priests of the various established Buddhist schools of Nichiren's day functioned as "evil friends," or negative influences, causing people to fall into the evil paths. Nichiren describes such people as "wardens of hell" who lead others toward the three evil paths and toward the nine worlds of the pre-Lotus Sutra teachings [which articulate a clear separation between the nine worlds and Buddhahood]. He further states that even in the Tendai school, which originally prized the Lotus Sutra, there are those who, while professing faith in the sutra's teachings, actually function as "wardens of hell" who lead people into the evil paths and into discarding the sutra.

From around 1275 to 1278, Nichiren intensified his criticism of Jikaku and Chisho,[35] patriarchs of the Tendai school who had created the fundamental cause for slander of the Lotus Sutra throughout Japan by incorporating esoteric doctrines of the True Word school into original Tendai teachings. These priests, who ought to have upheld the Lotus Sutra, instead corrupted the school's teachings and, as a result, became people who "destroy the Lotus Sutra" (see WND-1, 495).

In a time when people were profoundly influenced by these erroneous teachings and slander of the Law pervaded the land, Nichiren directly confronted the priests whom people looked up to as bastions of wisdom, denouncing them as the very source of this fundamental evil of slander. Since he is exerting himself in this struggle "no less fiercely than the Buddha and the devil king did in their battle,"[36] it is inevitable that the three obstacles and four devils will descend upon him with a vengeance.

The Ikegami brothers were among the loyal disciples who stood by Nichiren and shared the brunt of the attack by these hostile forces. In this letter, Nichiren strongly urges them again to continue fighting alongside him to spread the correct teaching.

Unity Is Key to Victory

Now you two brothers are like the hermit and the man of integrity. If either of you gives up halfway, you will both fail to achieve Buddhahood. (WND-1, 501)

You two wives should have no regrets even if your husbands do you harm because of your faith in this teaching. If both of you unite in encouraging your husbands' faith, you will follow the path of the dragon king's daughter and become a model for women attaining Buddhahood in the evil latter age. Insofar as you can act this way, no matter what may happen, Nichiren will tell the two sages, the two heavenly kings, the ten demon daughters, Shakyamuni, and Many Treasures to make you Buddhas in every future existence. (WND-1, 502)

The secret to faith for battling devilish functions is sharing the mentor's commitment and solidly uniting in purpose with fellow practitioners. Nichiren Daishonin emphasizes these key points in the closing passages of "Letter to the Brothers." First, he underscores the need for unity.

The most important thing for the Ikegami brothers was that they remain united. Devilish functions seek to create schisms. Had their father disowned both of them over religious differences, then it would simply have been a matter of them working together to clarify any misunderstanding with him. But in disowning only the elder, their father hoped to tempt the younger with the prospect of gaining the right of succession. It was clearly a scheme to drive a wedge between the two brothers and, as such, a manifestation of the workings of the devil king of the sixth heaven.

Only a positive united force could defeat these devilish functions. Hence, Nichiren tells the brothers, "If either of you gives up halfway, you will both fail to achieve Buddhahood." In other words, their unity represents an unassailable fortress to keep out devilish functions.

Further, he instructs the brothers' wives that they, too, must maintain courageous faith, writing: "You two wives should have no regrets even if your husbands do you harm because of your faith in this teaching. If both of you unite in encouraging your husbands' faith, you will follow the path of the dragon king's daughter and become a model for women attaining Buddhahood in the evil latter age."

Women's faith often proves decisive at a crucial moment. We should thus take Nichiren's words to heart. As for striving in faith for a happy and harmonious family, there is no need to be impatient with family members who do not practice Nichiren Buddhism. One person upholding faith in the Mystic Law is like a shining sun that illuminates all family members and loved ones, the benefit of their Buddhist practice extending to everyone. The most important thing is to pray and have absolute confidence that your efforts in faith will lead to their happiness.

In this letter, Nichiren writes that "women support others and thereby cause others to support them" (WND-1, 501), and he urges the Ikegami brothers' wives to unite in encouraging their husbands' faith. If they wisely maintain unwavering faith, they can definitely triumph over the onslaughts of devilish functions and achieve the boundless state of Buddhahood, which also encompasses their entire family. From his letters to the Ikegami brothers, we can surmise that the wives' prudent support of their husbands in accord with Nichiren's guidance played a significant role in the father, Ikegami Yasumitsu,[37] eventually taking faith in the correct teaching.

A Victorious Life Guided by the Principle of the Heart Being Most Important

A passage in the Six Paramitas Sutra says to become the master of your mind rather than let your mind master you. Whatever trouble occurs, regard it as no more than a dream, and think only of the Lotus Sutra. (WND-1, 502)

As Nichiren Daishonin declares, "It is the heart that is important" ("The Strategy of the Lotus Sutra," WND-1, 1000). The human heart or mind can give supreme dignity and nobility to life. At the same time, it can fall into the depths of depravity if it succumbs to the impulses of fundamental darkness or ignorance. Transforming the human heart is the foundation for all lasting change.

If we base ourselves on our own fickle, ever-changing hearts, we cannot make our way up steep ridges buffeted by the fierce winds of devilish functions. We must set our sights on the solid and unshakable summit of attaining Buddhahood and continually seek to master our minds. This is the meaning of the passage "Become the master of your mind rather than let your mind master you."

Becoming the master of one's mind ultimately means basing oneself on the unwavering foundation of the Law. Herein lies the importance of sutras or writings containing the teachings of the Buddha who has awakened to and spreads the Law. For us, as practitioners of Nichiren Buddhism, mastering our minds means basing ourselves on the Gohonzon and Nichiren's writings. And in Buddhism, it is the teacher or mentor who puts the teachings into practice that helps us connect to the Law. Mastering our minds means having a sincere seeking spirit in faith based on the oneness of mentor and disciple, and not being ruled by arrogant egoism or self-centeredness.

Nichiren highlights the importance of living with inner mastery—mastery based on the Law—in the following: "Whatever trouble occurs, regard it as no more than a dream, and think only of the Lotus Sutra." When viewed in terms of the infinite scale of eternity, any event or phenomenon is as fleeting as a passing dream. The Law, in contrast, is eternal. Allowing oneself to be defeated by devilish functions and straying from the Law will be a cause for everlasting regret. In this passage, Nichiren urges his followers to "think only of the Lotus Sutra," to focus only on kosen-rufu and to remain steadfast in their faith for the sake of eternal victory.

In the present age, we of the SGI have been dedicating ourselves to mastering our minds through single-minded commitment to the Lotus Sutra (Nam-myoho-renge-kyo). As a result, we are showing magnificent actual proof of victory. There are now countless heroic members—ordinary people exerting themselves valiantly in their Buddhist practice—in Japan and around the world. They are truly treasures of kosen-rufu and treasures of humanity. Basing themselves on the Law and embodying the spirit of the oneness of mentor and disciple, they have transformed their karma and established a life state of unshakable happiness. At the same time, they work tirelessly to contribute to the prosperity of their societies and to world peace, leading lives of unsurpassed meaning dedicated to happiness for both themselves and others. We have entered an age when leading thinkers in Japan and around the globe are praising our noble members' efforts.

***

Faith Based on the Oneness of Mentor and Disciple

Nichiren's teaching was especially difficult to believe at first, but now that my prophecies have been fulfilled, those who slandered without reason have come to repent. Even if in the future other men and women become my believers, they will not replace you in my heart...

This letter was written particularly for Hyoe no Sakan. It should also be read to his wife and to Tayu no Sakan's. (WND-1, 502)

At the end of this writing, Nichiren Daishonin reiterates the importance of his followers striving with the same spirit and commitment as he.

The workings of the human heart are infinitely diverse. Some people, upon seeing his predictions come true, regretted and retracted their earlier criticism of Nichiren and his followers. There were also many who let fear of persecution cause them to abandon their faith in his teachings. Some of these individuals ended up being even more abusive and antagonistic than those who had been hostile from the beginning.[38]

Weakness, cowardice, treachery—the human heart can be truly frightening. No doubt this is what prompted Nichiren to write to the Ikegami brothers and their wives, who remained true to the path of mentor and disciple, "Even if in the future other men and women become my believers, they will not replace you in my heart." These followers who persevered on the great path of kosen-rufu, undaunted by raging tempests and unfazed by those who abandoned their faith, are true disciples, he says in words of the highest praise. The mentor-disciple bond is one of life's supreme treasures.

President Toda once said: "To soar serenely in the skies of attaining Buddhahood in this lifetime, we must launch headlong into the fierce winds of adversity. Faith that remains undefeated by any hardship is what enables us to build a palace of eternal happiness in our lives. There is no obstacle that we cannot surmount with faith."

His towering conviction epitomizes the Soka Gakkai spirit, the *shakubuku* spirit of refuting error and clarifying what is right, and the spirit to battle devilish functions.

Faith is of utmost importance. In another letter, Nichiren tells the Ikegami brothers, "The three obstacles and four devils will invariably appear, and the wise will rejoice while the foolish will retreat."[39]

When our faith is that of "the wise who rejoice," the fierce winds of the three obstacles and four devils will merely disperse the clouds of karma that hang over us. A rainbow of great joy will definitely appear in the clear blue skies of our hearts. Confident that the sunlight of truth, happiness and victory will then shine forth brilliantly, let us boldly challenge all obstacles.

The disciples' victories over the three obstacles and four devils are the greatest wish and joy of mentors in the realm of Buddhism.

This lecture was originally published in the June 2009 issue of the Daibyakurenge, *the Soka Gakkai's monthly study journal.*

NOTES

[1] Great Teacher T'ien-t'ai (538–97): Also known as Chih-i. The founder of the T'ien-t'ai school in China. His lectures were compiled in such works as *The Profound Meaning of the Lotus Sutra*, *The Words and Phrases of the Lotus Sutra* and *Great Concentration and Insight*. He spread the Lotus Sutra in China and established the doctrine of "three thousand realms in a single moment of life."

[2] *Great Concentration and Insight:* One of T'ien-t'ai's three major works, this writing clarifies the principle of three thousand realms in a single moment of life, based on the Lotus Sutra, and elucidates the method of meditation for observing one's mind and realizing this principle within oneself.

[3] Three thousand realms in a single moment of life: A doctrine developed by the Great Teacher T'ien-t'ai of China based on the Lotus Sutra; the principle that all phenomena are contained within a single moment of life and that a single moment of life permeates the three thousand realms of existence (the entire phenomenal world). In "Letter to the Brothers," Nichiren Daishonin writes, "It was the Great Teacher T'ien-t'ai Chih-che who not only clarified the Buddha's teachings, but also brought forth the wish-granting jewel of a single moment of life comprising three thousand realms from the repository of the five characters of Myoho-renge-kyo and bestowed it on all people in the three countries [of India, China and Japan]" (WND-1, 501). And in *The Record of the Orally Transmitted Teachings,* Nichiren states that the principle of three thousand realms in a single moment of life is none other than Nam-myoho-renge-kyo (see p.99 and p.238).

[4] Greed, anger and foolishness: The three poisons, or fundamental evils inherent in life that give rise to human suffering. In Nagarjuna's *Treatise on the Great Perfection of Wisdom,* the three poisons are regarded

as the source of all illusions and earthly desires. The three poisons are so called because they pollute people's lives and work to prevent them from turning their hearts and minds to goodness.

[5] Devil king of the sixth heaven: Also, "devil king" or "heavenly devil." The king of devils, who dwells in the highest or the sixth heaven of the world of desire. He is also named Freely Enjoying Things Conjured by Others, the king who makes free use of the fruits of others' efforts for his own pleasure. Served by innumerable minions, he obstructs Buddhist practice and delights in sapping the life force of other beings. The devil king is a personification of the negative tendency to force others to one's will at any cost.

[6] Concentration and insight: The entire system of meditation set forth by the Great Teacher T'ien-t'ai in *Great Concentration and Insight*, the ultimate goal of which is to perceive "the region of the unfathomable," that is, the unification of the three truths within one's mind or the three thousand realms in a single moment of life. "Concentration" means focusing one's mind on one point without any

distractions, and "insight" means seeing all things as they are, or perception that penetrates the ultimate reality, or true aspect, of all phenomena.

[7] Nine worlds: The nine worlds are contrasted with the world of Buddhas to indicate the realm of delusion and impermanence. They are the worlds or realms of hell, hungry spirits, animals, *asuras,* human beings, heavenly beings, voice-hearers, cause-awakened ones and bodhisattvas.

[8] Tendai school: The Japanese counterpart of the Chinese T'ien-t'ai (Jpn Tendai) school of Buddhism, founded in the early ninth century by the Japanese priest Dengyo (767–822), also known as Saicho. But because of a tolerant attitude toward the erroneous teachings of other schools, including the True Word, Pure Land (Nembutsu) and Zen, by Nichiren's time, it could no longer be considered strictly based on the Lotus Sutra.

[9] The seven other schools are the three Hinayana schools of Dharma Analysis Treasury, Establishment of Truth and Precepts, and the four Mahayana schools of Dharma Characteristics, Three Treatises, Flower Garland and True Word.

[10] Wardens of hell: Demons in Buddhist mythology who torment transgressors who have fallen into hell. They work for King Yama, the king of hell who is said to judge and determine the rewards and punishments of the dead.

[11] This refers to the attainment of Buddhahood by the eight-year-old dragon king's daughter, which is described in "Devadatta," the 12th chapter of the Lotus Sutra. Daughter of Sagara, one of the eight great dragon kings. She conceives the desire for enlightenment upon hearing Bodhisattva Manjushri preach the Lotus Sutra. She then appears in front of the assembly described in the Lotus Sutra and instantaneously attains Buddhahood in her present form.

[12] Two sages: Bodhisattva Medicine King and Bodhisattva Brave Donor. In "Dharani," the 26th chapter of the Lotus Sutra, they vow to protect the sutra's practitioners.

[13] Two heavenly kings: Hearer of Many Teachings (Skt Vaishravana) and Upholder of the Nation (Dhritarashtra). Two of the four heavenly kings that serve the god Shakra and protect the four quarters of the world. In "Dharani,"

the 26th chapter of the Lotus Sutra, Hearer of Many Teachings and Upholder of the Nation pledge to protect those who embrace the sutra.

[14] Ten demon daughters: Ten female protective deities who appear in the Lotus Sutra as the "daughters of *rakshasa* demons" or the "ten rakshasa daughters." In the sutra's 26th chapter, "Dharani," they vow to guard and protect the sutra's practitioners, saying that they will inflict punishment on any who trouble them.

[15] Many Treasures Buddha: A Buddha depicted in the Lotus Sutra. Many Treasures appears, seated within his treasure tower, in order to lend credence to Shakyamuni's teachings in the sutra. According to "The Emergence of the Treasure Tower," the 11th chapter of the Lotus Sutra, Many Treasures Buddha lives in the World of Treasure Purity in the east. While still engaged in bodhisattva practice, he pledges that, even after entering nirvana, he will appear with his treasure tower in order to attest to the validity of the Lotus Sutra, wherever it might be taught.

[16] Six Paramitas Sutra: A sutra translated into Chinese in 788 by Prajna, a monk from northern India. It explains in detail the six *paramitas,* or six kinds of practice, that bodhisattvas must carry out to attain enlightenment.

[17] A similar passage also appears in the Nirvana Sutra, "May I be the master of my mind and not let my mind become my master!" ("Letter to Renjo," WND-2, 5).

[18] In his 1260 treatise "On Establishing the Correct Teaching for the Peace of the Land," Nichiren predicted that the calamities of internal strife and foreign invasion would befall Japan because of the country's slander of the Law. These prophecies were fulfilled by a revolt within the ruling Hojo clan, known as the February Disturbance of 1272 (also the Hojo Tokisuke Disturbance) and by the Mongol invasion of 1274.

[19] Three obstacles and four devils: Various obstacles and hindrances to the practice of Buddhism. The three obstacles are (1) the obstacle of earthly desires, (2) the obstacle of karma and (3) the obstacle of retribution. The four devils are (1) the hindrance of the five

components, (2) the hindrance of earthly desires, (3) the hindrance of death and (4) the hindrance of the devil king.

[20] Translated from Japanese. *Makiguchi Tsunesaburo* (Tsunesaburo Makiguchi), edited by Fusahiro Misaka (Tokyo: Seikyo Shimbunsha, 1973), p.456.

[21] Fundamental darkness: The most deeply rooted delusion inherent in life, said to give rise to all other delusions. Fundamental darkness means the inability to see or recognize the truth, particularly the true nature of one's life. Nichiren interprets fundamental darkness as ignorance of the ultimate Law, or ignorance of the fact that one's life is essentially a manifestation of the Law, which he identifies as Nammyoho-renge-kyo.

[22] The "Resonance" chapter of volume 21 of President Ikeda's book *The New Human Revolution* explains: "'Establishing the correct teaching' means to inspire others to embrace the ideals of Buddhist humanism as represented in the principles of human revolution and respect for the sanctity of life. And the effort to bring this about is kosen-rufu, the ultimate objective of which is 'the

peace of the land,' or in other words, the realization of a peaceful and prosperous society." See also July 24, 2009, *World Tribune*, p. B.

[23] Bodhisattvas of the Earth: The innumerable bodhisattvas who appear in "Emerging from the Earth," the 15th chapter of the Lotus Sutra, and are entrusted by Shakyamuni with the task of propagating the Law after his passing. In "Supernatural Powers of the Thus Come One," the 21st chapter of the sutra, these bodhisattvas, led by Bodhisattva Superior Practices, vow to spread the Buddha's teaching in the saha world in the evil age of the Latter Day of the Law.

[24] Three powerful enemies: Three types of arrogant people who persecute those who propagate the Lotus Sutra in the evil age after Shakyamuni Buddha's death, described in a twenty-line verse section of "Encouraging Devotion," the 13th chapter of the Lotus Sutra. The Great Teacher Miao-lo (711–82) of China summarizes them as arrogant lay people, arrogant priests and arrogant false sages.

[25] On September 8, 1957, Mr. Toda put forth a declaration calling for a ban on

the testing and use of nuclear weapons. Issued at a Soka Gakkai youth division athletic event held in Yokohama, Kanagawa Prefecture, it has become the starting point of the Soka Gakkai's activities for peace.

[26] Ikegami brothers: Leading disciples of Nichiren. The elder brother, Munenaka, was twice disowned by their father, who was a follower of Ryokan, the chief priest of Gokuraku-ji, a temple of the True Word Precepts school. Ryokan was hostile to Nichiren. The father tempted Munenaga, the younger brother, to abandon his faith in Nichiren's teaching and take his brother's place as the next head of the family.

[27] Observing the mind: To perceive or awaken to the ultimate reality inherent in one's life. Also, the method of practice that makes this possible.

[28] Fundamental nature of enlightenment: Also, Dharma nature. The unchanging nature inherent in all things and phenomena. It is identified with the fundamental Law itself, the essence of the Buddha's enlightenment, or ultimate truth.

[29] A boar rubbing against a golden mountain and making it shine more brightly is described in Nagarjuna's *Treatise on the Great Perfection of Wisdom*. It is used here as a metaphor for the faith of practitioners of the Lotus Sutra being strengthened by the onslaughts of the three obstacles and four devils.

[30] *Kalakula* (Skt): Imaginary insects that were said to swell rapidly in a strong wind. They are described in Nagarjuna's *Treatise on the Great Perfection of Wisdom*. Though their bodies are very small, the kalakula feed on the wind, swelling to an enormous size and consuming everything around them.

[31] Changing poison into medicine: The principle that earthly desires and suffering can be transformed into benefit and enlightenment by virtue of the power of the Law. This phrase is found in a passage from Nagarjuna's *Treatise on the Great Perfection of Wisdom*, which mentions "a great physician who can change poison into medicine." In this passage, Nagarjuna compares the Lotus Sutra to a great physician because the sutra opens the possibility of attaining Buddhahood to persons of the two

vehicles—voice-hearers and cause-awakened ones—who in other teachings were condemned as having scorched the seeds of Buddhahood. The Great Teacher T'ien-t'ai says in *The Profound Meaning of the Lotus Sutra*: "That persons of the two vehicles were given the prophecy of their enlightenment in this [Lotus] sutra means that it can change poison into medicine." This phrase is often cited to show that any problem or suffering can be transformed eventually into the greatest happiness and fulfillment in life.

[32] Five components (Skt *pancha-skandha*): Also, five components of life, five aggregates, or five *skandhas*. The five components are: form, perception, conception, volition and consciousness. Buddhism holds that these constituent elements unite temporarily to form an individual living being. Together they also constitute one of the three realms of existence, the other two being the realm of living beings and the realm of the environment.

[33] *The Treatise on the Great Perfection of Wisdom*: A comprehensive commentary on the Great Perfection of Wisdom

Sutra. Its authorship is traditionally attributed to Nagarjuna. The treatise is highly valued as a reference in the general study of Mahayana thought. Nagarjuna was a Mahayana scholar of southern India who wrote many important treatises, including *The Treatise on the Middle Way,* and had a major impact on the development of Buddhist thought in China and Japan. Nichiren identifies Nagarjuna as a successor who correctly understood Shakyamuni's true intent.

[34] Translated from Japanese. Tsunesaburo Makiguchi, *Makiguchi Tsunesaburo zenshu* (Collected Writings of Tsunesaburo Makiguchi) (Tokyo: Seikyo Shimbunsha, 1987), vol.10, pp.152–53.

[35] Jikaku (794–864), also known as Ennin, was the third chief priest of Enryaku-ji, the head temple of the Tendai school in Japan. A disciple of the school's founder Dengyo, Jikaku journeyed in 838 to China, where he studied Sanskrit and Esoteric Buddhism. During his time, the Tendai school incorporated Esoteric Buddhism into its original doctrines. Chisho (814–91), also known as Enchin, was the fifth chief priest of Enryaku-ji.

He contributed to the development of Tendai Esotericism, which Jikaku had begun. Nichiren harshly refutes both Jikaku and Chisho as erroneous teachers who destroyed the teachings of Dengyo and led people astray.

[36] In "On Repaying Debts of Gratitude," Nichiren writes: "Today those who slander the Law fill the entire country, and I, Nichiren, attack them, strong in my determination to uphold what is right and just. We battle no less fiercely than the asuras and the god Shakra, or the Buddha and the devil king" (WND-1, 716).

[37] Ikegami Yasumitsu: A loyal follower of Ryokan, chief priest of a temple in Kamakura, Gokuraku-ji, of the True Word Precepts school. Yasumitsu strenuously opposed the beliefs of his sons, Munenaka and Munenaga. He disowned the elder Munenaka in 1275 and again in 1277. In doing so, Yasumitsu was in effect provoking a rift between the two sons, tempting the younger Munenaga to trade his beliefs for the right to inherit his father's estate. Supported by Nichiren's guidance and encouragement, however, Munenaga

upheld his faith together with his brother, and in 1278, after twenty-two years of practice, their united efforts finally inspired their father to accept faith in Nichiren's teachings.

[38] In "Letter to the Brothers," Nichiren writes: "Among those who believed at first, many later discarded their faith, fearing that society would reject them. Among these are some who oppose me more furiously than those who slandered from the beginning" (WND-1, 502).

[39] In "The Three Obstacles and Four Devils," Nichiren writes: "There is definitely something extraordinary in the ebb and flow of the tide, the rising and setting of the moon, and the way in which summer, autumn, winter, and spring give way to each other. Something uncommon also occurs when an ordinary person attains Buddhahood. At such a time, the three obstacles and four devils will invariably appear, and the wise will rejoice while the foolish will retreat" (WND-1, 637).

CHAPTER 7

"THE SUPREMACY OF THE LAW—PART I OF 3

THE LOTUS SUTRA IS THE GREAT SHIP FOR THE ENLIGHTENMENT OF ALL PEOPLE

Passage for Study in This Lecture

When Buddhism had not yet been introduced in China, the writings of such sages as the Three Sovereigns,[1] the Five Emperors,[2] and the Three Kings,[3] T'ai-kung Wang,[4] Tan the Duke of Chou,[5] Lao Tzu, and Confucius were called the canons or classics. Through these teachings, the people learned propriety and came to understand the debt of gratitude they owed their parents, and a clear distinction was drawn between the ruler and the ruled, so that the country was governed wisely. The people obeyed the

leaders who followed these teachings, and heaven answered their prayers...

When the Buddhist scriptures were first brought to China from India, some people said that they should be accepted, while others said they should be rejected. A conflict arose, and the ruler summoned the two groups to meet and debate the issue. The adherents of non-Buddhist teachings were defeated by the supporters of Buddhism. (WND-1, 612)

***

In contrast, the Mahayana sutras are like those huge vessels that, carrying ten or twenty people and loaded with large quantities of cargo, can sail from Kamakura[6] as far as Tsukushi or Mutsu Province.[7]

But the ship of the true Mahayana sutra is incomparably greater than those huge ships that are the other Mahayana sutras. Loaded with a hoard of rare treasures and carrying a hundred or a thousand passengers, it can sail all the way to the land of Korea. The sutra called the Lotus Sutra of the one vehicle is like this. Devadatta[8] was the most evil man in the entire land of Jambudvipa, but the Lotus Sutra predicted that he would become the Thus Come One Heavenly King. Although

Ajatashatru[9] was a wicked king who killed his own father, he was among those present when the Lotus Sutra was preached, and after hearing only a verse or a phrase, formed a connection with the sutra [that would enable him to attain enlightenment in the future]. The dragon king's daughter,[10] a woman with a reptile's body, attained Buddhahood by listening to Bodhisattva Manjushri[11] preach the Lotus Sutra. Furthermore, the Buddha designated the evil era of the Latter Day of the Law as the very time for the Lotus Sutra to be propagated, and bequeathed it to the men and women of that impure age. The Lotus Sutra, the teaching of the one vehicle,[12] is then a sutra as great and as powerful as the ships of the China trade...

Moreover, there is superiority and inferiority not only among the sutras, but also among their adherents. The various teachers of the True Word school,[13] who believe in the Mahavairochana Sutra, are like fire being put out by water, or dew being blown away by the wind when confronted in debate by the votary of the Lotus Sutra. If a dog barks at a lion, its bowels will rot. The asura demon who shot an arrow at the sun had his head

> split into seven pieces. The True Word teachers are like the dog or the asura, while the votary of the Lotus Sutra is like the sun or the lion. (WND-1, 612–13)
>
> ***
>
> As you know, before the Mongol attack, the arrogance of the people of our day knew no bounds. Since the tenth month of last year, however, none of them has dared to assume a haughty attitude, for as you have heard, Nichiren alone predicted this foreign invasion. If the Mongols attack our country again, none of the people will have the courage to face them ... In battles soldiers regard the general as their soul. If the general were to lose heart, his soldiers would become cowards. (WND-1, 613)

LECTURE

The voices of the people have genuine power. The lively advance of the people can move society. Nothing is mightier than the power of the people. And nothing is as formidable or as indestructible as their solidarity. No one is a match for it. This is true in any time and place.

The Buddhism of Nichiren Daishonin is a religion for ordinary people, aimed at opening an era of the people and helping everyone gain true happiness. For us, as its practitioners, the realization of happiness for all people is not an abstract theory but a concrete goal that we can achieve by focusing on each individual. By helping one person become happy through faith in the Mystic Law, we can show actual proof of the validity of Nichiren Buddhism as a truly humanistic religion.

Achieving an ideal society must ultimately begin with each individual undergoing a great human revolution, or inner transformation. Nichiren sought to foster such people, and to do so, he taught that faith is a necessary and indispensable requirement.

Anyone who seeks to attain Buddhahood in this lifetime and carries out faith aimed at achieving human revolution can establish a firmly grounded self. We can develop a state of life that allows us to actualize happiness for ourselves and others. We can forge ahead undaunted by adversity and enhance our capacity for creating value out of every situation. Faith in Nichiren Buddhism enables us to cultivate an inner state of absolute freedom, undefeated by karmic challenges. It is the means by which we can polish our lives.

This time, we will study "The Supremacy of the Law," a writing Nichiren composed when Japan faced the very real threat of a second invasion by Mongol forces. The times were also characterized by great confusion in society and a prevalence of misguided beliefs and erroneous teachings. In this letter of encouragement,

Nichiren urges the recipient—referred to here only as the mother of Oto—to practice the correct teaching of the Lotus Sutra even more strongly and develop into a person of genuine faith. Ultimately, in a time of turmoil, the only thing we can rely on is our faith in the Mystic Law.

The woman who received this letter was a sincere disciple of the Daishonin. Together with her young daughter, Oto, she traveled all the way from Kamakura to visit him in exile on Sado Island. Because of her dedication, Nichiren bestowed upon her the Buddhist name Sage Nichimyo (Sun Wonderful).[14] What kind of guidance and encouragement did he offer this admirable woman? Through carefully studying this letter, we can glean important essentials of faith.

Sharing a Common Desire for People's Happiness

When Buddhism had not yet been introduced in China, the writings of such sages as the Three Sovereigns, the Five Emperors, and the Three Kings, T'ai-kung Wang, Tan the Duke of Chou, Lao Tzu, and Confucius were called the canons or classics. Through these teachings, the people learned propriety and came to understand the debt of gratitude they owed their parents, and a clear distinction was drawn between the ruler and the ruled, so that the country was governed wisely. The

people obeyed the leaders who followed these teachings, and heaven answered their prayers...

When the Buddhist scriptures were first brought to China from India, some people said that they should be accepted, while others said they should be rejected. A conflict arose, and the ruler summoned the two groups to meet and debate the issue. The adherents of non-Buddhist teachings were defeated by the supporters of Buddhism. (WND-1, 612)

Nichiren Daishonin tells the Sage Nichimyo that the Lotus Sutra is an incomparably noble teaching. He outlines the characteristics of the different Buddhist sutras, referring in particular to the essence of the Mahayana sutras, of which, he points out, the Lotus Sutra is the highest. His message is that those who uphold the Lotus Sutra in the present troubled age are infinitely respectworthy—and, more specifically, that Nichimyo is a remarkable woman for practicing this supreme teaching as his disciple.

Nichiren begins by explaining how Buddhism spread in China. First, he notes that the various respected teachings prevalent in China before the arrival of Buddhism also had the power to benefit the people in the respective times in which they were propagated.

The birth of almost all religions or spiritual traditions can be traced back to a wish for people's happiness. My mentor, second Soka

Gakkai president Josei Toda, often used to say he was certain that if the founders of various religious traditions—including Nichiren Daishonin, Shakyamuni, Jesus, Muhammad and so forth—gathered together in one room for a discussion, they would quickly arrive at a common understanding.

When top leaders—be it of an organization or a nation—meet face-to-face, they can easily convey their thoughts and make swift decisions. This is because their reasoning is guided by a strong sense of responsibility. In the realm of religion, too, when responsible people sit down and talk together frankly and open-mindedly, they are certain to find common ground.

It was Mr. Toda's view that the founders of universal religions in particular—irrespective of the differences in the times and societies in which they lived and in their particular approach or methodology—would be sure to find agreement in their shared wish to rid humankind of misery.

The problem, however, is that later heirs to these religious traditions invariably lose sight of the founder's original goal of people's happiness. Forgetting the intense struggles waged by the founder, they become increasingly preoccupied with ritual and formality. Eventually, they succumb to self-interest and personal ambition, denigrating the lay believers, the ordinary people. One of the most conspicuous examples of this is the Nichiren Shoshu priesthood, which is notorious for its blatant disregard for the welfare of its lay believers. By acting against Nichiren's spirit, it has degenerated into a school that espouses erroneous teachings.

The reason Nichiren vigorously refuted the other established Buddhist schools of his day was that their priests had turned their backs on Buddhism's original purpose and obscured the teaching of universal enlightenment that holds the key to the happiness of all people. He always made the happiness of the people his criterion. Because his actions were "solely for the sake of the nation, for the sake of the Law, for the sake of others" ("The Rationale for Writing 'On Establishing the Correct Teaching for the Peace of the Land,'" WND-1, 164) and "for the sake of all living beings" ("Letter to Hojo Tokimune," WND-2, 315), he dared to remonstrate with the ruler and refute the erroneous teachings of the other Buddhist schools. He was unable to ignore the situation where, because of the misguided priests of these schools, people's grief grew increasingly deeper (see "The Letter of Petition from Yorimoto," WND-1, 809).

In another writing, Nichiren declares that even wise individuals unaware of the teachings of Buddhism who came to the aid of those suffering and put an end to their anguish could be considered emissaries of the Buddha (see "The Kalpa of Decrease," WND-1, 1121–22).[15] While they may not have thought of themselves as such, the wisdom of Buddhism resided in their hearts.

In "The Supremacy of the Law," too, Nichiren first explains how, before the arrival of Buddhism in China, the writings or teachings of numerous sages and ideal rulers provided positive guidelines for the people to live by and contributed to the creation of a peaceful, well-ordered society.

Among the values they taught, he notes, was propriety, including respect for one's parents and the ruler. Here, of course, Nichiren isn't recommending that we embrace a feudal morality. But back in those days, a way of life based on a system of mutual obligations and a code of behavior centering on respect for one's parents, teachers and sovereign served as a crucial foundation for a society that was mutually beneficial for everyone.

External rules and standards alone, however, are insufficient to help people gain mastery over various human desires and impulses. So when Buddhism, with its more profound teachings and insights into human nature and existence, arrived in China, it eventually gained wide acceptance.

Buddhism is a teaching that enriches our lives and helps us develop outstanding character and humanity. Employing the profound wisdom of Buddhism that is the starting point of human revolution, we can greatly contribute to our own happiness as well as the happiness of others, which is the original purpose of all religions. Any religious tradition that forgets to put people first invariably grows self-righteous and dogmatic.

Ideally, the adherents of the various world religions should strive in a spirit of friendly competition to lead others to happiness. As Soka Gakkai members, we need to ponder how best to convey to people everywhere the true value of Nichiren Daishonin's humanistic Buddhism, which is based on the Lotus Sutra's lofty ideal of universal enlightenment. Today, as global pioneers of an age of humanistic competition, we are working hard to develop ourselves and also foster others. We are noble trailblazers spreading a religion for all humankind in the twenty-first century. Let's advance confidently with this pride.

The Great Ship of the Lotus Sutra

In contrast [to the Hinayana sutras], the Mahayana sutras are like those huge vessels that, carrying ten or twenty people and loaded with large quantities of cargo, can sail from Kamakura as far as Tsukushi or Mutsu Province.

But the ship of the true Mahayana sutra is incomparably greater than those ships that are the other Mahayana sutra. Loaded with a hoard of rare treasures and carrying a hundred or a thousand passengers, it can sail all the way to the land of Korea. The sutra called the Lotus Sutra of the one vehicle is like this. (WND-1, 612–13)

Nichiren Daishonin first acknowledges the positive role played by Confucian and other non-Buddhist teachings in ancient China and then highlights the ultimate superiority of Buddhism. Next, he explains that the Buddhist teachings themselves are also ranked according to merit. He says some Buddhist sutras "were superior in content or more profound than others" (WND-1, 612).

The expression "superior in content or more profound" doesn't mean, for instance, that certain sutras are utterly worthless; rather, it indicates each sutra's relative merit in terms of the whole, in that each has meaning or relevance corresponding to the time and the capacity of the people when it was preached. This means that when a more profound teaching appears in response to the time and people's capacity, then the pre-existing teachings become shallow and inferior in comparison.

As clarified in this writing, Nichiren bases his evaluation of the different sutras on the criteria of how many people they are capable of leading to happiness and also whether they can serve as a means to free all humankind from suffering.

He offers an easily accessible comparison, likening the respective Buddhist teachings categorized as Hinayana, provisional Mahayana and true Mahayana (the Lotus Sutra) to boats or ships of different sizes. The Hinayana sutras, he says, are like small boats that can carry only two or three passengers and a modest amount of cargo and are unable to travel far from shore. The provisional Mahayana sutras are like large ships that can carry ten to twenty people and a substantial payload and make lengthy journeys from one part of Japan to another. But superior is the ship of the Lotus Sutra (the sutra of the Buddha's true teaching). It is like a great oceangoing vessel that can carry hundreds of passengers, hold a cargo of rare treasures and travel as far away as the Korean Peninsula.

The Daishonin thus offers a list of objective criteria—(1) passenger capacity, (2) maximum range and (3) cargo capacity. Of these: "passenger capacity" corresponds to the number or scope of people that the sutra's teaching can lead to enlightenment; "maximum range" corresponds to the depth and richness of the state of life one can attain through continued practice of the sutra's teaching; and "cargo capacity" corresponds to the efficacy of the sutra's teaching and the depth of wisdom and insight it contains.

In short, the Lotus Sutra, by expounding the principle of the "mutual possession of the Ten Worlds,"[16] is the only teaching that reveals that all people possess within them the potential to become Buddhas. By bringing forth our inner Buddhahood, we attain enlightenment. The Lotus Sutra, therefore, is the great ship for all humankind, possessing infinite passenger capacity and unlimited range.

Moreover, this ship is available to us not only in this lifetime alone. The great ship of the Lotus Sutra, a teaching that enables us to actualize indestructible happiness, will also take us across the sea of the sufferings of birth and death. That is why Shakyamuni declares: "This sutra can save all living beings ... It is like ... someone finding a ship in which to cross the water" (LSOC, 327–28).

Nichiren wished first and foremost to give Nichimyo the confidence and peace of mind of knowing that those who embrace faith in the Mystic Law will definitely attain a state of absolute happiness.

The Lotus Sutra's Revolutionary Teaching of the Enlightenment of Women

Devadatta was the most evil man in the entire land of Jambudvipa [the whole world], but the Lotus Sutra predicted that he would become the Thus Come One Heavenly King. Although Ajatashatru was a wicked king who killed his own father, he was among those present when the Lotus Sutra was preached, and after hearing only a verse or a phrase, formed a connection with the sutra [that would enable him to attain enlightenment in the future]. The dragon king's daughter, a woman with a reptile's body, attained Buddhahood by listening to Bodhisattva

Manjushri preach the Lotus Sutra. Furthermore, the Buddha designated the evil era of the Latter Day of the Law as the very time for the Lotus Sutra to be propagated, and bequeathed it to the men and women of that impure age. The Lotus Sutra, the teaching of the one vehicle, is then a sutra as great and as powerful as the ships of the China trade. (WND-1, 613)

In this next section, Nichiren Daishonin touches on the enlightenment of evil people and women. The sutras expounded prior to the Lotus Sutra (such as the provisional Mahayana sutras) held that evil people and women were incapable of attaining Buddhahood. Many practitioners therefore felt resigned to that unfortunate fate; but the Lotus Sutra firmly dispels such disconsolation by proclaiming broadly that all people have the potential for Buddhahood.

The power of the Lotus Sutra's teaching is such that it can enable even evil people like Devadatta and King Ajatashatru to attain enlightenment. Devadatta was a former disciple who turned on Shakyamuni Buddha and committed many grave offenses, including causing disunity in the Buddhist Order.[17] As a result, he is said to have fallen into the hell of incessant suffering while still alive. Ajatashatru, meanwhile, was the king of Magadha who, at Devadatta's instigation, arrested and deposed his father, King Bimbisara, in order to seize the throne for himself. He also plotted to assassinate Shakyamuni.

Above all, the Lotus Sutra teaches the enlightenment of women, who in the pre-Lotus Sutra teachings had been scorned and despised. The dragon king's daughter, hearing Manjushri preach the Lotus Sutra—the "secret teaching of the attainment of Buddhahood in one's present form"[18]—instantly manifests the life state of a Buddha. In doing so, she scored a victory for the happiness of women everywhere.

The enlightenment of the dragon king's daughter might seem to have no relevance to the enlightenment of men. But Nichiren writes, "All living beings are the dragon king's daughter as an essential or intrinsic quality" (OTT, 230). The enlightenment of the dragon king's daughter, in other words, is a vital precondition for the enlightenment of all people, because it serves as actual proof of the principle of "attaining Buddhahood in one's present form." It could be said to symbolize the enlightenment of all humankind.

The reason Nichiren mentions Devadatta and the dragon king's daughter here is that in the next passage, he explains that the Lotus Sutra was bequeathed to the men and women of the evil age of the Latter Day of the Law. The Lotus Sutra is a teaching that can lead people of all capacities to enlightenment in even the most terrible times and impure lands. Nam-myoho-renge-kyo—the teaching of sowing[19] at the heart of the Lotus Sutra—serves as the cause or catalyst that unlocks the Buddha nature inherent in the lives of all people, no matter who they are.

Nichimyo must have gained incredible courage from Nichiren's confident assertion that the Lotus Sutra is a teaching for the men and women of the Latter Day.

President Toda wrote: "No matter how advanced civilization might become, there will be no true happiness for humanity in a world where nations ignore morality and engage in endless power struggles. In the unfortunate event of a nuclear war breaking out, the inhabitants of our planet will be headed for certain destruction. I am convinced that it is precisely for this present age that Nichiren Daishonin bequeathed to us a great religion that can prevent the destruction of humankind."[20]

Memories of my mentor's unquenchable passion and enthusiasm for kosen-rufu live on in my heart. We must keep moving forward in our undertaking. How disappointed Nichiren would be if our movement ever ground to a halt. It would signal an age in which humanity slips back into barbarism. Let us therefore continue to forge ahead with unshakable conviction in our noble endeavor of ending the interminable cycle of misery and suffering that has plagued humankind.

Genuine Leaders Work for People's Happiness

Moreover, there is superiority and inferiority not only among the sutras, but also among their adherents. The various teachers of the True Word school, who believe in the Mahavairochana Sutra, are like fire being put out by water, or dew being blown away by the wind when confronted in debate by the votary of the Lotus Sutra. If a dog barks at a lion, its bowels will rot. The asura demon who shot an arrow at the sun had his head split into seven pieces. The True Word teachers are like the dog or the asura, while the votary of the Lotus Sutra is like the sun or the lion. (WND-1, 613)

In this section, Nichiren Daishonin asserts that the practitioners of the different sutras can also be ranked in a corresponding manner to the sutras themselves.

In one writing, he cites T'ien-t'ai's *The Words and Phrases of the Lotus Sutra*, "Since the Law is wonderful, the person is worthy of respect" ("The Person and the Law," WND-1, 1097). In another writing, he himself asserts, "If the Law that one embraces is supreme, then the person who embraces it must accordingly be foremost among all others" ("Questions and Answers about Embracing the Lotus Sutra," WND-1, 61).

The true measure of human beings and of the depth and breadth of their lives is found in their wisdom, the beliefs and philosophy from which that wisdom derives, and to what extent they have embodied or actualized their ideals.

Nichiren notes that there is a world of difference between the votary of the Lotus Sutra and the priests of the True Word school. In a debate, the former would prevail as easily as water extinguishes fire or wind blows away the dew.

Why does he single out the True Word priests for criticism? We can assume it was because at that time, the entire country was relying heavily on the priests of this school to offer up incantations and prayers for the defeat of the Mongol forces. Also, the esoteric True Word school enjoyed unsurpassed influence and prestige in Japanese society during Nichiren's day. Even the Tendai school, originally based on the Lotus Sutra, gradually fell under the influence of the esoteric doctrines and rituals of the True Word school. Beguiling people with the mystique of their incantations and prayers, the priests of various schools, especially the True Word school, ingratiated themselves with those in power, gaining patronage and protection.

It was exactly the opposite of the behavior of the votary of the Lotus Sutra, who, in accord with the sutra's teachings, championed the cause of universal enlightenment and remonstrated with the ruling authorities to get them to abandon their erroneous tenets.

The people of Nichiren's day should have been asking these questions about the established

Buddhist schools: Did they benefit the people or merely seek to bolster their own authority and power? Did they lead people to happiness or consign them to misfortune? Did they combat the devilish nature of power or collude with it? But, sadly, the people had no way of knowing the true nature of these schools.

Nichiren scornfully notes that the priests of these various Buddhist schools give the appearance of being "most dignified and wise" (WND-1, 613) but that this has no substance in reality. In other words, they deceive people with their seeming virtue and wisdom. Frauds are skilled at duping people. That is why the only real solution lies with people becoming wiser.

In order to awaken people so that they can make prudent decisions, Nichiren continues his blistering castigation. He says: "If a dog barks at a lion, its bowels will rot. The asura demon who shot an arrow at the sun had his head split into seven pieces."[21] The True Word priests with their aberrant views, he states, are exactly like these dogs and *asura* demons. To protect the correct teaching, he speaks out boldly and incisively against erroneous teachings that not only spell suffering for the people but can easily put the entire country on the path to ruin.

Without deeply engraving in our hearts Nichiren's solemn determination to protect the Law, we cannot be regarded as genuine disciples. This passage vividly conveys Nichiren's noble commitment to keep on fighting, even if entirely alone, to protect the Lotus Sutra and defend the spirit of Shakyamuni Buddha.

Supporting those who work for the people's welfare, but denouncing those who discriminate against the people; being open to ideals that benefit humanity, but rejecting those that inflict suffering—this is the spirit of genuine humanism. Because this was the spirit with which he fought, the Daishonin, the votary of the Lotus Sutra, is "like the sun or the lion."

Let us also live out our lives like lions and the shining sun. The lion is the fearless king of beasts. The sun brightly illuminates society and the world and fills people's hearts with hope.

As the Japanese author and critic Mimpei Sugiura observed: "Since World War II, the Soka Gakkai has devoted itself to awakening the people. Human beings can only be polished in company with other human beings."[22] To calmly surmount all storms of criticism and abuse and go out among the people to help others gain wisdom and insight—this is the essence of our Soka movement for human revolution. It is none other than the struggle to achieve peace and prosperity in society through widely spreading the humanistic ideals and principles of Buddhism, just as Nichiren instructs.

In this writing, he conveys to Nichimyo his towering conviction that lions are dauntless and the sun invincible, and that through faith in the Mystic Law, we can open the way to a life of good, happiness and victory.

The Times Demand a Leadership Revolution

As you know, before the Mongol attack, the arrogance of the people of our day knew no bounds. Since the tenth month of last year [October 1274, when the first Mongol invasion occurred], however, none of them has dared to assume a haughty attitude, for as you have heard, Nichiren alone predicted this foreign invasion. If the Mongols attack our country again, none of the people will have the courage to face them ... In battles soldiers regard the general as their soul. If the general were to lose heart, his soldiers would become cowards. (WND-1, 613)

In July 1260, Nichiren Daishonin completed his treatise "On Establishing the Correct Teaching for the Peace of the Land," in which he predicted that, unless the correct teaching was followed, the country would soon suffer internal strife and foreign invasion. These were the only two calamities among the so-called "three calamities and seven disasters"[23] that had not yet assailed Japan. Nichiren presented this treatise as a remonstration to Hojo Tokiyori, the retired regent but still the most powerful figure in Japan's ruling clan.

Neither the ruler nor the general populace, however, paid serious attention to his pointed warnings. They even refused to give his words credence after a delegation of emissaries from the Mongol empire arrived on Japanese shores. On the contrary, jealous priests of the other Buddhist schools and deluded government authorities conspired to have the Daishonin executed at Tatsunokuchi.[24] Thus, as a result of the widespread slander of the correct teaching in society, he says, the heavenly deities—the protective forces of the universe—abandoned the country, and because of this, his prediction of foreign invasion came true. In October 1274, the year before "The Supremacy of the Law" was written, the Mongol forces attacked Japan for the first time.

Before coming to see the Mongol forces as a real and present threat, the people had been blithely confident and unconcerned. But once the country was actually attacked, they were thrown into fear and confusion. "None of them," Nichiren writes, "has dared to assume a haughty attitude." And he even goes so far as to say that should the Mongol forces attack again, there would probably be no one brave enough to face them head-on (see WND-1, 613).

Further, in April 1275, a few months before this letter was written, another Mongol delegation arrived. The country was again in turmoil. The government, which ultimately beheaded the envoys (in September of that year), hastened to step up its security and defense measures. It requested Buddhist temples and Shinto shrines throughout the land to pray for the defeat of the foreign invaders.

"Nichiren alone predicted this foreign invasion"—he was the only one who perfectly apprehended the situation based on the keen insight of Buddhism and had repeatedly warned that the two remaining calamities would occur. It is just as he says when he writes, "Three times now I have gained distinction by having such [prophetic] knowledge"[25] ("The Selection of the Time," WND-1, 579).

Starting with the submission of "On Establishing the Correct Teaching," he remonstrated with the authorities three times,[26] persevering amid unrelenting persecution and great hardships. This arose from his compassionate desire to save all people from suffering. It was an unprecedented struggle to fundamentally transform the deeply ingrained societal mentality that prevented people from properly distinguishing right from wrong.

At the time of the Mongol invasion, those who until then had been haughty and arrogant were suddenly petrified. Notes Nichiren, "All ... have become cowards" (WND-1, 613). Nevertheless, reflecting his compassionate resolve to lead every person to happiness, he declares: "In battles soldiers regard the general as their soul. If the general were to lose heart, his soldiers would become cowards."

Japan had to weather an unprecedented national calamity. At precisely such a time, there was a critical need for leaders with proper insight and courage. But the top rulers of the military government had lost the ability to make correct decisions and were consumed with fear. In terms of diplomacy, summarily beheading the envoys of another country could not be considered a normal or sane course of action.

Nichiren says that just as frontline soldiers under a general who shows cowardice in battle will lose courage, so those ruled by errant leaders will grow fearful and fainthearted. It was the same with Japan during World War II. A deplorably misguided group of leaders brought the country to ruin. People led by foolish leaders are truly unfortunate.

"We mustn't permit this situation where people suffer the direst distress because of inept and incompetent leaders! Now is the time for a leadership revolution!"—this was the essence of the Daishonin's fervent resolve to keep fighting based on his unwavering commitment to the welfare of the people, which is evident in this writing.

Where, then, could the country find a true leader, a truly "great general," who could lead it out of this difficult situation? In challenging Ryokan of Gokurakuji [a temple in Kamakura], a prominent priest of the True Word Precepts school, to a public debate, the Daishonin proclaimed, "I, Nichiren, am the foremost votary of the Lotus Sutra in all of Japan, a great general who can defeat the forces of the Mongol nation"

("Letter to Ryokan of Gokuraku-ji," WND-2, 324). We can discern here his supreme life state—his profound awareness that he alone could truly save the country from this threat of national calamity.

Let us therefore take as a guideline for leadership the words: "In battles soldiers regard the general as their soul. If the general were to lose heart, his soldiers would become cowards." Mr. Makiguchi underlined this passage in his copy of Nichiren's writings, and he constantly embodied it in his own behavior. Mr. Toda and I, too, amid major struggles for kosen-rufu, read this passage together with our fellow members as a source of strength and inspiration for our advance.

The more troubled the times, irrespective of the challenge, the more crucial is the attitude and resolve of those in leadership positions. Are the leaders energetic? Are they brimming with enthusiasm, a passionate fighting spirit? Are they filled with a fearless and tenacious determination to win in the face of even the most difficult trials?

Courage inspires courage. One wave gives rise to a thousand in a ripple effect that powerfully spreads through the entire organization until everyone is emboldened, finally producing an overwhelming ground-swell toward victory. Everything hinges on the leaders.

This year [2009] marks the bicentennial of the birth of Abraham Lincoln, the sixteenth U.S.

president. The well-known American poet of the people, Walt Whitman, sang the slain leader's praises—in one poem calling him, "O Captain! my Captain!"[27] and in another describing him as:

Gentle, plain, just and resolute—under whose cautious hand,
Against the foulest crime in history known in any land or age,
Was saved the union of These States.[28]

Whitman paid moving tribute to Lincoln who, as a pioneer of democracy, had steered the ship of his nation toward the realization of a great ideal.

As practitioners of Nichiren Buddhism, we are continuing our epic voyage of kosen-rufu aboard the great ship of the Soka Gakkai in order to lead all people of the Latter Day to happiness. In a well-loved Soka Gakkai song, we find the line "This ship is on a sure course to historic achievement."[29] Accordingly, let us create a glorious, indestructible history as trailblazers in this noblest of human endeavors we aspire to fulfill.

This lecture was originally published in the July 2009 issue of the Daibyakurenge, *the Soka Gakkai's monthly study journal.*

NOTES

[1] Three Sovereigns: Also called the Three Rulers. Fu Hsi, Shen Nung and Huang Ti (Yellow Emperor), legendary rulers of ancient China. They are usually regarded as having invented fishing, farming and medicine, respectively. In his writings, Nichiren Daishonin often refers to Shen Nung and Huang Ti as masters of medicine, and refers to the reigns of Fu Hsi and Shen Nung as an age in which an ideal society was realized.

[2] Five Emperors: The five legendary sage emperors in China who are said to have reigned after the Three Sovereigns. There are three different sets of Five Emperors in the classics. One of them lists Shao Hao, Chuan Hsü, Ti Kao, T'ang Yao and Yü Shun.

[3] Three Kings: Founders of the three dynasties, Hsia, Yin (Shang) and Chou, in China. They are King Yü of the Hsia dynasty, King T'ang of the Yin dynasty and King Wen of the Chou dynasty. They are said to have realized model governments.

[4] T'ai-kung Wang: A general who served King Wen, the founder of the Chou dynasty of China. During the Yin (Shang)

dynasty, he was living in seclusion but emerged to lead the army of King Wen at the latter's request. After Wen's death, he served King Wu, Wen's successor, and fought valorously to defeat King Chou of the Yin dynasty.

[5] Tan the Duke of Chou: A younger brother of King Wu, the founder of the Chou dynasty (circa 1100–256BCE). After assisting his brother in the task of overthrowing the Yin (Shang) dynasty and founding a new rule, he continued to be closely involved in the affairs of government. When King Wu died and his son Ch'eng, who was still a child, came to the throne, the Duke of Chou acted as regent for the young ruler. He has been revered over the centuries by Confucianists as a model of correct government and propriety.

[6] Kamakura: The seat of the Japanese military government during Nichiren Daishonin's day. Located in present-day Kanagawa Prefecture.

[7] Tsukushi was located in what is part of present-day northern Kyushu, while Mutsu Province was located in the northeastern part of Japan that corresponds roughly to the present-day Tohoku region.

[8] Devadatta: A cousin and disciple of Shakyamuni. Out of arrogance, however, he eventually became an enemy of Shakyamuni and committed many grave offenses, including disrupting the Buddhist Order and attempting to kill the Buddha. As a result, Devadatta is said to have fallen into hell alive. In the Lotus Sutra, however, Shakyamuni predicts that Devadatta will attain enlightenment in the future as a Buddha named Heavenly King. This illustrates the principle that even evil persons have the potential for enlightenment.

[9] Ajatashatru: A king of Magadha in India in the time of Shakyamuni. At the urging of Devadatta, he gained the throne by arresting and deposing his father, King Bimbisara, a follower of Shakyamuni. He also made attempts on the lives of the Buddha and his disciples. Later, he converted to Buddhism out of remorse for his evil acts and supported the First Buddhist Council in its compilation of Shakyamuni's teachings.

[10] Dragon king's daughter: Also, the dragon girl. The eight-year-old daughter of Sagara, one of the eight great dragon kings said to dwell in a palace at the

bottom of the sea. In "Devadatta," the 12th chapter of the Lotus Sutra, the dragon girl conceives the desire for enlightenment upon hearing Bodhisattva Manjushri preach the Lotus Sutra in the dragon king's palace. She then appears in front of the assembly of the Lotus Sutra and instantaneously attains Buddhahood in her present form. The dragon girl's enlightenment is a model for the enlightenment of women and reveals the power of the Lotus Sutra to enable all people equally to attain Buddhahood just as they are.

[11] Manjushri: A bodhisattva who appears in the sutras as the leader of the bodhisattvas of the theoretical teaching and is regarded as symbolic of the perfection of wisdom.

[12] One vehicle: Also, single vehicle, Buddha vehicle, one Buddha vehicle, one vehicle of Buddhahood or supreme vehicle. Refers to the Buddha's highest or true teaching that can carry or lead all people to enlightenment; in other words, the Lotus Sutra.

[13] True Word (Jpn Shingon) school: A Buddhist school in Japan established by Kobo (774–835), also known as Kukai,

that follows the esoteric doctrines and practices found in the Mahavairochana and Diamond Crown sutras, its two fundamental scriptures. The name *true word* is the rendering in Chinese of the Sanskrit mantra (meaning secret word or mystic formula). In the True Word school, this indicates the words that Mahavairochana Buddha is said to have uttered. The chanting of these secret words is one of the school's basic esoteric rituals for the attainment of enlightenment. In 804 Kobo traveled from Japan to Ch'ang-an, where he studied Esoteric Buddhism under Huikuo. In 806 he returned to Japan with numerous Buddhist scriptures, esoteric mandalas and ritual implements, and in 809 entered the capital, Kyoto, where he advocated the supremacy of Esoteric Buddhism.

[14]　In "Letter to the Sage Nichimyo," Nichiren writes: "You are the foremost votary of the Lotus Sutra among the women of Japan. Therefore, following the example of Bodhisattva Never Disparaging, I bestow on you the Buddhist name Sage Nichimyo" (WND-1, 325). The Sage Nichimyo is thought to

be the same person referred to elsewhere in his writings as the "mother of Oto" (WND-2, 1030).

[15] In "The Kalpa of Decrease," citing the example of ancient Chinese leaders who restored peace and order to the realm, the Daishonin writes: "Though these men lived before the introduction of Buddhism, they helped the people as emissaries of Shakyamuni Buddha, the lord of teachings. And though the adherents of the non-Buddhist scriptures were unaware of it, the wisdom of such men contained at heart the wisdom of Buddhism" (WND-1, 1121–22).

[16] Mutual possession of the Ten Worlds: The principle that each of the Ten Worlds possesses the potential for all ten within itself. "Mutual possession" means that life is not fixed in one or another of the Ten Worlds but can manifest any of the ten—from hell to the state of Buddhahood—at any given moment. The important point of this principle is that all beings in any of the nine worlds possess the Buddha nature. This means that every person has the potential to manifest Buddhahood, while a Buddha also possesses the nine worlds

and in this sense is not separate or different from ordinary people.

[17] Causing disunity in the Buddhist Order: The Buddhist Order means the community of believers who practice and propagate the Law. To disrupt the unity of practitioners is counted as one of the five cardinal sins, the most serious offenses in Buddhism.

[18] In "Hell Is the Land of Tranquil Light," Nichiren writes, "This teaching [of the Lotus Sutra] is of prime importance, but I will impart it to you just as Bodhisattva Manjushri explained the secret teaching of the attainment of Buddhahood in one's present form to the dragon king's daughter" (WND-1, 457).

[19] Teaching of sowing: "Sowing" refers to the process by which the Buddha sows in people's lives the seed or fundamental cause for attaining enlightenment. The entity of the teaching of sowing is Nam-myoho-renge-kyo.

[20] Translated from Japanese. Josei Toda, "Soka Gakkai no rekishi to kakushin" (The History and Conviction of the Soka Gakkai), in *Toda Josei zenshu* (Collected

Writings of Josei Toda) (Tokyo: Seikyo Shimbunsha, 1983), vol.3, p.112.

[21] These are references from ancient Indian folklore.

[22] Translated from Japanese. Article by Mimpei Sugiura, November 18, 1999, *Seikyo Shimbun*.

[23] Three calamities and seven disasters: Catastrophes described in various sutras. The three calamities occur at the end of a kalpa. There are two types: the three greater calamities of fire, water and wind, which destroy the world, and the three lesser calamities of high grain prices or inflation (especially that caused by famine), warfare and pestilence, from which human society perishes. The seven disasters include war and natural disasters and are generally held to result from slander of the correct teaching. They are mentioned in the Medicine Master, Benevolent Kings and other sutras. They differ slightly according to the source. Nichiren combined these two different types of calamities in a single phrase to explain the disasters besetting Japan in his time. In his 1260 treatise "On Establishing the Correct Teaching for the Peace of the Land," he

states, based on the sutras, that they occur because both the rulers and the populace turn against the correct teaching.

[24] This refers to the Tatsunokuchi Persecution. On September 12, 1271, powerful figures in the government unjustly arrested Nichiren and led him off in the middle of the night to a place called Tatsunokuchi on the outskirts of Kamakura, the seat of government, where they tried to execute him under cover of darkness. The execution attempt failed, and, about a month later, the Daishonin was exiled to Sado Island.

[25] Three instances of gaining distinction: Also known as the "three-time gaining of distinction" or "three-time distinction." This refers to Nichiren making accurate predictions at the time of each of his three remonstrations with the ruling authorities. The first instance was his prophecy of internal strife and foreign invasion made on submitting "On Establishing the Correct Teaching for the Peace of the Land" on July 16, 1260. The second was his second prophecy of internal strife and foreign invasion made in his remonstration to Hei no Saemon,

when the latter came to arrest him on the evening of September 12, 1271, at the time of the Tatsunokuchi Persecution. And the third instance was his prophecy of foreign invasion made in his final remonstration to Hei no Saemon on April 8, 1274, after returning to Kamakura from his exile on Sado Island.

[26] The occasions of the three remonstrations are identical to those described as the three instances of gaining distinction. See footnote 25.

[27] Walt Whitman, "O Captain! My Captain!" in *Leaves of Grass* (London: Everyman's Library, 1968), p.282.

[28] Walt Whitman, "Memories of President Lincoln," in *Leaves of Grass* (London: Everyman's Library, 1968), p.283.

[29] A line from the song, "Kofu ni hashire" (Onward to Kosen-rufu).

CHAPTER 8

"THE SUPREMACY OF THE LAW"—PART 2 OF 3

LEADING A LIFE OF PRINCIPLE AND CONVICTION TOGETHER WITH ONE'S MENTOR

Passage for Study in This Lecture

Women regard their husband as their soul. Without their husband, they lack a soul. Nowadays, even married women find it difficult to get along in the world. Though you have lost your soul, you lead your life more courageously than those who have one. Furthermore, because you maintain your faith in the gods and you revere the Buddha, you are indeed a woman who surpasses others...

Certainly the heavenly gods will protect you, and the ten demon daughters[1] will have compassion on you. The Buddha promised in the Lotus Sutra that, for women, the sutra will

serve as a lantern in the darkness, as a ship when they cross the sea, and as a protector when they travel through dangerous places[2]...

Furthermore, human beings have two heavenly gods who always accompany them, just as a shadow follows the body. One is named Same Birth and the other Same Name. Perched on one's left and right shoulders, they protect one [by reporting all of one's deeds to heaven]. Therefore, heaven never punishes those who have committed no error, let alone people of merit.

That is why the Great Teacher Miao-lo[3] stated, "The stronger one's faith, the greater the protection of the gods."[4] So long as one maintains firm faith, one is certain to receive the great protection of the gods. I say this for your sake. I know your faith has always been admirable, but now you must strengthen it more than ever. Only then will the ten demon daughters lend you even greater protection. You need not seek far for an example. Everyone in Japan, from the sovereign on down to the common people, without exception has tried to do me harm, but I have survived until this day. You should realize that this is because, although I am alone, I have firm faith.

If a boat is handled by an unskilled steersman, it may capsize and drown everyone aboard. Likewise, though someone may have great physical strength, if he lacks a resolute spirit, even his many abilities will be of no use. In this country, there may be many wise people, but they cannot utilize their wisdom because they are governed by foolish leaders...

At that time, those who declared they would not see or listen to me will join their palms together and take faith in the Lotus Sutra. Even the adherents of the Nembutsu and Zen schools will chant Nam-myoho-renge-kyo...

When I was about to be beheaded, the World-Honored One of Great Enlightenment took my place. It is the same in the present as it was in the past. All of you are my lay supporters, so how can you fail to attain Buddhahood? (WND-1, 613–15)

LECTURE

Through the power of faith in the Mystic Law, those who have suffered the most can attain the greatest happiness. Nichiren Buddhism enables those who have triumphed over hardship and adversity to become inspiring leaders who can help many others.

Nichiren Daishonin sought to enable all his followers to become genuine practitioners of the Mystic Law. He lived among the ordinary people and endeavored to foster authentic disciples capable of realizing happiness for themselves and others. This letter, "The Supremacy of the Law," is infused throughout with his compassionate wish that its recipient, Nichimyo, and her daughter, Oto, lead truly happy lives and, toward that end, develop the strong faith that would allow them to resiliently weather any challenge presented by the evil times in which they lived. The Daishonin's words also paint a vivid image of how sincerely Nichimyo had striven thus far in following his guidance and devoting herself to the path of faith.

For Nichimyo, and many of Nichiren's other women followers, the answer to such fundamental questions as "What is a correct way of life?" and "How can I lead a truly meaningful existence?" was to advance together with this great teacher of Buddhism who, despite momentous obstacles, remained steadfast in his principles and convictions. In this and numerous other writings, he unstintingly commends the faith of his female disciples. Such praise is no doubt inspired by his fervent hope that each without exception would enjoy a happy and victorious life.

My mentor, second Soka Gakkai president Josei Toda, used to say, "When mothers everywhere are happy, we will have true peace in the world." I share exactly the same sentiment, and I have consistently acted with the belief that the alliance of Soka women—leading happy and winning lives—will have a profound impact on the world and contribute to the creation of a new age of women.

This part of my lecture on "The Supremacy of the Law" will focus on the essentials of faith Nichiren outlines in order for us to be victors in life and experts in the art of happiness.

Victory Lies in Striving With the Same Commitment as Our Mentor

Women regard their husband as their soul. Without their husband, they lack a soul. Nowadays, even married women find it difficult to get along in the world. Though you have lost your soul, you lead your life more courageously than those who have one. Furthermore, because you maintain your faith in the gods and you revere the Buddha, you are indeed a woman who surpasses others... Certainly the heavenly gods will protect you, and the ten demon daughters will have compassion on you. (WND-1, 613–14)

"Women regard their husband as their soul. Without their husband, they lack a soul"

(WND-1, 613), writes Nichiren Daishonin in thirteenth-century feudal Japan. "Soul" here can be interpreted as meaning support, mainstay or sustenance.

Epidemics and famines were rampant throughout the land, and the threat of a second Mongol invasion loomed over the populace. It must have been arduous for Nichimyo to survive amid these troubled times without a husband to support and protect her. Yet, she did not give in to self-pity or despair. Undaunted by circumstances, she applied herself steadfastly to her Buddhist practice, just as Nichiren instructed.

"You are indeed a woman who surpasses others," he extols her. I believe these words of praise for Nichimyo can also be taken as inspiring encouragement for all women practitioners of Nichiren Buddhism. He assures Nichimyo that if she continues to earnestly chant Nam-myoho-renge-kyo, she can overcome all suffering and negative karma and go on to write a triumphant personal history. And these are not his only words of praise for her. Noting that she had journeyed to visit him during his exile on distant Sado Island, amid a time of intense persecution that saw many other followers abandon their faith, he exclaims, "It was almost too amazing to be true" (WND-1, 614).

Not only did Nichimyo travel to Sado, but, because of her seeking spirit and desire to repay her gratitude, after Nichiren was pardoned from exile and subsequently took up residence at

Mount Minobu,[5] she also visited him there. Nichiren warmly confirms that because of her sincere devotion, the protective forces of the universe will safeguard her and compassionately watch over her without fail.

The depth of our commitment to faith is revealed at a crucial moment. The touchstone is whether, when it really counts, we continue taking action in the same spirit as our mentor.

Viewed from the perspective of Buddhism, Nichiren's exile to Sado was simply a devious plot by hostile forces to drive a wedge between him and his followers. Devilish functions always seek to divide the forces of the Buddha.

The Soka Gakkai is the community of believers accomplishing the Buddha's intent and decree in the modern day. Throughout our history, we have faced countless schemes by malevolent forces bent on breaking the unity of mentor and disciple. But such onslaughts, in fact, ultimately served to show who genuinely shared the mentor's commitment.

This was the case during World War II when the Japanese militarist government cracked down on the activities of the Soka Kyoiku Gakkai (or Value-Creating Education Society, forerunner of the Soka Gakkai) and jailed our first president, Tsunesaburo Makiguchi. While one after another of the top leaders of the organization betrayed and deserted Mr. Makiguchi, Josei Toda alone remained a loyal disciple to the end, sharing with him the ordeal of prison.

Later, on the second anniversary of Mr. Makiguchi's death, gazing tearfully at a photo of his deceased mentor, Mr. Toda voiced these now-famous words:

> In your vast and boundless compassion, you let me accompany you even to prison ... The benefit of this was coming to know my former existence as a Bodhisattva of the Earth[6] and to absorb with my very life even a small degree of the [Lotus] sutra's meaning. Could there be any greater happiness than this?[7]

Mr. Toda demonstrated how it is possible to triumph over all devilish functions, all adversity, when we devote ourselves to kosen-rufu with the same spirit as our mentor. Such efforts also enable us to develop an expansive state of life overflowing with good fortune and benefit.

It would seem evident from Nichimyo's dedicated commitment to practicing the Mystic Law alongside Nichiren that she placed complete trust in him as a true teacher of Buddhism and a person genuinely fighting for the welfare and happiness of all humankind. The women of Soka are carrying on the noble spirit of faith exhibited by Nichimyo.

Nichiren says, "Though no one else came to visit me, you, a woman, not only sent me various offerings, but personally made the journey to see me" (WND-1, 614). In terms of our activities today, this is comparable to solidly uniting our hearts with our mentor and realizing victorious achievements on the grand stage of kosen-rufu. The mentor-disciple relationship is not defined by physical distance. It ultimately comes down to the commitment and actions of the disciple.

***

"Buddhism Is About Winning"

The Buddha promised in the Lotus Sutra that, for women, the sutra will serve as a lantern in the darkness, as a ship when they cross the sea, and as a protector when they travel through dangerous places...

Furthermore, human beings have two heavenly gods who always accompany them, just as a shadow follows the body. One is named Same Birth and the other Same Name. Perched on one's left and right shoulders, they protect one [by reporting all of one's deeds to heaven]. Therefore, heaven never punishes those who have committed no error, let alone people of merit. (WND-1, 614)

Based on a passage in "Former Affairs of the Bodhisattva Medicine King," the 23rd chapter of the Lotus Sutra, Nichiren Daishonin explains that the sutra will serve as "a lantern in the darkness," "a ship when they cross the sea" and "a protector when they travel through dangerous places,"[8] emphasizing that it alone teaches that women can attain enlightenment.

Another passage in the "Medicine King" chapter describes a profound benefit of the Lotus Sutra as follows: "It can cause living beings to cast off all distress, all sickness and pain. It can unloose all the bonds of birth and death" (LSOC, 328). How wonderful it is to encounter the Lotus Sutra! How immense are the benefits of practicing it!

Actually, the benefits described in the "Medicine King" chapter are not limited to women. They apply to all living beings. In this letter to Nichimyo, however, Nichiren especially adds "for women." These words convey his wish to warmly encourage Nichimyo, giving her confidence that, in light of the sutra, her future happiness is assured. Buddhism is the foremost ally of all who are suffering.

Next, the Daishonin refers to the heavenly gods Same Birth and Same Name who, according to Buddhist lore, reside from birth on a person's shoulders. They keep a constant record of that person's good and bad deeds, and take turns to report to heaven. Since one or the other is always keeping track, their records are detailed and precise. And because of their constant reporting, there is no chance for omission or evasion. Nichiren is therefore confirming to Nichimyo that the heavenly deities are fully aware of her meritorious actions, large and small.

The law of cause and effect is strict and impartial. Cunning and deviousness do not get one far in the realm of Buddhism. Sincere, honest efforts, on the other hand, will all return to us in the form of good fortune and benefit. Those who have striven earnestly for kosen-rufu will absolutely be protected. Responsible, dedicated people will certainly be rewarded. This is my conclusion based on more than sixty years of practice.

Throughout his writings, Nichiren emphasizes that inconspicuous efforts, or struggles of which no one else is aware, will definitely produce benefit. For instance, he says: "Unseen virtue brings about visible reward" ("The Farther the Source, the Longer the Stream," WND-1, 940), "What is hidden turns into manifest virtue" ("The Three Kinds of Treasure," WND-1, 848) and "Though one's trustworthiness may at first go unnoticed, in time it will be openly rewarded" ("The Four Virtues and the Four Debts of Gratitude," WND-2, 636).

During the years I spent working for Mr. Toda, I devoted myself to countless behind-the-scenes struggles. When he faced the greatest adversity, I supported him in ways of which no one else was ever aware. Because of those efforts, I often couldn't attend Soka Gakkai meetings or activities. Some top leaders callously remarked, "Ikeda's quit practicing." But I wasn't swayed in the least, because I was confident that supporting and assisting Mr. Toda would lead to the advance of kosen-rufu.

One day, as I waged this solitary struggle, Mr. Toda said to me with a bright glint in his eyes: "Daisaku, Buddhism is about winning. Let's fight like men, giving it our all as long as we live. Life is eternal. Evidence of our dedicated efforts will definitely appear in some form in this lifetime."

Now I understand that it is exactly as he said. The words of this great teacher of kosen-rufu are free of error. The causes for the tremendous actual proof manifested as the present global spread of kosen-rufu can be found in my selfless struggles as a youth to develop our movement. And I can state unequivocally that everything I am or have achieved today is the good fortune and benefit resulting from having done my utmost to support and protect Mr. Toda. Such is the realm of Buddhism.

The teachings of the Lotus Sutra constitute a direct path by which ordinary people of deep seeking spirit can attain absolute happiness. How inspiring Nichimyo must have found Nichiren's explanation of the great and unmistakable benefits of practicing this sutra.

The Spirit of Always Moving Forward From the Present Moment

That is why the Great Teacher Miao-lo stated, "The stronger one's faith, the

greater the protection of the gods." So long as one maintains firm faith, one is certain to receive the great protection of the gods. I say this for your sake. I know your faith has always been admirable, but now you must strengthen it more than ever. Only then will the ten demon daughters lend you even greater protection. (WND-1, 614)

Citing a passage from the Great Teacher Miao-lo, Nichiren Daishonin emphasizes that those with firm faith in the Mystic Law are certain to be protected by the Buddhist gods. This is an assurance that the protective forces of the universe will safeguard all who devote themselves to kosen-rufu with unshakable commitment.

Buddhist scriptures describe the mind as changing "eight million four thousand times" in a single day.[9] This suggests just how changeable the human mind can be. The mind can also be swayed by evil influences. It is extremely difficult to forge a mind that will remain constant amid the tempests of fundamental darkness or ignorance that rage in the polluted Latter Day of the Law. Firm faith or courageous resolve to persevere in upholding the correct teaching is therefore of vital importance.

We cannot move the heavenly deities to action with a weak or passive attitude in faith. The protective workings of these benevolent universal forces arise in response to prayers and actions infused with an unwavering determination to win and never be defeated by hardship.

In the above passage from "The Supremacy of the Law," Nichiren tells Nichimyo, "I say this for your sake." He is already well aware that Nichimyo is a woman of strong faith. But he takes this opportunity to teach her the key to establishing an even more unassailable Buddhist practice. First, he pays tribute to her commitment to seeking the correct path of Buddhism, which has been clear in her actions so far. He writes, "I know your faith has always been admirable." He then gives her this guidance, "But now you must strengthen it more than ever."

Nichiren in no way implies here that Nichimyo—who has shown herself to be a dedicated disciple by visiting him at both Sado and Minobu—lacked seeking spirit or gratitude. He urges her to strengthen her faith even more in order to teach her a cornerstone of Buddhist practice. This, in other words, is the spirit of always moving forward and continually growing—further today than yesterday, further tomorrow than today.

Nichiren Buddhism teaches the mystic principle of the true cause[10]—meaning that a fresh cause can be made at each moment—and emphasizes the present and the future. No matter how admirably we may have exerted ourselves in our Buddhist practice in the past, if we allow our efforts to grind to a halt in the present, we will eventually stop growing in faith. As the saying goes, "Not advancing is regressing."

Of course, people sometimes cannot be as active as they'd like due to illness or the infirmities of old age. And circumstances sometimes place restrictions on people's efforts for kosen-rufu. But irrespective of our situations, the important thing is not to slacken in our resolve; if we do, we cannot be said to have the firm faith that Nichiren proclaims is so necessary. No matter how hard we might have struggled in the past, if we stop practicing, then all our efforts will have been in vain.

In the latter part of this letter, too, he urges Nichimyo, "Strengthen your resolve more than ever" (WND-1, 615). Indeed, we find such encouragement throughout his writings.

An ever-fresh resolve and unflagging dedication—this has been the Soka Gakkai spirit since the pioneering days of our movement. "Forward, forward—ever forward!"—this is the motto of kosen-rufu.

Having firm faith means bravely confronting adversity, not retreating under any circumstance. Those who are weak and indecisive at a crucial moment cannot hope to bring forth the protection of the heavenly deities.

The Great Teacher T'ien-t'ai[11] discusses the importance of strong resolve using the following analogy. If the lord of a castle is resolute, his men will also be confident. But if the lord is fainthearted, his men will be fearful and anxious.[12]

No matter what daunting hardships we face, we must keep pressing forward. We must forge ahead with the determination to strengthen our faith day by day and month after month, as Nichiren exhorts (see "On Persecutions Befalling the Sage," WND-1, 997).

In the above passage, I keenly sense Nichiren's great compassion for Nichimyo's welfare. Precisely because of their tumultuous times, he wanted to teach her the true essence of faith so that she could lead a life of absolute victory. He wished for all his followers to become genuine disciples, people of invincible and indestructible faith.

Self-reliant Disciples Taking Initiative To Spread the Correct Teaching

You need not seek far for an example. Everyone in Japan, from the sovereign on down to the common people, without exception has tried to do me harm, but I have survived until this day. You should realize that this is because, although I am alone, I have firm faith. (WND-1, 614)

Nichiren Daishonin says, "You need not seek far for an example." In other words, he confidently asserts that he himself is the perfect example of a person who practices the Mystic

Law with firm faith and is unfailingly protected by the heavenly deities as a result.

Ever since submitting "On Establishing the Correct Teaching for the Peace of the Land"[13] to the country's most powerful figure (in July 1260), Nichiren had encountered life-threatening persecution. He had written this treatise of remonstration out of the wish to relieve the suffering and misery of all people of the Latter Day of the Law. But from that time on, he says, "Everyone in Japan, from the sovereign on down to the common people, without exception has tried to do me harm." The entire populace was turned against him and clamored for his death. Nevertheless, he managed to survive. What is the reason for this? He clearly explains, "Because, although I am alone, I have firm faith." This passage deeply resonates in my heart.

The Daishonin stood entirely alone, outnumbered by hostile and antagonistic forces. Yet he declared that victory is not decided by numbers but by one's own heart or resolve. His statement "Because ... I have firm faith," which was backed by the conviction of his experience, encapsulates several key ingredients of faith. These include an unwavering commitment to the great vow for kosen-rufu, the courageous and vigorous determination to fight against evil and wrongdoing, and the spirit of compassion to lead others to enlightenment. Because of his strong faith in the Lotus Sutra and his dauntless, lionlike courage, Nichiren could emerge triumphant over all obstacles.

How reassuring Nichimyo must have found the Daishonin's invincible conviction. By attributing his survival to firm faith, he may also have wanted to communicate to his disciple the powerful and infinitely noble potential residing in the depths of each person's life.

One reason he describes his own struggles in his writings, I believe, is his wish for the emergence of genuine disciples of unwavering resolve. Throughout, he calls on followers to strive in the same spirit as he has. In sharing details of his own struggles, Nichiren shows us that if we emulate his spirit and efforts, we can develop the same dauntless state of life.

The Buddha's great wish is to "make all persons equal to me, without any distinction between us" (LSOC, 70)—that is, to help everyone gain the same enlightened state of being he has attained. This reflects the Buddhist view that all people possess the same boundless potential as the Buddha.

Buddhism, a teaching of universal enlightenment, began with Shakyamuni's decision to stand up alone and share with others the truth to which he had become enlightened. Likewise, the widespread propagation of the Mystic Law in the Latter Day began with Nichiren standing up alone and declaring the establishment of his teaching, Nam-myoho-renge-kyo. And the Soka Gakkai began with the first three presidents—united in the bonds of mentor and disciple—each standing up and taking personal initiative to spread Nichiren Buddhism. During their respective periods of leadership, the Soka Gakkai reactivated the flow of kosen-rufu, secured the foundations for future development and brought about the brilliant flowering of worldwide kosen-rufu.

To share the same spirit as our mentor means to take action and strive in our Buddhist practice with the same standalone spirit. This constitutes true oneness of mentor and disciple.

Nichiren sought to foster admirable, self-reliant disciples who would persevere in spreading the Mystic Law, whether or not others joined them. Nichimyo must have been deeply moved by the Daishonin's encouragement in this letter and inspired to deepen her commitment to strive with a standalone spirit for kosen-rufu.

Buddhism teaches the principle of "three thousand realms in a single moment of life." Nichiren exemplifies how our inner resolve or determination at each moment plays a powerful role in bringing about victory. A courageous, resolute spirit is contagious. Courageous people awaken courage within others.

In the next passage, Nichiren indicates that the entire country of Japan had become infected by fear.

The Central Role of Women in Building Peace

If a boat is handled by an unskilled steersman, it may capsize and drown everyone aboard. Likewise, though someone may have great physical strength, if he lacks a resolute spirit, even his many abilities will be of no use. In this country, there may be many wise people, but they cannot utilize their wisdom because they are governed by foolish leaders…

At that time [when the Mongols attack again], those who declared they would not see or listen to me will join their palms together and take faith in the Lotus Sutra. Even the adherents of the Nembutsu and Zen schools will chant Nam-myoho-renge-kyo. (WND-1, 614–15)

While encouraging Nichimyo with the profound hope that she would stand up confidently on her own and forge ahead with strong faith, Nichiren Daishonin also directs his gaze at the societal state of affairs. Here, he castigates the country's incompetent ruling officials, highlighting, based upon the leadership philosophy and ideals found in the Lotus Sutra, how leaders ought to behave.

Faced with an imminent second Mongol invasion, the land was filled with despair and fear. How could Japan steer clear of this impending disaster? First, Nichiren says that if the person at the ship's helm is unskilled at sailing, everyone on board may lose their lives. Next, he says that if people are fainthearted, then no matter how strong they may be physically, they cannot make full use of their abilities. In this way, he seeks to drive home that the country's problems can only be overcome if its leaders have proper wisdom and dauntless courage.

In "On Establishing the Correct Teaching for the Peace of the Land," he emphasizes the paramount need for the country's leaders to change. If the leaders become wise, the entire country will change. Bringing peace to the land ultimately hinges on a leadership revolution—a revolution in the hearts and minds of leaders themselves.

The calamity of foreign invasion would never have occurred in the first place, in Nichiren's view, had the country's rulers promptly heeded his advice and governed the land in accord with correct principles. But not only did they ignore his warnings, they actively persecuted him. And even after the Mongol forces attacked, the rulers were incapable of making the right decisions for the country's future.

Amid these circumstances, Nichiren deliberately conveyed to his followers his unshakable confidence that kosen-rufu can definitely be achieved. Even while living at Minobu, he wrote tirelessly, proclaiming the correct teaching with an indomitable lion's roar.

In this writing, he states that if the Mongols were to attack again, people throughout the land would likely open their eyes at last and realize that he had been right in his assertions and embrace faith in the Mystic Law. This is in accord with the principle that "when great evil occurs, great good follows."[14] Because grave slander of the Law pervaded the entire country, the great correct Law was sure to spread. Nichiren declares to Nichimyo that there would surely come a time when those who refused to heed him would all join in chanting Nam-myoho-renge-kyo, even the Nembutsu and Zen schools' adherents.

On rereading this letter, I am again impressed by Nichiren's painstaking efforts to always explain the supreme Buddhist philosophy from various perspectives to his women followers, thereby demonstrating an egalitarianism far ahead of his times. His writings can be seen as teaching a sound view of self, of life, of society and of the universe for living a valuable and meaningful existence. He explains Buddhist principles and history, clarifies what is true and erroneous in terms of doctrine, indicates the supreme worth and nobility of each person irrespective of gender, and teaches a philosophy of transformation. Consistent with his assertion that there should be no discrimination between men or women (see "The True Aspect of All Phenomena," WND-1, 385), Nichiren strove to give all his followers an unsurpassed education.

The objective of Buddhism is the happiness of all people. In times of war and conflict, it is mothers and children who suffer the most. I cannot forget my own mother's crushing grief when she heard news of my older brother's death in the war. The foremost duty of Buddhists is to create a safe and peaceful world for mothers and children everywhere. Toward that end, we have to change the fundamental nature of human society, moving away from a culture of war and greed to a culture of building peace.

And women can play a central role in this process. When women of great courage, optimism and wisdom join together, society will change profoundly. When a united force of fearless women emerges, the times will change dramatically. When women with the rich sensitivity and deep compassion of nurturers and protectors of life rise into action, human society will be transformed on a fundamental level.

Buddhism is a teaching for fostering genuinely awakened people—men and women, young and old—who are capable of translating ideals into reality for the happiness of themselves and others.

Each Person's Victory Contributes to the Eternal Flow of Kosen-rufu

When I was about to be beheaded, the World-Honored One of Great Enlightenment took my place. It is the same in the present as it was in the past. All of you are my lay supporters, so how can you fail to attain Buddhahood? (WND-1, 615)

A passage in "The Teacher of the Law," the 10th chapter of the Lotus Sutra, states that those who uphold the Lotus Sutra are supported by Shakyamuni, who will carry them on his shoulders.[15] Based on this, Nichiren Daishonin declares that Shakyamuni protected him by taking his place at the time of the Tatsunokuchi Persecution.

Just prior to this passage, he related the legend of how Kumarayana,[16] the father of Kumarajiva,[17] was carried to safety on the back of a statue of Shakyamuni. "It is the same in the present as it was in the past," Nichiren says, emphasizing that whether in the past of Kumarayana's time or in the present of his own time, the principles of Buddhism are the same, and genuine Lotus Sutra practitioners will be protected. And he proclaims that, according to the same principle, Nichimyo will be kept safe by all Buddhas and heavenly deities throughout the universe and will attain Buddhahood without fail.

Nichiren stood up alone and initiated the struggle to bring peace and prosperity to the land by establishing the right ideals and principles of Buddhism. Many humble, ordinary people—including female followers like Nichimyo—joined him in that endeavor. And we are carrying on this noble struggle today around the globe. People who stand up for their convictions are strong. They will never be daunted by storms of persecution.

The renowned French writer Victor Hugo declared: "No matter what momentary tyrants may do, they are opposed by the eternal essence"[18] and "There is no position higher than giving one's life for the sake of justice."[19] He also said: "It is time for the human conscience to awaken ... Come, consciences, up! Wake up, it is time!"[20]

The foundation of worldwide kosen-rufu has been firmly secured. People everywhere are waiting to encounter the inspiring ideals of Soka humanism.

The victory of each of us is becoming increasingly important. The victory of each of us will contribute to the eternal flow of the great river of kosen-rufu.

This lecture was originally published in the August 2009 issue of the Daibyakurenge, *the Soka Gakkai's monthly study journal.*

NOTES

[1]   Ten demon daughters: Ten female protective deities who appear in the Lotus Sutra as the "daughters of rakshasa demons" or the "ten rakshasa daughters." In the sutra's 26th chapter, "Dharani," they vow to guard and protect the sutra's practitioners, saying that they will inflict punishment on any who trouble the latter.

[2] See LSOC, 328.

[3] Miao-lo (711–82): A patriarch of the T'ien-t'ai school in China. He is revered as the school's restorer. His commentaries on T'ien-t'ai's three major works are titled *The Annotations on "The Profound Meaning of the Lotus Sutra," The Annotations on "The Words and Phrases of the Lotus Sutra"* and *The Annotations on "Great Concentration and Insight."*

[4] From *The Annotations on "Great Concentration and Insight."*

[5] Mount Minobu: Located in present-day Yamanashi Prefecture, Japan. Nichiren Daishonin lived there during the later years of his life, from May 1274 through September 1282, just prior to his death. There, he devoted himself to educating his disciples, directing propagation efforts and writing doctrinal treatises.

[6] Former existence as a Bodhisattva of the Earth: In "Emerging from the Earth," the 15th chapter of the Lotus Sutra, Shakyamuni calls forth from beneath the earth countless disciples to whom he entrusts the propagation of the Mystic Law in the Latter Day of the Law. These are the Bodhisattvas of the Earth. In prison, Josei Toda awoke to his identity

as a Bodhisattva of the Earth, and upon his release, he undertook the great struggle to achieve kosen-rufu.

[7] Translated from Japanese. Josei Toda, *Toda Josei zenshu* (Collected Writings of Josei Toda) (Tokyo: Seikyo Shimbunsha, 1983), vol.3, p.386.

[8] The "Former Affairs of the Bodhisattva Medicine King" chapter states: "This [Lotus] sutra can save all living beings. This sutra can cause all living beings to free themselves from suffering and anguish. This sutra can bring great benefits to all living beings and fulfill their desires ... It is like ... someone finding a ship in which to cross the water, a sick man finding a doctor, someone in darkness finding a lamp" (LSOC, 327–28).

[9] This is used to describe how the human mind is constantly changing in response to various external causes or conditions. In "On the Attainment of Buddhahood by Women," Nichiren writes: "The sutra texts tell us that a single person in the course of a single day has eight million four thousand thoughts. All of these various thoughts produce karma that will lead to rebirth in the three evil paths [i.e.,

the realms of hell, hungry spirits and animals]" (WND-2, 307).

[10]   Mystic principle of the true cause: Nichiren Buddhism directly expounds the true cause for enlightenment as Nam-myoho-renge-kyo, which is the Law of life and the universe. It teaches a way of Buddhist practice of always moving forward from this moment on based on this fundamental Law.

[11]   T'ien-t'ai (538–97): Also known as Chih-i. The founder of the T'ien-t'ai school in China. His lectures were compiled in such works as *The Profound Meaning of the Lotus Sutra, The Words and Phrases of the Lotus Sutra* and *Great Concentration and Insight*. He spread the Lotus Sutra in China and established the doctrine of "three thousand realms in a single moment of life."

[12]   The eighth volume of T'ien-t'ai's *Great Concentration and Insight* states, "If the ruler of a walled city is unbending, then those who guard the city will remain firm; but if the ruler is cowardly, then those who guard the city will grow fearful."

[13]   "On Establishing the Correct Teaching for the Peace of the Land": One of

Nichiren's five major writings. He submitted this treatise to Hojo Tokiyori, the retired regent but still the most powerful figure in Japan's ruling clan. In it, he predicts that unless people of the day quickly took faith in the correct teaching, then internal strife and foreign invasion—two of the seven disasters that had yet to take place—would occur without fail.

[14] In "Great Evil and Great Good," Nichiren writes: "Great events never have minor omens. When great evil occurs, great good follows. Since great slander already exists in our land, the great correct Law will spread without fail" (WND-1, 1119).

[15] The Lotus Sutra states, "[Persons who read and recite the Lotus Sutra] are borne upon the shoulders of the Thus Come One" (LSOC, 201).

[16] Kumarayana (n.d.): Lived in the fourth century and was the son of a minister of an Indian kingdom but forsook his position to enter the Buddhist Order at a time when Buddhism was on the verge of decline. He left India and crossed the Pamir range to the north, traveling toward China. According to legend,

when Kumarayana left India, he brought with him a statue of Shakyamuni. It is said that he carried the statue during the day, and at night the statue carried him.

[17] Kumarajiva (344–413): A Buddhist scholar and translator of Buddhist scriptures into Chinese. He studied Buddhism from a young age and later actively spread the Mahayana teachings. In 401, at the invitation of Yao Hsing, ruler of the Later Ch'in dynasty of ancient China, Kumarajiva made his way to the capital Ch'ang-an, where he immersed himself in the translation of Buddhist scriptures. His prodigious body of translated works includes the Lotus Sutra.

[18] Translated from French. Victor Hugo, *Pendant l'exil: 1852–1870* (During the Exile: 1852–1870), in *Actes et paroles* (Acts and Words) (Paris: Albin Michel, 1938), vol.2, p.6.

[19] Ibid., 24.

[20] Translated from French. Victor Hugo, *Napoléon le petit* (Napoleon the Little), in *Victor Hugo oeuvres complètes: histoire* (The Complete Works of Victor Hugo:

History), edited by Shiela Gaudon (Paris: Robert Laffont, 1987), pp.8–9.

CHAPTER 9

"THE SUPREMACY OF THE LAW—PART 3 OF 3"

FAITH THAT GROWS STRONGER IS THE KEY TO ETERNAL VICTORY

> The Passage for Study in This Lecture
>
> No matter whom you may marry, if he is an enemy of the Lotus Sutra, you must not follow him. Strengthen your resolve more than ever. Ice is made of water, but it is colder than water. Blue dye comes from indigo, but when something is repeatedly dyed in it, the color is better than that of the indigo plant.[1] The Lotus Sutra remains the same, but if you repeatedly strengthen your resolve, your color will be better than that of others, and you will receive more blessings than they do. (WND-1, 615)
>
> ***

The people of Japan, by becoming enemies of the Lotus Sutra, have brought ruin on themselves and their country. And because I proclaim this, I am called arrogant by those of little understanding. But I do not speak out of arrogance. It is simply that if I did not speak out I would not be the votary of the Lotus Sutra. Moreover, when my words prove later to be true, people will be able to believe all the more readily. And because I write this down now, the people of the future will recognize my wisdom.

[*The Annotations on the Nirvana Sutra* states,] "One's body is insignificant while the Law is supreme. One should give one's life in order to propagate the Law." Because my body is insignificant, I am struck and hated, but because the Law is supreme, it will spread without fail. If the Lotus Sutra spreads, my mortal remains will be respected, and if my remains are respected, they will benefit the people. Then I will come to be revered as highly as Great Bodhisattva Hachiman is now. You should understand that, at that time, the men and women who supported me will be honored as greatly as Takenouchi and Wakamiya.[2]

The benefits that come from opening the eyes of even one blind person are beyond description. How then is it possible to describe the benefits that derive from opening the blind eyes of all the Japanese people, and from giving the gift of sight to all human beings throughout Jambudvipa and the other three continents?[3]...

I may be a foolish man, but I am surely not inferior to a fox or a demon. The noblest people in the present age are in no way superior to Shakra or the boy Snow Mountains,[4] yet because of my low social position, they have rejected my wise words. That is why the country is now on the brink of ruin. How lamentable! And what I find even sadder is that I will be unable to save those disciples of mine who have pitied my sufferings.

If anything at all happens, please come over here. I will welcome you. Let us die of starvation together among the mountains. And I would imagine that your daughter, Oto, has become a fine, intelligent girl. I will write you again. (WND-1, 615–16)

LECTURE

The mentor-disciple relationship is the foundation of Nichiren Buddhism. When mentor and disciple are united in purpose, they can accomplish anything. In both our own human revolution and in the challenge to establish the correct teaching for the peace of the land, steadfastly adhering to the path of mentor and disciple is the direct path to absolute victory.

The Lotus Sutra speaks of "following and learning from these teachers [of the Law]."[5] To have the opportunity to follow an exemplary teacher of kosen-rufu and learn about the tenets and practice of Buddhism—surely there is no greater happiness in life than this. With this spirit, I dedicated myself to serving and supporting my mentor, second Soka Gakkai president Josei Toda.

One profoundly encouraging aspect of the path of mentor and disciple as taught in Buddhism is that the mentors themselves manifest and embody the essence of the Buddhist teachings in their own lives as ordinary human beings. By setting a personal example of the dignity and nobility inherent in human life, they inspire others and spur them to walk the same illustrious path. Following the lead of the mentors, these awakened disciples proceed in the same spirit to take action to make a difference in the world.

As long as we carry on the noble cause and struggles of our mentors in faith, Buddhism will continue to spread throughout the world and illuminate people's hearts as a teaching for the enlightenment of all humankind.

"The Supremacy of the Law" can be viewed as a writing in which Nichiren Daishonin outlines the struggle he was waging against the entire country of Japan. At the time this letter was written, news of the death and destruction wrought by a Mongol invasion had spread throughout the land, leaving everyone terrified at the prospect of a second invasion. This letter contained the Daishonin's bold assertion that it was time for the whole populace, gripped by fear and anxiety, to accept a truly humanistic philosophy as its mainstay.

Many in society probably assumed that Nichiren, having moved to Mount Minobu, had retired from the world. But this was incorrect; he had never let up in his spiritual struggle. On the contrary, through his example, he taught his disciples the dauntless spirit of ceaseless challenge to the very end. It must have been extremely inspiring for his followers to learn of his undiminished fighting spirit through his letters. His spiritual vigor and dynamism would have left a deep and lasting impression in their hearts.

No doubt Nichimyo, the recipient of this letter, was inspired to practice with fresh determination in response to the Daishonin's urging that she always advance together with him, come what may.

In "The Supremacy of the Law," Nichiren teaches us a crucial key to faith for persevering on the path of the oneness of mentor and disciple—namely, continuously working to strengthen our resolve.

Repeatedly Strengthening Our Resolve Causes Our Benefit To Multiply

No matter whom you may marry, if he is an enemy of the Lotus Sutra, you must not follow him. Strengthen your resolve more than ever. Ice is made of water, but it is colder than water. Blue dye comes from indigo, but when something is repeatedly dyed in it, the color is better than that of the indigo plant. The Lotus Sutra remains the same, but if you repeatedly strengthen your resolve, your color will be better than that of others, and you will receive more blessings than they do. (WND-1, 615)

Faith in the Mystic Law serves as our compass for navigating the rough seas of life and society. Living as we do in the defiled age of the Latter Day of the Law, it is all the more important that we are not swayed by negative influences but make faith the center of our daily life and existence.

Nichiren Daishonin tells Nichimyo that no matter whom one marries, that partner should not be followed in matters of faith if he or she is opposed to the Lotus Sutra's teachings. True happiness will forever elude us if we lose sight of the correct path of faith.

Next, he urges Nichimyo to strengthen her resolve in faith more than ever. By maintaining strong faith, we can turn back the tide of any adversity. That is why developing an ever-stronger foundation in faith is the ultimate source of victory.

Nichiren then cites examples from the natural world. Ice, for instance, is frozen water, but it is very different from water in terms of hardness and coldness. Blue dye, meanwhile, comes from the leaves of the indigo plant, but fabric or yarn repeatedly soaked in that dye will become a shade of blue much deeper than the color of the leaves.

Drawing a parallel with these phenomena, the Daishonin writes, "The Lotus Sutra remains the same, but if you repeatedly strengthen your resolve, your color will be better than that of others, and you will receive more blessings than they do." As these words indicate, through faith that grows ever stronger, we will enjoy increasing energy and vibrancy both mentally and physically, while benefit will manifest itself ever more clearly in our lives. By repeatedly strengthening our faith, we can bring forth the indestructible, diamondlike state of Buddhahood within us.

Nichiren uses analogies such as the following to describe this great transformation: "Wood is vulnerable to fire, but sandalwood cannot be burned.[6] Fire is extinguished by water, but the fire that cremated the Buddha's remains could not be quenched.[7] Although flowers are scattered by the wind, those that bloom in the heavens of purity do not wither"[8] (WND-1, 615).

By continually reaffirming our commitment to faith, our lives in this transient existence become adorned with the everlasting and indestructible treasures of eternity, happiness, true self and purity.[9] Constantly fortifying our faith becomes the key to establishing such a state of life.

Repeatedly strengthening one's resolve, or faith, therefore, means persevering in one's Buddhist practice. It means being undaunted by obstacles or, rather, using obstacles as an impetus to summon forth even stronger faith and to polish one's life even more.

While all of us who practice Nichiren Buddhism embrace faith in the same Lotus Sutra (the Mystic Law) and the Gohonzon, it is the strength of our faith that determines the outcome. The stronger the faith we summon, the greater the benefits we will experience, and the more expansive and fulfilled the life state we will achieve. Aware of this truth, our members around the world are showing wonderful actual proof of the power of faith.

Throughout his writings, the Daishonin calls on his followers to ceaselessly forge their faith. For example, he says to Shijo Kingo:[10] "Strengthen your power of faith more than ever" ("Happiness in This World," WND-1, 681) and "You must summon up the great power of faith more than ever" ("The Strategy of the Lotus Sutra," WND-1, 1000). He also praised the lay nun of Kubo[11] for her "ever-strengthening faith" ("False Official Documents," WND-2, 877), while encouraging the lay nun Ueno[12] to "strive even more earnestly in faith" ("Hell Is the Land of Tranquil Light," WND-1, 457). In this way, Nichiren urges even followers of exemplary faith to keep strengthening their resolve all the more. Put another way, the spirit to keep striving even harder is the essence of faith and the fundamental key to practicing Nichiren Buddhism.

Both Nichiren and Shakyamuni exerted themselves with an ever-fresh and unflagging commitment, living with a fighting spirit to the very end. The same can be said of Tsunesaburo Makiguchi and Josei Toda, the first two Soka Gakkai presidents. And I now want to teach this essential spirit of faith to my disciples.

Life, in one sense, is a constant battle against deadlock. As long as we are alive, as long as we continue challenging ourselves, difficult obstacles will block our way forward. If life were all smooth sailing, if we never encountered setbacks, that itself would be a sign of stagnation.

I am reminded of the time in my youth when Mr. Toda's businesses fell into financial crisis, and I worked desperately to solve the situation. On seeing how exhausted I was by my efforts, Mr. Toda encouraged me, saying: "Faith is a never-ending battle against deadlock. It is a struggle between the Buddha and devilish functions—between negative and positive forces. That is why we say, 'Buddhism is about winning.'"

All of us at times feel stuck or at an impasse in our lives or undertakings. But it is precisely when we are deadlocked that our faith is put to the test; such a time represents a decisive moment to seize victory. The important thing is to always keep our minds focused on moving forward. The challenge of triumphing over obstacles will itself become the cause for substantially expanding our state of life. If we actively grapple with our problems, we can definitely change inside and transform our karma.

Any time we become stuck, then, is actually an opportunity to realize victory. And ever-stronger faith is what gives us the power to break through such deadlocks. This is true both in terms of our individual struggles and the larger struggles of society.

Broadly speaking, deadlock arising on the level of society, the economy or a country as a whole points to a clear limitation of the ideals or philosophy that guide or underlie them. In fact, it is at such times that a new philosophy emerges. The burgeoning of powerful new ideas can transform deadlock into an opportunity to build a better society.

Shakyamuni says: "Hasten to do good, restrain your mind from evil. The mind of one who is sluggish about doing good finds amusement in evil."[13]

Everything lies before us. Everything comes down to an inner struggle. It is one's mind, one's heart, that is important.
Protecting the Law Means Steadfastly Proclaiming the Truth

The people of Japan, by becoming enemies of the Lotus Sutra, have brought ruin on themselves and their country. And because I proclaim this, I am called arrogant by those of little understanding. But I do not speak out of arrogance. It is simply that if I did not speak out I would not be the votary of the Lotus Sutra. Moreover, when my words prove later to be true, people will be able to believe all the more readily. And because I write this down now, the people of the future will recognize my wisdom. (WND-1, 615)

The Nirvana Sutra states, "Rely on the Law and not upon persons" ("Conversation between a Sage and an Unenligthtened Man," WND-1, 102). Nichiren Daishonin always waged his struggle based on the Law. Accordingly, he was very strict about distinguishing between correct and erroneous Buddhist teachings. When considering a particular teaching, he would ask: "Is this a correct teaching that seeks to actualize the Buddhist ideal of universal enlightenment? Or is it an erroneous teaching that distorts this fundamental principle and causes people suffering?" He clarified what was true and what was false, safeguarding the correct teaching and refuting erroneous teachings. This is the way in which Nichiren strove to protect the Law.

The people of Japan at the time, having been swayed by negative influences, discarded the Lotus Sutra and placed their faith in provisional Buddhist teachings that rejected the principle of universal enlightenment. Hence, Nichiren's lament, "The people of Japan, by becoming enemies of the Lotus Sutra, have brought ruin on themselves and their country."

If things continued as they were, the country would suffer complete destruction. To avert this catastrophe, he had remonstrated with the country's rulers and tirelessly proclaimed the truth—especially escalating his efforts after submitting his treatise "On Establishing the Correct Teaching for the Peace of the Land"[14] (in July 1260). He was fully aware that his actions would invite great persecution, but this deterred him not in the least, because he was solely concerned with protecting the Law and leading all people to enlightenment.

One criticism leveled against Nichiren by his contemporaries was that he was "arrogant" or "conceited." In "The Supremacy of the Law," he writes, "Because I proclaim this [the truth], I am called arrogant by those of little understanding." Dwelling in an island country where people's thoughts were filled with jealousy (see "How Those Initially Aspiring to the Way," WND-1,

873), the Daishonin faced a relentless storm of slander and abuse, but without retreating a step, he boldly continued to declare the truth.

He rejects the criticism that he is arrogant, clarifying his intent. He points out first that the Lotus Sutra is the foremost teaching and that if he failed to thoroughly warn people of the ruinous consequences their hostility to the sutra could have for the country, then he would not be its votary. To broadly proclaim the Lotus Sutra's greatness and take a firm stand against its enemies are the actions of a genuine votary. Those who lack this fighting spirit and are ruled by fear do not qualify as votaries.

Nichiren also rejects criticism from another perspective, explaining that he is motivated by the desire to chronicle the truth for the future. Leaving a written record of his predictions of internal strife and foreign invasion coming to pass would help people of future times to appreciate his immense foresight and wisdom.

He clarifies, however, that the fulfillment of his predictions is not an indication of his own ability but rather is proof of the accuracy of Buddhism's correct teaching. In his treatise "The Selection of the Time," Nichiren discusses the three times he gained distinction by having such prophetic knowledge.[15] He writes: "It was not I, Nichiren, who made these three important pronouncements. Rather it was in all cases the spirit of the Thus Come One Shakyamuni that had taken possession of my body. And having personally experienced this, I am beside myself with joy" (WND-1, 579).

If the truth were preserved, people of discernment and insight in later generations would surely applaud Nichiren's efforts and take action in the same spirit. Successors to his spiritual legacy would carry on his work and create a groundswell of humanism led by ordinary people. And in fact, we of the SGI, sharing bonds of mentor and disciple with the first three presidents, have inherited Nichiren Daishonin's spirit. We have launched a movement of confident, awakened individuals dedicated to the cause of worldwide kosen-rufu, the Buddha's wish and decree—a movement that is now an unstoppable force around the globe.

No matter what slander or criticism we might encounter, if we continue to speak out and leave a clear record of the truth, our victory will be assured. During the early years of the Soka Gakkai's history, the number of defamatory articles in the print media about our organization increased in direct proportion to our phenomenal membership growth in Japan. This was in exact accord with the sutra's prediction that its practitioners would encounter slander and abuse in the evil age after the Buddha's passing.

Mr. Toda remained unperturbed by these events, remarking calmly: "They write sensational articles about us because they know it will boost their sales ... They can't possibly surprise us with anything they write, because they haven't the least clue what they're writing about."[16] And he declared: "We of the Soka Gakkai have faith; we have the Gohonzon. Everything we have achieved is a result of the benefit of our faith in the Gohonzon ... Faith is at the heart of everything. Remaining steadfast in our Buddhist practice is what matters."[17]

With this invincible conviction, the Soka Gakkai has achieved victory after victory. Irrespective of the times or circumstances, we will win in the end as long as we never discard our faith.

Truly Noble Are Those Who Uphold and Propagate the Law With Selfless Dedication

[The Annotations on the Nirvana Sutra states,] "One's body is insignificant while the Law is supreme. One should give one's life in order to propagate the Law." Because my body is insignificant, I am struck and hated, but because the Law is supreme, it will spread without fail. If the Lotus Sutra spreads, my mortal remains will be respected, and if my remains are respected, they will benefit the people. Then I will come to be revered as highly as Great Bodhisattva Hachiman is now. You should understand that, at that time, the men and women who supported me will be honored as greatly as Takenouchi and Wakamiya. (WND-1, 615)

The ultimate spirit of faith in Buddhism is summed up in the following words: "One's body is insignificant while the Law is supreme. One should give one's life in order to propagate the Law."

"One's body is insignificant while the Law is supreme"—which can also be expressed as "valuing the Law more highly than one's life"—refers to the spirit of ceaselessly protecting and propagating the correct teaching. Similarly, "One should give one's life in order to propagate the Law" refers to devoting oneself selflessly to spreading the Law. Nichiren Daishonin indicates to Nichimyo that he has always dedicated himself to his struggle with precisely this commitment.

He also declares that he is undeterred by any criticism because his body is insignificant and that he is unafraid of any hostility because the Law itself is supreme. Consequently, he says, there is not the slightest doubt that the correct teaching will spread.

The Law, the ultimate truth or reality, is eternal and indestructible. Accordingly, if there are individuals willing to give their all to spreading the Law, kosen-rufu can definitely be realized. On the other hand, if there is no one willing to spread the Law with such a selfless, ungrudging spirit, then kosenrufu will end up an empty dream.

Who was it that strove all out for Buddhism? Nichiren and his followers. If the Mystic Law is great, then those who spread it are also great.

The Daishonin says that if, through his selfless efforts, he succeeds in propagating the Law, then his life will be forever adorned with the immeasurable benefit that derives from that action. He also promises that the disciples who have supported him throughout will likewise enjoy everlasting good fortune and benefit. This confident declaration that Nichiren and his disciples dedicating their lives to widely propagating the Mystic Law are unimaginably noble must have deeply moved and inspired Nichimyo anew.

Let us, too, embrace the Daishonin's wholehearted commitment to protecting and propagating the Law as the guiding spirit of kosen-rufu and make it the foundation of our own Buddhist practice. This is the Soka Gakkai spirit.

Naturally, selfless dedication to propagating the Law in Nichiren Buddhism in no way indicates a feudalistic self-annihilation or self-sacrifice for some greater public good. Buddhism's purpose is to help all people attain genuine happiness and thereby transform the karma of humankind. On an individual level, by sharing the Mystic Law with others, we can change our own karma and fundamentally transform our state of life. Such efforts represent the surest and most direct path to realizing happiness for ourselves and others.

The SGI is striving for kosen-rufu in the same spirit of selfless dedication to the Law as

Nichiren. And, just as he declares that his disciples will be greatly honored by future generations, all who practice with the SGI will likewise command eternal respect and admiration.

In light of the principles of Buddhism, each SGI member is a unique and amazing individual possessing the noblest of missions.

Great Benefits Derive From Opening the Eyes of People Throughout the World

The benefits that come from opening the eyes of even one blind person are beyond description. How then is it possible to describe the benefits that derive from opening the blind eyes of all the Japanese people, and from giving the gift of sight to all human beings throughout Jambudvipa and the other three continents? (WND-1, 615)

This passage indicates the great benefits obtained by those who promote kosen-rufu with selfless dedication.

To embrace faith in the Lotus Sutra means to open one's eyes. It means removing the veil of illusion that has kept one's eyes closed and seeing the truth and essence of all things.

The benefit that comes from opening the eyes of even one person blinded by illusion is incalculable. How vast, then, is the benefit of opening the eyes of all people in the country of Japan! And how even more indescribable is the benefit of opening the eyes of all humankind! Nichiren Daishonin accomplished this momentous undertaking, which he had vowed to fulfill (by establishing the means by which all people could attain enlightenment).

He speaks of "giving the gift of sight to all human beings throughout Jambudvipa and the other three continents." From these words, we can discern the lofty life state of the Daishonin, who took the lead of kosen-rufu from a global perspective.

Today, just as 700 years ago, humankind is in need of a fundamental guiding philosophy that can serve to awaken or "open the eyes" of the people. Such a philosophy is found in the Lotus Sutra's teachings of universal enlightenment and respect for all people. This philosophy holds that when we rise above differences of ethnicity and culture and discard all barriers, we come to see that all people inherently possess the same noble Buddha nature and have been born in this world to fulfill their highest potential. Every person is worthy of supreme respect. And when each person brings his or her innate Buddhahood to shine to the fullest, the world will change. A great human revolution in the life of just one person can change the world's destiny.

It is the SGI that is spreading the humanistic Buddhism of Nichiren Daishonin, based on the Lotus Sutra's ideals of the sanctity of life and the nobility of all people. Our movement represents an unprecedented effort to open the eyes of people around the globe—an undertaking we are determined to continue until all humanity has been awakened and misfortune and misery have been eradicated from the face of the earth.

"Already Soka Gakkai is a world affair"[18]—declared British historian Arnold J. Toynbee several decades ago, in a foreword he contributed to volume one of the English edition of my novel *The Human Revolution*. He also wrote:

> Nichiren ... loved his country, but his horizon and his concern were not bounded by Japan's coasts. Nichiren held that Buddhism, as he conceived it, was a means of salvation for his fellow human beings everywhere. In working for the human revolution, Soka Gakkai is carrying out Nichiren's mandate.[19]

Further, after commenting on the legacy of our first and second presidents, Tsunesaburo Makiguchi and Josei Toda, Dr. Toynbee made the following observations:

> What have been the causes of Soka Gakkai's triumphant postwar success? The fundamental cause was the faith with which this community and its leaders in our time have been inspired by the founder, Nichiren, whose spirit is still potent in the seventh century after his death. This faith had given them the courage and constancy to endure persecution, and the sincerity that they have demonstrated by their endurance has

opened their countrymen's hearts and minds to this teaching and has helped to win Soka Gakkai its huge increase in numbers.[20]

Dr. Toynbee's words reflect a profound understanding of our movement. He was a person of keen insight.

Let us continue this dramatic and joyful march of the people. Deeply reflecting on the expansive life state of Nichiren, who aspired for the realization of worldwide kosen-rufu, let us continue moving forward, always maintaining our direct connection to him and basing ourselves on his writings. This is the honorable mission of the SGI, which is determined to take responsibility for the future of our world.

"In Matters of Buddhism, the Words of the Sutras Are What Must Come First"

I may be a foolish man, but I am surely not inferior to a fox or a demon. The noblest people in the present age are in no way superior to Shakra or the boy Snow Mountains, yet because of my low social position, they have rejected my wise words. That is why the country is now on the brink of ruin. How lamentable! (WND-1, 616)

People throughout the land relentlessly harassed and persecuted Nichiren Daishonin, who was striving valiantly as a "sovereign, teacher, and parent"[21] to the country. Some maligned him because of his low social position. In several writings, Nichiren describes others disparaging him as a "person of humble position" ("On Establishing the Correct Teaching for the Peace of the Land," WND-1, 17) or a "person of no more than humble station in life" ("Conversation between a Sage and an Unenlightened Man," WND-1, 109). But he was proud of his origins, describing himself as the "son of commoner parents" ("Condolences on a Deceased Husband," WND-2, 766), or as "born poor and lowly to a chandala[22] family" ("Letter from Sado," WND-1, 303). The malicious words of those who spoke ill of Nichiren only exposed their own ugly snobbery and prejudice.

In "The Supremacy of the Law," Nichiren dismisses their jeers by citing the examples of Shakra who respectfully learned Buddhism from a fox,[23] and the boy Snow Mountains who took a demon as his teacher to discover the Buddha way (see WND-1, 616). He rebukes his critics by saying that to devalue a teaching based on the teacher's outward status is to reject the conduct of such admirable models of seeking spirit as Shakra and Snow Mountains.

In "Conversation between a Sage and an Unenlightened Man," Nichiren states: "In matters of Buddhist doctrines one cannot jump to conclusions simply on the basis of the eminence of the person involved. The words of the sutras are what must come first" (WND-1, 109). In Buddhism, the standard is always the superiority and depth of the teaching and not the social status of the person who teaches or spreads it. "Don't judge people based on their dress or appearance. You cannot possibly tell from such things how someone will turn out in the future or what mission they might have." This was Mr. Toda's strict injunction.

Social position, titles, academic degrees and the like are irrelevant in the realm of the Soka Gakkai. Truly respectworthy are those who have a seeking spirit in faith. Furthermore, it is vital that we treasure those who take action for kosen-rufu. These must forever remain our guiding principles.

Citadels of the People Built Through the Bonds of Mentor and Disciple

And what I find even sadder is that I will be unable to save those disciples of mine who have pitied my sufferings.

If anything at all happens, please come over here. I will welcome you. Let us die of starvation together among the mountains. And I would imagine that your daughter, Oto, has become a fine, intelligent girl. I will write you again. (WND-1, 616)

"How lamentable!" (WND-1, 616) Nichiren Daishonin says regarding those who slandered him. At the same time, he expresses deep sadness over the plight of disciples who had striven alongside him, a reflection of his great compassion and concern for them. He knew that, as inhabitants of a country receiving general punishment for its slander of the Law, they could not avoid being caught up in the confusion that swirled through society. This concern for others is the fundamental spirit of Nichiren Buddhism. The Daishonin's concern was of such sensitivity and breadth that it deeply touched people's hearts. That concern is the very essence of his teaching, which places the utmost importance on human conduct.

He also extends his all-embracing compassion to Nichimyo and her daughter. "I would imagine that your daughter, Oto, has become a fine, intelligent girl," he tells her. And he urges the two to join him at Minobu should the Mongols invade. "I will welcome you," he says warmly. "Let us die of starvation together among the mountains." Such are the lengths to which Nichiren goes to encourage this sincere follower caring for her young child.

Buddhism is not sentimentalism, self-pity or shallow sympathy. Nichiren spoke of "giving the gift of sight to all human beings throughout Jambudvipa and the other three continents" (WND-1, 615). As these words indicate, he dedicated his life to widely propagating the Mystic Law and expounding the correct teaching with the world as his stage, and he steadfastly refused to be defeated by the life-threatening persecutions that assailed him. He possessed the resolute strength to uphold the truth without wavering and the warmth to embrace all people.

The vigorous spirit to refute falsehood and the compassion to embrace others, in other words, are two sides of the same coin. Genuine humanism lies in having both qualities.

The Daishonin and Nichimyo shared a pure and solid bond of mentor and disciple. Nichiren had forged such spiritual bonds with many followers. No devilish power or authority could sever these bonds, which had survived countless hardships and persecutions. The unity of people bound by the shared commitment of mentor and disciple in faith is the great, eternally indestructible foundation of kosen-rufu.

We have built magnificent citadels of the people all around the globe. But we have just begun. Before us lies the true stage for propagating the Law in order to bring happy smiles to the faces of many new Nichimyos and Otos—mothers and children—throughout the world.

Goethe declared that life is a constant struggle. He wrote:

This is the highest pitch of wisdom:
He alone deserves his life and liberty
Who every day must fight for them...

Such a swarming I should like to see,
Stand on a free ground with a people who are free.[24]

Mr. Makiguchi cherished the following saying from the Confucian classic *The Great Learning:* "Renew yourself each day, and do so day after day. Let there be daily renewal." Let's ready ourselves for fresh challenges! Everything lies before us.

In closing, I present to you these words of indomitable conviction by Mr. Toda, which remain forever engraved in my heart: "The Soka Gakkai will transform this troubled world we live in. Let's rouse our courage, unite and forge ahead on the great path of kosen-rufu!"

—With my prayers especially for the happiness of the noble women's division and young women's division members in Japan and throughout the world.

This lecture was originally published in the September 2009 issue of the Daibyakurenge, *the Soka Gakkai's monthly study journal.*

NOTES

[1] This is based on a passage in the Chinese classic *Hsün Tzu:* "Learning should never cease. Blue comes from the indigo plant but is bluer than the plant itself. Ice is made of water but is colder than water ever is" (New York: Columbia University Press, 1963, 1996, p.15). In another

writing, Nichiren Daishonin says: "[The Great Teacher] T'ien-t'ai states, 'From the indigo, an even deeper blue.' This passage means that, if one dyes something repeatedly in indigo, it becomes even bluer than the indigo leaves. The Lotus Sutra is like the indigo, and the strength of one's practice is like the deepening blue" ("Hell Is the Land of Tranquil Light," WND-1, 457).

[2] Takenouchi is a legendary general and statesman who is said to have played an active part in Empress Jingu's expedition to Korea and later served her son, Emperor Ojin. Ojin was deified after death and referred to as Great Bodhisattva Hachiman. Wakamiya refers to Great Bodhisattva Hachiman of Tsurugaoka Hachiman Shrine in Kamakura.

[3] According to the ancient Indian cosmology, the world consists of four continents, including Jambudvipa.

[4] The boy Snow Mountains: The name of Shakyamuni Buddha in a previous lifetime when he was practicing austerities. Deciding to test Snow Mountain's resolve, the god Shakra appeared before him in the form of a hungry demon and recited half a verse from a Buddhist teaching. The

boy begged the demon to tell him the second half of the verse. The demon agreed, but demanded flesh and blood in payment. Snow Mountains gladly promised to offer his own body to the demon, who in turn gave him the latter half of the teaching. When the boy was about to fulfill his promise and jumped from a tall tree into the demon's mouth, the demon changed back into Shakra and caught him. He praised Snow Mountains for his willingness to give his life for the Law.

[5] "Teacher of the Law," the 10th chapter of the Lotus Sutra, states: "If you stay close to the teachers of the Law, you will speedily gain the bodhisattva way. By following and learning from these teachers you will see Buddhas as numerous as Ganges sands" (LSOC, 208).

[6] Sandalwood is prized as fragrant wood. Legend has it that sandalwood could not be burned by fire, but the source of such references is unclear. In a similar vein, certain Buddhist texts state that people would not be burned by fire if they rubbed their bodies with the fragrance of sandalwood.

[7] The Epilogue to the Mahaparinirvana Sutra states that when Shakyamuni's cremation

pyre was doused with water in the form of rain created by the dragon deities of the threefold world, the fire, instead of going out, only grew more intense.

[8] "The heavens of purity" refers to the five heavens of purity, or the five highest heavens in the world of form. According to *The Great Commentary on Abhidharma*, these heavens are free from the three major calamities—fire, water and wind. Hence, flowers that bloom there will not wither.

[9] Eternity, happiness, true self and purity are known as the four virtues. Describing the noble qualities of the Buddha's life, the four are explained as follows: "eternity" means unchanging and eternal; "happiness" means tranquillity that transcends all suffering; "true self" means true and intrinsic nature; and "purity" means free of illusion or mistaken conduct.

[10] Shijo Kingo (1230–1300): One of Nichiren's leading followers. His full name and title were Shijo Nakatsukasa Saburo Saemon-no-jo Yorimoto. As a samurai retainer, he served the Ema family, a branch of the ruling Hojo clan. Shijo Kingo was well versed in both

medicine and the martial arts. He is said to have converted to Nichiren's teaching around 1256. When Nichiren was taken to Tatsunokuchi to be beheaded in 1271, Shijo Kingo accompanied him, resolved to die by his side.

[11] The lay nun of Kubo (n.d.): A follower of Nichiren Daishonin who lived in Suruga Province. She appears to have been a sincere believer who frequently sent offerings to him.

[12] The lay nun Ueno (d. 1284): A lay follower of Nichiren. She was the wife of Nanjo Hyoe Shichiro, the steward of Ueno Village in Suruga Province. The couple had nine children, including Nanjo Tokimitsu. Her husband died of illness in 1265, while she was pregnant with their last child. She went on to raise her children alone while maintaining faith in the Daishonin's teachings.

[13] *The Dhammapada: Sayings of the Buddha,* translated by Thomas Cleary (New York: Bantam Books, 1994), p.43.

[14] "On Establishing the Correct Teaching for the Peace of the Land": One of Nichiren's five major writings. He submitted this treatise to Hojo Tokiyori, the retired regent but still the most

powerful figure in Japan's ruling clan, on July 16, 1260. In it, he predicts that unless people quickly took faith in the correct teaching, then of the three calamities and seven disasters, the two that had yet to occur—internal strife and foreign invasion—would happen without fail.

[15] Three instances of gaining distinction: Also known as the "three-time gaining of distinction" or "three-time distinction." This refers to Nichiren making accurate predictions at the time of each of his three remonstrations with the ruling authorities. The first instance was the prophecy of internal strife and foreign invasion that he made in his treatise "On Establishing the Correct Teaching for the Peace of the Land," submitted on July 16, 1260. The second was the prophecy of internal strife and foreign invasion that he made in remonstrating with Hei no Saemon, when the latter had come to arrest him on the evening of September 12, 1271, at the time of the Tatsunokuchi Persecution. The third instance was the prophecy of foreign invasion that the Daishonin made in his final

remonstration with Hei no Saemon on April 8, 1274, after returning to Kamakura from exile on Sado Island.

[16] Translated from Japanese. Josei Toda, *Toda Josei zenshu* (Collected Writings of Josei Toda) (Tokyo: Seikyo Shimbunsha, 1989), vol.4, pp.581–83.

[17] Ibid., 582–83.

[18] Daisaku Ikeda, *The Human Revolution* (New York & Tokyo: Weatherhill, 1972), vol.1, p. xi.

[19] Ibid., xi–xii.

[20] Ibid., x.

[21] With the words, "I, Nichiren, am sovereign, teacher, and father and mother to all the people of Japan" ("The Opening of the Eyes," WND-1, 287), Nichiren declared that he possessed the three virtues—sovereign, teacher and parent—in the Latter Day of the Law. The three virtues are the benevolent functions of Buddhas. The virtue of sovereign is the power to protect all living beings, the virtue of teacher is the wisdom to instruct and lead them to enlightenment, and the virtue of parent is the compassion to nurture and support them.

[22] *Chandala:* A class of untouchables, below the lowest of the four castes in the ancient Indian caste system. People in this class handled corpses, butchered animals and carried out other tasks associated with death or the killing of living things. Nichiren declared himself to be a member of the chandala class because he was born to a fisherman's family.

[23] This story is found in *The Annotations on "Great Concentration and Insight."* When a fox on Mount Shita, a place in India, was chased by a lion, it accidentally fell into a dry well and remained there for three days. On the brink of starvation, it resolved to dedicate itself to the Buddhist Law and recited a verse expressing its desire to expiate its past offenses. When the fox's voice reached the god Shakra on the summit of Mount Sumeru, Shakra rescued it and asked it to preach the Law to him and the other heavenly deities.

[24] Johann Wolfgang von Goethe, *Faust, Part II,* translated and edited by David Constantine (London: Penguin Books Ltd., 2009), p.237.

CHAPTER 10

"THE THREE KINDS OF TREASURE"—PART 1 OF 3

THE ESSENCE OF BUDDHISM LIES IN ONE'S "BEHAVIOR AS A HUMAN BEING"

The Passage for Study in This Lecture

I have received various articles from your messenger, including a white quilted robe and a string of coins, and the goods mentioned in Toki's letter.[1] The persimmons, pears, and fresh and dried seaweed are particularly welcome.

I am most grieved over your lord's illness. Although he has not professed faith in the Lotus Sutra, you are a member of his clan, and it is thanks to his consideration that you are able to make offerings to the sutra. Thus, these may become prayers solely for your lord's recovery. Think of a small tree under a large one, or grass by a great river. Though they do not receive rain or water directly, they nonetheless thrive, partaking of dew from the large tree or drawing moisture from the river. The same holds true with the relationship between you and your lord. To give another example, King Ajatashatru[2] was an enemy of the Buddha. But because Jivaka,[3] a minister in the king's court, believed in the Buddha and continually made offerings to him, the blessings accruing from his actions are said to have returned to Ajatashatru.

Buddhism teaches that, when the Buddha nature manifests itself from within, it will receive protection from without. This is one of its fundamental principles. The Lotus Sutra says, "I have profound reverence for you."[4] The Nirvana Sutra states, "All living beings alike possess the Buddha nature." Bodhisattva Ashvaghosha's[5] *Awakening of Faith in the Mahayana* says, "Because the true abiding Law invariably permeates one's life and exerts its influence, illusions are instantly extinguished, and the Dharma body manifests itself." Bodhisattva Maitreya's[6] *Treatise on the Stages of Yoga Practice* contains a similar statement. What is hidden turns into manifest virtue.

> The heavenly devil[7] knew about this from before, and he therefore possessed your colleagues, causing them to invent that preposterous lie in order to prevent you from making offerings to the Lotus Sutra. Since your faith is profound, however, the ten demon daughters[8] must have come to your aid and caused your lord's illness. He does not regard you as his enemy, but since he once acted against you by giving credit to the false accusations of your colleagues, he has become seriously ill, and the malady persists.
>
> Ryuzo-bo,[9] whom these people count on as their pillar of strength, has already been toppled, and those who spoke falsely of you have contracted the same disease as your lord. Because Ryokan[10] is guilty of a much graver offense, it is more than likely that he will meet with or cause a bad accident. Surely he will not escape unharmed. (WND-1, 848)

LECTURE

Buddhism manifests in one's behavior. The Law is invisible to the eye, but it can be discerned in the conduct of those who correctly practice the Buddhist teachings. This is because their actions exemplify the great merit of the Law.

In this respect, it is essential that SGI leaders actively go out and meet with people, engage in one-to-one dialogue with them, share in their joys and sorrows, and work and move forward together with them. Leaders not only need to offer inspiring encouragement and give people courage to challenge problems and hardships; they must also stand up to error and injustice themselves while warmly protecting, guiding and caring for everyone. Buddhism does not exist apart from such committed action on the part of real, living human beings.

A person who prays more than anyone else and works harder than anyone else to propagate the Mystic Law is a genuine leader in Buddhism. *Buddha* is another name for someone of dedicated action. As long as there are efforts by devoted individuals to help others attain enlightenment, Buddhism will eternally shine as a living religion. If, on the other hand, such efforts were to disappear, Buddhism would become a dead religion, pallid and lifeless.

Shakyamuni and Nichiren Daishonin each left behind an exemplary model of behavior as individuals committed to leading others to enlightenment. They continually went among the people and engaged in dialogue to awaken the innate Buddha nature within each person.

Of course, human behavior takes numerous forms, and it also reflects the Ten Worlds—the life states from hell to Buddhahood. The human behavior that is the focus of my discussion here, however, specifically refers to the highest behavior or humanistic conduct—conduct that reflects the life state of Buddhahood and thus shows respect for all people. It also encompasses all efforts directed toward positive personal growth and to the happiness of both oneself and others in the actual realm of the nine worlds. And especially in terms of respectful conduct aimed at awakening people to their Buddha nature, it refers to the behavior of Bodhisattva Never Disparaging.[11] It also indicates the behavior in his efforts to battle evil and promote good for the happiness of all people. This is the exact same behavior of each of us in the SGI, the Bodhisattvas of the Earth[12] making efforts for kosen-rufu.

Buddhism shines the spotlight on individuals who, just as the Buddha does, show through their actions unceasing respect for people.

For the next three installments, we will study "The Three Kinds of Treasure." In this letter addressed to Shijo Kingo, dated September 1277, Nichiren teaches his loyal disciple the importance of being a person of wisdom and how crucial one's behavior can be in a time of adversity.

How should we correctly conduct ourselves as Buddhists? How can we take strong and wise action to break through any hardship? Nichiren answers these questions, explaining the essential way of life for Buddhist practitioners.

Let us deeply internalize the Daishonin's guidance on how to live with wisdom, using it as a source of inspiration for our own victory in life and in our efforts for kosen-rufu.

Sincerity and Integrity Are the Springboard for Overcoming Adversity

I have received various articles from your messenger, including a white quilted robe and a string of coins, and the goods mentioned in Toki's letter. The persimmons, pears, and fresh and dried seaweed are particularly welcome. (WND-1, 848)

Shijo Kingo had been undergoing severe trials. In an earlier letter, Nichiren Daishonin quoted him as saying that great hardships had showered down on him like rain (see "The Difficulty of Sustaining Faith," WND-1, 471). Three years prior (in 1274), Kingo had tried to convert his lord, Ema Mitsutoki,[13] to the Daishonin's teaching, but this only resulted in Ema marginalizing Kingo. From that time on, spiteful fellow retainers spread false accusations about Kingo and tarnished his good name. Attempts were even made on Kingo's life. Ema's disfavor also continued, causing tremendous hardship for Kingo and his family. This hardship took various forms, most conspicuously his being ordered to relinquish his existing fief and accept a smaller one. Throughout his struggles, Kingo faithfully followed Nichiren's detailed guidance and tenaciously persevered in his Buddhist practice.

Then, as a consequence of spurious accusations leveled against him in connection with an alleged incident at the Kuwagayatsu Debate[14] of June 1277, Kingo suddenly found himself in danger of having all his lands confiscated. Ema pressed him to recant his faith in the Lotus Sutra or else be stripped of his fief. But Kingo chose faith without the slightest hesitation or doubt. He immediately sent a pledge to this effect to Nichiren. And the swift reply he received contained the famous lines: "This life is like a dream. One cannot be sure that one will live until tomorrow. However wretched a beggar you might become, never disgrace the Lotus Sutra" ("A Warning against Begrudging One's Fief," WND-1, 824).

Another consistent piece of advice Nichiren gave Shijo Kingo was to not be fawning or servile.[15] Servility is tantamount to destroying one's own dignity or self-esteem. Even worse, behaving in a cowardly or servile manner toward devilish functions will prevent one's Buddhahood from shining forth.

We must firmly stand up to devilish functions that bring misery to people. When confronted by people of dignity and integrity, devilish functions will always make a fast retreat. This is just like foxes fleeing when they hear the mighty roar of the lion king or like darkness vanishing the instant the sun comes out.

Let us live with unshakable confidence and pride and without the least servility. The Daishonin repeatedly teaches his followers that this is where the true brilliance of human dignity is to be found.

What is admirable about Shijo Kingo is how he always sought Nichiren's guidance and followed it unerringly. Because he strove in a spirit of oneness with his mentor, he could triumph magnificently over all obstacles. The mentor-disciple relationship is the driving force for victory in life and in kosen-rufu. This is an eternally unchanging principle of Buddhism.

When Shijo Kingo faithfully put his mentor's instructions into practice, profoundly determined never to disgrace the Lotus Sutra or behave servilely, his situation changed dramatically. It happened that Ema became seriously ill, and Kingo, who was knowledgeable in medicine, was called on to treat him. He was thus presented with a great opportunity to win back his lord's trust. This was only a few months after the threat of having his fiefs confiscated.

But the outcome of this chance to improve his relationship with his lord was still very uncertain. And Kingo's trying circumstances remained unchanged, with no immediate solution in sight. He still faced hostility from fellow retainers as well as continuing discord with his brothers. Meanwhile, the underhanded scheming of Ryokan of Gokuraku-ji, a temple in Kamakura, and others aimed at discrediting Kingo also continued unabated.

Yet, precisely because significant developments were taking shape—including glimmerings of a positive turnaround—it was crucial that Shijo Kingo not grow overconfident or negligent. He would need to proceed carefully and cautiously toward resolving the situation. And it was imperative that he pay even greater attention to the people and things around him and secure victory through his wise behavior. This is the concrete guidance that the Daishonin offers Shijo Kingo in this letter, advising him in detail on how to view and challenge the situation confronting him.

The letter begins with the Daishonin expressing his appreciation for the offerings he has received. From this passage, we see that Shijo Kingo had sent a sizable parcel of sincere offerings, along with a letter entrusted to his care by fellow practitioner Toki Jonin. No doubt, concern for Nichiren's well-being in the remote mountains of Minobu as winter was approaching prompted Kingo to send him so many items. Nichiren confirms that the goods have arrived safely and warmly thanks Kingo for his generosity, adding that the foodstuffs are "particularly welcome." Here we can sense the deep heart-to-heart exchange between them as mentor and disciple.

Having received news of the latest developments in Kingo's situation, Nichiren offers him pertinent advice on daily conduct. He also praises Kingo for his victory achieved through faith, saying, "Is not his [your lord's] regard for you due to the aid of the Lotus Sutra?" (WND-1, 850). At the same time, concerned that Kingo would become the target of increasing envy and be placed in even greater danger, Nichiren warns him to be extremely careful and avoid rash or indiscreet behavior. He also teaches him that maintaining personal integrity and realizing victory are crucial in opening the way forward in the different challenging situations he faces.

This letter shines throughout with profound passages that have given encouragement and sustenance to countless members:

> More valuable than treasures in a storehouse are the treasures of the body, and the treasures of the heart are the most valuable of all. (WND-1, 851)

***

> The purpose of the appearance in this world of Shakyamuni Buddha, the lord of teachings, lies in his behavior as a human being. (WND-1, 852)

***

The wise may be called human, but the thoughtless are no more than animals. (WND-1, 852)

The Daishonin explains to his embattled disciple that the key to breaking through adversity ultimately lies in wise action and one's own humanity. This applies not only to Shijo Kingo. Our actions, as well, reflect our faith and determine victory or defeat in our Buddhist practice.

Each passage in this writing is imbued with Nichiren's profound compassion to encourage each follower as his first priority. As a Buddhist, no action is more exalted than that of raising other human beings, fostering capable people.

Founding Soka Gakkai president Tsunesaburo Makiguchi once encouraged a youthful educator. Hailing from a rural area in Japan, the young man was embarrassed by his accent and thus found it difficult to voice his opinions in front of others. Mr. Makiguchi told him:

> Even if your pronunciation is poor or you have an accent, it is important for you to be yourself and do your best. Every person is endowed with wonderful potential. Go ahead and volunteer to make a presentation. This will benefit you. At the same time, your giving a presentation will also benefit the other teachers and, by extension, contribute to the growth of the children in their charge. Thus your action will result in good. Soka education means

doing our utmost to create value that constitutes benefit and good.

"Be yourself and do your best"—this tenet of humanistic education is consistent with the humanistic principles of Buddhism, because humanistic behavior on the part of a genuine Buddhist practitioner leads to the creation of the highest possible value.

Helping people develop their humanity is the hallmark of Buddhism. I have always believed that Nichiren's key message to Shijo Kingo in this letter is that the correct path of Buddhist practice lies in continuing efforts to improve one's character and develop one's humanity. In other words, it lies in continually striving to undergo one's human revolution.

The Wise Always Have Appreciation for Their Benefactors

I am most grieved over your lord's illness. Although he has not professed faith in the Lotus Sutra, you are a member of his clan, and it is thanks to his consideration that you are able to make offerings to the sutra. Thus, these may become prayers solely for your lord's recovery. Think of a small tree under a large one, or grass by a great river. Though they do not receive rain or water directly, they nonetheless thrive, partaking of dew from the large tree or drawing moisture from the river. The same holds true with the relationship between you and your lord. To give another example, King Ajatashatru was an enemy of the Buddha. But because Jivaka, a minister in the king's court, believed in the Buddha and continually made offerings to him, the blessings accruing from his actions are said to have returned to Ajatashatru. (WND-1, 848)

Having followed in the footsteps of his father, Shijo Kingo was a second-generation samurai retainer of the Ema family, which was directly related to one of the Hojo regents who ruled the Kamakura military government. Both father and son had been loyal to the Ema family in times of grave peril.[16] It is therefore not difficult to imagine that his lord would have placed deep trust in Kingo. The latter only incurred his lord's disfavor after he tried to convert him to Nichiren Daishonin's teachings.

Subjected to unjustified harassment and disciplinary action, including transfer to another estate in a remote province, Kingo, it appears, even considered suing Ema. Nichiren, however, urges him to exercise restraint, writing in another letter from the same period: "As vassals, you, your parents, and your close relatives are deeply indebted to your lord" ("The Eight Winds," WND-1, 794); and "Even if he never shows you the slightest further consideration, you should not hold a grudge against your lord" (WND-1,

794). Ingratitude ranks among the very worst kind of human conduct, as it incurs evil karma.

Nichiren tells Shijo Kingo that rather than resenting his lord, who is directly bringing pressure to bear on him, he should focus on battling the real adversary—namely, the workings of the "three obstacles and four devils"[17] manifesting in Ema's actions. Far more deserving of blame, he points out, is Ryokan, whose villainous schemes were largely behind the persecution of the Daishonin's followers and the false assumptions made by Kingo's lord. He declares that Ryokan is the epitome of the group known as "arrogant false sages"—one of the three powerful enemies[18] of Buddhism. It is an admonition to recognize the true nature of such negative and obstructive forces.

Following Nichiren's guidance, Kingo conducted himself with wisdom and utmost sincerity in his daily life and interactions with others. As a result, when illness struck, Ema sought treatment from Shijo Kingo, who was renowned as an "excellent physician" ("On Prolonging One's Life Span," WND-1, 955).

Learning that Ema was unwell, Nichiren writes, "I am most grieved over your lord's illness." Even though on the surface Ema was the very person inflicting suffering on Shijo Kingo, a sincere Lotus Sutra practitioner, Nichiren was deeply concerned about his illness.

Regarding truth or error in terms of the Law or teaching, Nichiren Buddhism maintains a rigorous attitude, but when it comes to people's sufferings, it always has a spirit of tolerance and compassion. Nichiren would do whatever he could to help those suffering, even if they were people who slandered the Law. Thinking of their plight, he exclaimed, "How tragic, how pitiful...!" ("The Selection of the Time," WND-1, 578). At heart, he was indignant over human suffering (see "On Establishing the Correct Teaching for the Peace of the Land," WND-1, 7). The essence of Buddhism is found in the heartfelt wish for the happiness of each person.

My mentor, second Soka Gakkai president Josei Toda, shared the same spirit as the Daishonin. If people discarded their faith, he was filled with deep sorrow. "How tragic this is!" he once exclaimed. "It hurts as though a gimlet is boring into my heart!"

The Soka Gakkai has realized brilliant and unprecedented development because it has inherited this noble spirit to go out among the people and take action for their happiness.

In this writing, Nichiren points out that Ema, while not a Lotus Sutra practitioner himself, makes it possible for Shijo Kingo to give offerings to the sutra. Therefore, he says, the merit and good fortune Kingo acquires will also extend to Ema. Nichiren cites the example of a small tree beneath a large tree or grass on the banks of a great river. Though the small tree or the grass may not receive rain or water from the river directly, it will still thrive on the dew. He also notes that in Shakyamuni's day, a king named Ajatashatru was a great enemy of Buddhism but was ultimately protected because his physician, Jivaka, was a devoted follower of the Buddha.

In a family, too, if one person radiates the brilliance of the Mystic Law, then all family members, including those who do not practice Nichiren Buddhism, will be protected. Individuals can similarly illuminate their workplaces and their communities. That is how vast and immeasurable the benefit of the Mystic Law is. Accordingly, from the standpoint of our Buddhist practice, it is important that we ourselves, irrespective of what others may do, become like the large tree or the great river in this analogy.

Buddha Nature Manifesting Itself From Within and Bringing Forth Protection From Without

Buddhism teaches that, when the Buddha nature manifests itself from within, it will receive protection from without. This is one of its fundamental principles. The Lotus Sutra says, "I have profound reverence for you." The Nirvana Sutra states, "All living beings alike possess the Buddha nature." Bodhisattva Ashvaghosha's *Awakening of Faith in the Mahayana* says, "Because the true abiding Law invariably permeates one's life and exerts its influence, illusions are instantly extinguished, and the Dharma body

manifests itself." **Bodhisattva Maitreya's** *Treatise on the Stages of Yoga Practice* **contains a similar statement. What is hidden turns into manifest virtue. (WND-1, 848)**

Nichiren Daishonin explains a key Buddhist principle—the "Buddha nature manifesting itself from within and bringing forth protection from without." In other words, when we activate the Buddha nature inside us, it will cause the protective functions of life to work externally.

We possess this Buddha nature, and it is up to us to awaken to and manifest it. By practicing Nichiren Buddhism, the Mystic Law comes to permeate one's life and exert its influence (see WND-1, 848)—that is, our Buddha nature, once revealed, pervades our lives in the same way that burning incense imbues our clothing with its fragrance. Our Buddha nature emerges like a fragrance wafting in the breeze. And while we speak of receiving protection from the heavenly deities—the positive forces of the universe—the first step in that process is to embark on our own inner transformation.

In "How Those Initially Aspiring to the Way Can Attain Buddhahood through the Lotus Sutra," Nichiren writes:

> When we revere Myoho-renge-kyo inherent in our own life as the object of devotion, the Buddha nature within us is summoned forth and manifested by our chanting of Nam-myoho-renge-kyo. This is

what is meant by "Buddha." To illustrate, when a caged bird sings, birds who are flying in the sky are thereby summoned and gather around, and when the birds flying in the sky gather around, the bird in the cage strives to get out. When with our mouths we chant the Mystic Law, our Buddha nature, being summoned, will invariably emerge. The Buddha nature of Brahma and Shakra, being called, will protect us, and the Buddha nature of the Buddhas and bodhisattvas, being summoned, will rejoice. (WND-1, 887)

Chanting Nam-myoho-renge-kyo to the Gohonzon, the object of devotion in Nichiren Buddhism, is in fact the same as summoning forth and praising the Buddha nature inherent in our own lives and residing in all things in the universe. In response to the sound of our chanting, through which we reveal our Buddha nature, all benevolent forces throughout the universe move into action to protect us. This principle succinctly expresses the unique character of Nichiren Buddhism, which is completely different from faith that pins hope for salvation on some external power.

The concept of the Buddha nature manifesting itself from within indicates a power existing and generated from inside us. Buddhism is known as the "inner way." Therefore, we do not seek Buddhahood, or the life of the Buddha, outside ourselves. The life state of the Buddha, characterized by the four noble virtues—eternity, happiness, true self and purity—is found within our own mortal being that also experiences the delusions of earthly desires and the sufferings of birth and death. Nichiren Buddhism enables us to awaken and manifest the benefit of Buddhahood in our lives.

In other words, because we all possess the Buddha nature, when we chant Nam-myoho-renge-kyo with a clearly focused mind, the life of the Buddha is summoned forth from within and emerges. Manifesting our inner Buddhahood causes protection to arise from without. All this hinges on our inner focus or resolve.

In light of the principle of the Buddha nature manifesting itself from within and bringing forth protection from without, we can definitely change any situation or environment by transforming our fundamental mindset and revealing our Buddha nature. All fear vanishes the moment we fully believe that "I alone write the script for the drama of my life."

Next, Nichiren continues, "What is hidden turns into manifest virtue." Unseen virtue turns into conspicuous reward. To practice the Mystic Law is to proceed along the path of victory; all virtue will manifest in visible form without fail. When we forge ahead with this deep, unshakable conviction, our future will open up in wonderful ways we could never have imagined. This is the conviction and the declaration of Nichiren

Daishonin, the Buddha of the Latter Day of the Law.

As a matter of fact, SGI members around the world are constructing such confident states of life. They are models of respectful, humanistic conduct toward others. The Lotus Sutra's spirit of respect and reverence for all people is deeply ingrained in the lives of SGI members.

When someone is in trouble, we cannot simply look the other way. When someone appears to be struggling, we cannot help offering encouragement. When someone is suffering, we cannot help embracing them. Believing in the potential of all people, we actively pursue positive and meaningful interactions. SGI members' actions are the very embodiment of respect for others.

This in itself is proof of their having deeply cultivated the life state of Buddhas and bodhisattvas. There is no greater benefit. The fragrant breeze of happiness boundlessly caresses their being. SGI members are truly the heroes of the people. They are great champions of life.

Never Be Defeated by Lies and Defamation

The heavenly devil knew about this from before, and he therefore possessed your colleagues, causing them to invent that preposterous lie in order to prevent you from making offerings to the Lotus Sutra. Since your faith is profound, however, the ten demon daughters must

have come to your aid and caused your lord's illness. He does not regard you as his enemy, but since he once acted against you by giving credit to the false accusations of your colleagues, he has become seriously ill, and the malady persists. (WND-1, 848)

Devilish forces always spin lies. In this passage, Nichiren Daishonin indicates that devils invariably resort to fabrications and false accusations to discredit people.

The Chinese writer Lu Xun keenly observed, "There is also a weapon that kills without drawing any blood—false rumors."[19] To spread scurrilous lies and rumors—that is the essential character of devilish functions.

Nichiren says that the Tatsunokuchi Persecution,[20] the culminating persecution that nearly saw him beheaded, was due to "endless slanders" ("On Repaying Debts of Gratitude," WND-1, 728). Slander means a twisting of the facts to malign another person. Devilish functions constantly employ such means to persuade the powerful to bring down people of integrity and justice. This is the insidious, manipulative working of the devil king. Those who fall into the category of "arrogant false sages"—the most fearful of the three powerful enemies—also employ false accusations and misinformation to incite the ruling authorities to persecute the votary of the Lotus Sutra. In contrast to those who qualify as arrogant lay people or arrogant priests—the two other powerful enemies—arrogant false sages never personally come out into the open; they do not directly strike any blows. This is the true nature of the devil king of the sixth heaven.

In view of this principle, Nichiren asserts that such devilish functions are behind Shijo Kingo's present circumstances. In short, the devil king has influenced people connected to the Ema family, causing them to lie so that Kingo will come under fire.

Silently, imperceptibly, devilish functions wreak havoc and destruction in people's hearts. Having the wisdom to discern the true nature of such functions reduces them in power by half. Courage—which equates to the power of faith—is what ultimately defeats devilish functions.

Based on the principle of "the Buddha nature manifesting itself from within and bringing forth protection from without," Nichiren explains that because Shijo Kingo has manifested his inherent Buddha nature—because he has demonstrated strong faith—the ten demon daughters moved into action, causing Ema to fall ill. As I have touched on already, this development provided Kingo with an opportunity to break through his painful situation.

How the protective functions of the universe manifest will differ widely depending on the particular circumstances. In Kingo's case, protection appeared in the form of Ema falling ill—the result, Nichiren surmises, of Ema himself succumbing for a time to the deception of devilish forces. But because this event led Ema to regain his trust in Kingo, he, too, in keeping with the above principle, shared in the benefit of the Lotus Sutra. This clearly seems the result of Ema's own good fortune.

In the next passage, the Daishonin clarifies how, in contrast, those directly instigating these devilish workings in others would receive unmistakable retribution in their present existence.

Justice Is Proven by Realizing Victory

Ryuzo-bo, whom these people count on as their pillar of strength, has already been toppled, and those who spoke falsely of you have contracted the same disease as your lord. Because Ryokan is guilty of a much graver offense, it is more than likely that he will meet with or cause a bad accident. Surely he will not escape unharmed. (WND-1, 848)

Wrongdoers never prosper—good will always win out over evil in accord with the inexorable causal workings of the Mystic Law.

Ryuzo-bo, who was venerated by many of those ill-disposed toward Shijo Kingo, had already fallen ill in the epidemic, as had many other samurai who had slandered Shijo Kingo. Further, Nichiren says that Ryokan, who was engaged in base and evil machinations, was guilty of a much graver offense and would surely not escape unharmed.

If the Daishonin had not appeared, Ryokan would have continued to be revered by the public as a "living Buddha," his true ugly nature forever hidden from view. Humiliated by losing to Nichiren in a contest to pray for rain, Ryokan cunningly ingratiated himself even more with various influential figures and plotted to bring persecution down on Nichiren.

Even after Nichiren moved to Mount Minobu, the vain and self-serving Ryokan no doubt lived in constant fear of being exposed as a fraud, terrified of the noble and dignified forces of the Buddha. Whatever his outward bravado, he was surely trembling inside. The more he allowed himself to be ruled by negative impulses, the more conscious he would have been in the depths of his heart of his own wretchedness.

The French writer and poet Charles Péguy declared: "The triumph of demagogues is fleeting. But the ruin is eternal."[21] Instigators of lies and false assertions end up leading lives of eternal regret and spiritual defeat.

Around this same time, in addition to Shijo Kingo's triumph, the Ikegami brothers—two other key followers of Nichiren facing persecution for their beliefs—were also victorious. For Ryokan, who was intent on fomenting intrigues to oppress Nichiren's followers, these were certainly major setbacks. Ryokan's malicious schemes utterly failed—Nichiren's disciples dealing a powerful blow, as it were, to corrupt power.

"Though evils may be numerous, they cannot prevail over a single great truth" ("Many in Body, One in Mind," WND-1, 618). It all comes down to one great truth or good. When mentor and disciple unite, devilish functions can definitely be defeated. When this victory is secured, a new page opens.

It is no exaggeration to say that the drama enacted by Shijo Kingo is a brilliant testament to his having won because of his upright, humanistic behavior—in other words, the forces of the Buddha vanquishing all devilish forces.

The times today also call for humanism. Humanistic action will no doubt become increasingly important in the future. Mr. Toda once said, "You can talk about sincerity and integrity all you want, but unless your actions match your words, it's pointless." Our actions are what matter. The world is now waiting and yearning for the humanistic behavior that SGI members exemplify.

The stage for our endeavors is now opening ever wider before us as we move toward an age of the people, of women, of youth, of children, of peace, of culture, of education, of humanity and of life. The twenty-first century has only just begun. The time has come when the radiant light of our humanity, our humanistic behavior, will shine with ever-greater brilliance.

This lecture was originally published in the October 2009 issue of the Daibyakurenge, *the Soka Gakkai's monthly study journal.*

NOTES

[1] Toki refers to Toki Jonin, one of Nichiren Daishonin's leading followers. He lived in Shimosa Province (part of present-day Chiba Prefecture) and served as a retainer of Lord Chiba, the constable of that province.

[2] King Ajatashatru: A king of Magadha in India in the time of Shakyamuni Buddha. Incited by Devadatta, he gained the throne by killing his father. Later, however, Ajatashatru regretted his conduct deeply. Tormented by guilt, he broke out in virulent sores, and it was predicted that he would die. His physician and minister, Jivaka, persuaded him to repent his evil conduct and seek out the Buddha's teaching. Ajatashatru did so, overcame his illness and became a devout follower of the Buddha. He supported the First Buddhist Council in its compilation of Shakyamuni's teachings undertaken the year following Shakyamuni's death.

[3]   Jivaka: A skilled physician of the state of Magadha in India in Shakyamuni's time. At the royal court, Jivaka treated Bimbisara, the king of Magadha, and his son, Ajatashatru. He was also a devout Buddhist and patron of the Buddhist Order, and he treated Shakyamuni Buddha and his disciples, as well as the general citizenry.

[4]   LSOC, 308.

[5]   Ashvaghosha (n.d.): A second-century Mahayana scholar and poet of Shravasti in India. He at first criticized Buddhism but was later converted by Parshva. He led many people to the Buddha's teachings through his skill in music and literature. Ashvaghosha is known as the twelfth of Shakyamuni's twenty-four successors.

[6]   Maitreya: The founder of the Consciousness-Only school, thought to have been the teacher of Asanga and to have lived around 270–350 (350–430, according to another account).

[7]   Heavenly devil: Also, devil king of the sixth heaven or devil king. The king of devils, who dwells in the highest or the sixth heaven of the world of desire. He is also named Freely Enjoying Things Conjured by Others, the king who makes

free use of the fruits of others' efforts for his own pleasure. Served by innumerable minions, he obstructs Buddhist practice and delights in sapping the life force of other beings. The devil king is a personification of the negative tendency to force others to one's will at any cost.

[8] Ten demon daughters: Ten female protective deities who appear in the Lotus Sutra as the daughters of *rakshasa* demons or the ten rakshasa daughters. In "Dharani," the sutra's 26th chapter, they vow to guard and protect the sutra's practitioners, saying that they will inflict punishment on any who trouble the latter.

[9] Ryuzo-bo (n.d.): A Tendai priest who was expelled from Enryaku-ji, a temple on Mount Hiei and headquarters of the Tendai school, and later came to Kamakura where he won the patronage of Ryokan of Gokuraku-ji, a priest of the True Word Precepts school.

[10] Ryokan (1217–1303): Also known as Ninsho. A prominent priest of the True Word Precepts school in Japan. In 1267, with the patronage of the Hojo clan, Ryokan became chief priest of Gokuraku-ji, a temple in Kamakura.

Hostile to Nichiren Daishonin, he used his connections with powerful figures to harass the Daishonin and his followers, and was behind numerous persecutions that befell them.

[11] Bodhisattva Never Disparaging: A bodhisattva described in "Bodhisattva Never Disparaging," the 20th chapter of the Lotus Sutra. This bodhisattva—Shakyamuni in a previous lifetime—would bow to everyone he met and say: "I have profound reverence for you, I would never dare treat you with disparagement or arrogance. Why? Because you will all practice the bodhisattva way and will then be able to attain Buddhahood" (LSOC, 308). But he was attacked by arrogant people, who beat him with sticks and staves and threw stones at him. The sutra explains that his practice of respecting the Buddha nature of others became the cause for him to attain Buddhahood.

[12] Bodhisattvas of the Earth: Countless bodhisattvas whom Shakyamuni calls forth in "Emerging from the Earth," the 15th chapter of the Lotus Sutra. They are led by four great bodhisattvas—Superior Practices,

Boundless Practices, Pure Practices and Firmly Established Practices. In "Supernatural Powers," the 21st chapter, Shakyamuni entrusts these bodhisattvas with the essential teaching that they are to spread in the evil age after his passing.

[13] Ema Mitsutoki (n.d.): Also known as Hojo Mitsutoki. He was a devout follower of the priest Ryokan of the True Word Precepts school.

[14] Kuwagayatsu Debate: A debate held in Kuwagayatsu, Kamakura, in 1277, between Nichiren's disciple Sammibo and a priest named Ryuzo-bo, who was under the patronage of Ryokan of Gokuraku-ji. Ryuzo-bo was defeated by Sammi-bo. Kingo merely attended the debate as an observer and did not utter a word. Yet, it was alleged to Kingo's lord, Ema, that Shijo Kingo had burst into the debate with several confederates with weapons drawn and disrupted the proceedings.

[15] In "A Warning against Begrudging One's Fief," Nichiren advises Shijo Kingo: "Just as you have written in your letter, you must act and speak without the least servility. If you try to curry favor, the

situation will only worsen ... You must in no way behave in a servile fashion toward the magistrate" (WND-1, 824).

[16] A petition to Ema that Nichiren composed on Shijo Kingo's behalf explains the history of long and dedicated service by Kingo, and his father before him, to the Ema clan. Written as if Kingo were personally addressing Ema, it states: "When your father incurred the wrath of the authorities, his hundreds of retainers all shifted their allegiance; among them, my late father Yorikazu alone remained faithful to the end, accompanying him into exile to the province of Izu. Shortly before the battle that took place in Kamakura on the twelfth day of the second month in the eleventh year of the Bun'ei era, I, Yorimoto, was in the province of Izu, but no sooner had I received word at the hour of the monkey on the tenth day than I hastened alone over the Hakone pass and joined with seven others who vowed before you to put an end to their lives" ("The Letter of Petition from Yorimoto," WND-1, 811).

[17] Three obstacles and four devils: Various obstacles and hindrances to the practice of Buddhism. The three obstacles are (1) the obstacle of earthly desires, (2) the obstacle of karma and (3) the obstacle of retribution. The four devils are (1) the hindrance of the five components, (2) the hindrance of earthly desires, (3) the hindrance of death and (4) the hindrance of the devil king.

[18] Three powerful enemies: Three types of arrogant people who persecute those who propagate the Lotus Sutra in the evil age after Shakyamuni Buddha's death, described in the twenty-line verse section of "Encouraging Devotion," the 13th chapter of the Lotus Sutra. The Great Teacher Miao-lo (711–82) of China summarizes them as arrogant lay people, arrogant priests and arrogant false sages.

[19] Translated from Chinese. Lu Xun, *Lu Xun quanji* (The Complete Works of Lu Xun) (Beijing: Renmin Wenxue Chubanshe, 1996), vol.4, p.595.

[20] Tatsunokuchi Persecution: On September 12, 1271, powerful figures in the government unjustly arrested Nichiren Daishonin and led him off in the middle

of the night to a place called Tatsunokuchi on the outskirts of Kamakura, the seat of government, where they tried to execute him under cover of darkness. The execution attempt failed, and about a month later he was exiled to Sado Island.

[21] Translated from French. Charles Péguy, *Œuvres en prose complètes* (Complete Collection of Prose Works), edited by Robert Burac (Paris: Gallimard, 1988), vol.2, p.375.

CHAPTER 11

"THE THREE KINDS OF TREASURE"—PART 2 OF 3

"TREASURING EACH PERSON"—THE GUIDING SPIRIT OF OUR ACTIONS AS GENUINE PRACTITIONERS OF NICHIREN BUDDHISM

> The Passage for Study in This Lecture
>
> As things stand now, I have a feeling you are in danger. Your enemies are sure to make an attempt on your life. In backgammon, if two stones of the same color are placed side by side, they cannot be hit by an opposing stone. A cart, as long as it has two wheels, does not lurch all over the road. Likewise, if two men go together, an enemy hesitates to attack. Therefore, no matter what faults you may find with your younger brothers, do not let them leave you alone even for a moment.

Your face bears definite signs of a hot temper. But you should know that the heavenly gods will not protect a short-tempered person, however important they may think he or she is. If you should be killed, even though you might attain Buddhahood, your enemies would be delighted, but we would feel only grief. This would indeed be regrettable. While your foes busy themselves plotting against you, your lord places greater confidence in you than before. Therefore, although they appear to have quieted down, inwardly they are no doubt seething with hate. (WND-1, 848–49)

***

Probably you are well aware of it, but let me cite the Buddha's prediction about what the latter age will be like. In essence he states: "It will be a muddied age in which even sages will find it difficult to live. They will be like stones in a great fire, which for a while seem to endure the heat but finally char and crumble into ashes..." Thus the saying goes, "Do not remain in the seat of honor too long."

Many people have plotted to undo you, but you have avoided their intrigues and emerged victorious. Should you lose your composure now and fall into their trap, you will be, as people say, like a boatman who rows his boat with all his might only to have it capsize just before he reaches the shore, or like a person who is served no hot water at the end of his meal. (WND-1, 849)

***

But since you are hot-tempered by nature, you might not take my advice. In that case, it will be beyond the power of my prayers to save you.

Ryuzo-bo[1] and your elder brother plotted evil against you. Therefore, the heavenly gods so contrived it that the situation would develop exactly as you wished. Then how can you now dare to go against the wish of the heavenly gods? ... You must hurry and talk with these four men and report to me how the matter goes. Then I will fervently pray to the heavenly gods for your protection. (WND-1, 850)

LECTURE

In a discussion with representatives of a youth delegation from China, I was asked what had been the key to the Soka Gakkai's development. Without a moment's hesitation, I replied, "Our treasuring every one of our members." This is my conviction and my unwavering philosophy.

To treasure each person—this is the foundation of Nichiren Buddhism. As the saying goes, "One is the mother of ten thousand" ("Conversation between a Sage and an Unenlightened Man," WND-1, 131). The enlightenment of one person opens the way for all people to attain enlightenment. Nichiren Daishonin states, "When the dragon king's daughter[2] attained Buddhahood, it opened up the way to attaining Buddhahood for all women of later ages" ("The Opening of the Eyes," WND-1, 269). This is a case of "one example that stands for all the rest"[3] (WND-1, 269).

Each Soka Gakkai member embodies the entire Soka Gakkai. Wholeheartedly encouraging each individual member we encounter, therefore, will invigorate the entire organization. As long as open, one-to-one dialogue is fostered, our organization will continue to flourish. This means giving confidence to those feeling lost and confused, hope to those burdened with worries, courage to those sunk in despair, joy to those filled with sorrow, wisdom to those beset by hardships, strength and tenacity to those facing setbacks, peace of mind to those gripped by fear, and conviction to those stalled by uncertainty. Such a steady stream of encouragement becomes a powerful source of revitalization. It fosters bonds of joint commitment, of working together for a common cause. Through these supportive efforts, we actually take a step closer to happiness for both ourselves and others.

My mentor, second Soka Gakkai president Josei Toda, was a virtuoso in the art of giving personal guidance and encouragement in faith. In the early postwar years, the Soka Gakkai Headquarters had a branch office in a building in Tokyo's Ichigaya area. At the top of the stairs on the second floor, a small waiting room measuring about one hundred sixty square feet was always filled with members wishing to receive guidance from Mr. Toda. They were struggling with all kinds of worries—financial trouble, sickness, family discord and many other grave problems that defied description. But Mr. Toda would put these suffering people at ease, greeting them warmly and asking, "What's the matter?" Then, as if the floodgates had been opened, they would pour out their problems to him.

Mr. Toda always reassured them: "It's going to be all right!" "You'll definitely become happy by practicing Nichiren Buddhism." He also always cited Nichiren's writings when he gave encouragement, careful to explain: "This is what the Daishonin teaches. These aren't my words." All who came to see him were revitalized by his confident guidance and left with a new, purposeful spring in their step. While grappling with their own karmic challenges, they followed Mr. Toda's lead to become emissaries of happiness in their local areas, supporting and encouraging their fellow members and fostering many capable people for kosen-rufu.

We grew from one person to two, three, ten, a hundred, a thousand, ten thousand and so on—in this way, our alliance of people dedicated to the cause of good steadily spread to encompass all of Japan, so that now the country is veritably wreathed with "human flowers" (LSOC, 142) brimming with happiness. And it further spread across the entire world, giving rise to the magnificent global SGI network we have today.

It is evident in Nichiren's writings that he always based his guidance and encouragement on a keen understanding of the character and specific circumstances of whomever he was addressing. This is particularly apparent in "The Three Kinds of Treasure." His expressions of concern and meticulous advice throughout this letter overflow with his boundless compassion for his disciple Shijo Kingo, who was then facing the greatest challenge of his life.

Nichiren wrote this letter as if Kingo were sitting right in front of him, as if he were speaking to him in person, weighing Kingo's reactions to his words. In some places, he describes in detail how Kingo should conduct himself. Elsewhere, he deftly identifies key areas on which Kingo will need to focus toward carrying out his human revolution. And in still other places, he praises Kingo's selfless and ungrudging efforts for the sake of the Law. No doubt, various images of his loyal disciple would have come to mind as he composed this letter.

Giving personal guidance is an all-out, life-to-life interaction fueled by compassion and conviction. It is a struggle to apprehend the shifting emotions going through others' hearts moment to moment and to cut through the ignorance or darkness shrouding their lives. In the course of this exchange, we may see their expressions gradually change—for instance, conveying agreement, appearing self-reflective, looking more positive and upbeat, filled with a sense of relief and finally shining with fresh resolve. The process of offering guidance is a struggle to ignite a spark of courage and hope within others' lives that will give them the strength to overcome their negative karma and to share wisdom and advice based on the teachings of Buddhism with which they can defeat the devilish functions or obstacles they face.

For us, "The Three Kinds of Treasure"—a great source of encouragement for Shijo Kingo that helped him pave the way to ultimate victory—can be viewed as an instructive reference for giving guidance in faith.

***

Leaders Must Be Infinitely Thoughtful and Considerate

As things stand now, I have a feeling you are in danger. Your enemies are sure

to make an attempt on your life. In backgammon, if two stones of the same color are placed side by side, they cannot be hit by an opposing stone. A cart, as long as it has two wheels, does not lurch all over the road. Likewise, if two men go together, an enemy hesitates to attack. Therefore, no matter what faults you may find with your younger brothers, do not let them leave you alone even for a moment. (WND-1, 848–49)

Earlier in this letter, referring to the principle of the "Buddha nature manifesting itself from within and bringing forth protection from without,"[4] Nichiren Daishonin expresses great joy that Shijo Kingo's own strong faith above all had produced a major breakthrough toward positive resolution. A proactive and forward-looking attitude is key to ensuring a successful outcome. Carelessness is the greatest enemy. From this passage on, Nichiren gives Kingo detailed advice and words of caution.

Leaders in faith need to be extremely thoughtful and considerate. Leaders who strut around self-importantly while not paying attention to minor details are totally lacking in compassion and concern for others.

In another letter to Shijo Kingo, Nichiren writes, "An enemy will try to make you forget the danger so that he can attack" ("General Stone Tiger," WND-1, 952–53). When we are lulled into complacency and let our guard down, devilish functions will take advantage. That is why a word of warning or reminder to be careful can elicit the wisdom to defeat devilish functions; it can also help prevent accidents. To remain silent is irresponsible. For instance, brief reminders to people at the end of a meeting that they be careful going down the stairs or that they drive home safely are examples of our voices doing the compassionate work of the Buddha. This is humanistic behavior embodying the principles of Nichiren Buddhism.

In saying "As things stand now," Nichiren turns the focus to Kingo's course of action going forward. First, he expresses concern that Kingo's life is still in grave danger. Naturally, Kingo would have been aware that certain parties were actively seeking to eliminate him. But he may well have thought, *I'll be fine because I'm practicing Buddhism.* Here, Nichiren was most likely sounding a warning to sweep away any such complacency.

Next, he cites two examples: "In backgammon, if two stones of the same color are placed side by side, they cannot be hit by an opposing stone. A cart, as long as it has two wheels, does not lurch all over the road." He wishes to impress on Kingo the importance of having allies in order to successfully weather the present crisis. Specifically, Nichiren instructs him to cultivate cordial relations with his younger brothers, even if they have made mistakes in the past and have various shortcomings. He further points out that if Kingo is always accompanied by his brothers, his enemies will refrain from attacking him.

The reason for the Daishonin's strong insistence that Kingo under no circumstances travel alone was that the situation still remained so tense that he might be ambushed at any moment. He is deliberately strict here, because Kingo has just overcome one difficult hurdle by obtaining an opportunity to regain his lord's trust, putting him at a most crucial juncture.

When I read this passage, I am deeply struck by the immense compassion of the Daishonin who is concerned above all for the safety and well-being of his followers.

Faith Is a Struggle With Our Own Inner Darkness

Your face bears definite signs of a hot temper. But you should know that the heavenly gods will not protect a short-tempered person, however important they may think he or she is. If you should be killed, even though you might attain Buddhahood, your enemies would be delighted, but we would feel only grief. This would indeed be regrettable. (WND-1, 849)

"Your face bears definite signs of a hot temper," Nichiren Daishonin says. There's no way of knowing whether Shijo Kingo looked short-tempered all the time, or whether his current tribulations simply caused him to appear grim and tense. In any case, the Daishonin's description likely captures a key aspect of Kingo's personality. Kingo tended to be extremely single-minded and acted with a zealous sense of right and wrong. But this could sometimes work to his disadvantage. Therefore, Nichiren tells him bluntly that the Buddhist gods will not protect someone who is short-tempered (see WND-1, 849).

Of course, when it comes to attaining Buddhahood, there is certainly no discrimination based on personality. Anyone's personality can shine brightly when illuminated by the Mystic Law. And it is by fully utilizing each person's unique personality that our movement for kosen-rufu can achieve perfect and harmonious development.

We can surmise, however, that Nichiren purposely adopts a stern tone here in order to dispel Kingo's innate darkness. Ignorance gives rise to dark impulses and fuels negative tendencies. Everyone has areas he or she needs to challenge to accomplish their own human revolution. The important thing is that we confront our overarching shortcoming and strive to achieve positive development and growth. Through continually challenging ourselves and ceaselessly striving to move forward, we can grow in faith and expand our state of life.

Sometimes Buddhist teachers may give their disciples strict guidance out of a desire for them to realize their tremendous potential. This is because genuine mentors cherish and care for their disciples. Often their strictness is aimed at breaking through the negative tendencies or devilish functions at work in a disciple's life.

In the case of Shijo Kingo, there was a very real danger that his hot temper might get the better of him and exacerbate the situation. Carried away by their own views of right and wrong, people often forget to be circumspect or consider others' feelings, causing friction and resentment. Nichiren worried that with Kingo, it could create an opening for devilish forces to take advantage; hence, the reason for his unvarnished words.

Nichiren further points out that if Kingo were to antagonize others and lose his life as a result, his enemies would rejoice while his fellow practitioners of the Mystic Law would be filled with sorrow. Here, the Daishonin teaches Kingo that his victory does not stop with him alone but is deeply connected to the victory of the entire community of Nichiren's followers. Consequently, he advises Kingo to exercise the utmost care and take precautions for his own safety.

An Evil Age Rife With Jealousy

While your foes busy themselves plotting against you, your lord places greater confidence in you than before. Therefore, although they appear to have

quieted down, inwardly they are no doubt seething with hate. (WND-1, 849)

Nichiren Daishonin next turns his attention to those around Shijo Kingo and how they might feel about recent developments. Kingo had gained even greater trust from Ema than before. This would have been intolerable for those elements eager to bring about his downfall. Consequently, Nichiren notes that while these hostile forces may seem unperturbed on the outside, they are surely seething inside with hate.

He understood the nuances of Kingo's situation. He also deeply recognized the frightening human tendency to malign and tear others down out of jealousy, rivalry and resentment. This tendency is all the more apparent in the strife-filled saha world of the Latter Day of the Law, an evil age when people are swayed by greed, anger, foolishness, arrogance and doubt.[5]

Nichiren himself had consistently triumphed in the struggle against the three powerful enemies of Buddhism—arrogant false sages represented by corrupt and jealous priests in the thrall of devilish functions, along with arrogant priests and arrogant lay people in league with them.

There is nothing more fearful than a life consumed by jealousy. Male jealousy or rivalry can be especially frightening. Mr. Toda often said, "Male jealousy is pitch black." In terms of inner state of mind, jealousy is a manifestation of fear and insecurity, a projection of one's own weakness.

A quote by the Japanese intellect Kiyoshi Miki has stayed with me since my youth. He said: "Jealousy is always insidious ... Rather than prompting people to raise themselves to the same level as the person they are jealous of, it usually spurs them to bring that person down to their own level."[6] He also noted, "Jealousy comes from insecurity."[7]

There is nothing to fear once we realize that jealousy lies at the heart of all attempts to obstruct the progress of the community of believers that correctly upholds the Buddha's teachings. The important thing is that we have courage combined with wisdom and mindful behavior. Our behavior as human beings, as taught in Buddhism, is the key to victory.

The Daishonin then continues to caution Shijo Kingo in exhaustive detail and depth:

> So you should at all times behave unobtrusively in their presence. Pay greater respect to the other retainers of the clan than you have in the past. For the time being, when the sons of members of the Hojo clan are visiting your lord, refrain from calling on him, even if he should summon you...
>
> If those sons of the Hojo clan or the wives of those in power should inquire about your lord's illness, no matter who the person may be, get down on your

knees, place your hands properly, and reply thus: "His malady is entirely beyond my poor skill to cure. But no matter how often I decline, he insists that I treat him. Since I am in his service, I cannot help but do as he says." Leave your sidelocks uncombed, and refrain from wearing well-starched court dress, bright quilted robes, or other colorful clothing. Be patient, and continue in this way for the time being. (WND-1, 849)

The guidance here is probably so detailed because Nichiren was thoroughly familiar with the tendencies that might inadvertently trip Kingo up—tendencies that Kingo also recognized about himself as well as shortcomings of which he was unaware.

Of course, Buddhism is a teaching that enables each of us to live with complete freedom. It gives us the power to act with unconstrained energy and cheerfulness. But as "for the time being" indicates, Buddhism also means exercising the utmost care, prudence and wisdom in our conduct at crucial moments. At such times, it is vital that we bring forth wisdom most appropriate to the situation and create the greatest possible value. We must, therefore, remain unswayed in the depths of our lives, while at the same time flexibly respond to whatever develops. This is the Buddhist wisdom of the Middle Way.

A Wise Person Triumphs Amid Life's Harsh Realities

Probably you are well aware of it, but let me cite the Buddha's prediction about what the latter age will be like. In essence he states: "It will be a muddied age in which even sages will find it difficult to live. They will be like stones in a great fire, which for a while seem to endure the heat but finally char and crumble into ashes..." Thus the saying goes, "Do not remain in the seat of honor too long."

Many people have plotted to undo you, but you have avoided their intrigues and emerged victorious. Should you lose your composure now and fall into their trap, you will be, as people say, like a boatman who rows his boat with all his might only to have it capsize just before he reaches the shore, or like a person who is served no hot water at the end of his meal. (WND-1, 849)

In his letters, Nichiren Daishonin repeatedly encourages Shijo Kingo to live wisely, citing as examples the conduct of various wise people in ages past. When we have a goal or a model to aspire to, we can uncover fresh potential and achieve positive development and growth very rapidly.

In this writing, Nichiren notes that even sages find it difficult to live in this evil latter age, and he offers guidance to enable Kingo to take action with deep, unfaltering commitment. "Do not remain in the seat of honor too long," he says. Here, he warns Kingo not to get carried away just because his lord has asked him to treat his illness.

Through earnest efforts in exact accord with Nichiren's guidance, Kingo had overcome the tense situation with his lord, showing actual proof of victory based on strong faith. It is a reality of life and society, however, that the seeds of future defeat are often sown in times of victory—just as the seeds of future victory may be sown in times of defeat. Nichiren points out that should Kingo lose his composure now and fall into the trap of those plotting against him (see WND-1, 849)—that is, should he foolishly antagonize others and make matters worse by losing his temper, thereby playing into the hands of his enemies—then all his efforts to achieve a positive outcome will have been in vain.

Nichiren uses the examples of a "boatman who rows his boat with all his might only to have it capsize just before he reaches the shore" and a "person who is served no hot water at the end of his meal" to encourage Kingo to live out his life as a person of wisdom. These passages comprise a crucial lesson underscoring the importance of persevering in our Buddhist practice to the very end. Through ceaseless challenge and exertion, we can bring our lives to completion with supreme fulfillment. We mustn't grow lax along the way. To achieve a state of life imbued with the four noble virtues—eternity, happiness, true self and purity[8]—throughout past, present and future, we have to continue forging ahead with vigor, optimism and joy.

Here, Nichiren offers Kingo detailed advice about various safety precautions out of his wish that his disciple might triumph over all hardships and complete his Buddhist practice unaffected by life's vicissitudes—the "eight winds."[9] He writes:

> While you are in your lord's residence, if you stay in the room assigned to you, nothing will happen. But on your way to work at dawn or returning from it at dusk, your enemies are bound to be lying in wait for you. Also, be very careful in and around your house in case someone should be hiding beside the double doors, inside the family sanctuary, under the floor, or in the space above the ceiling. This time your foes will use even more cunning in their plots than before. In the end, no one will be more dependable in an emergency than the night watchmen of Egara in Kamakura. However disagreeable it may be to you, you should associate with them amicably. (WND-1, 849–50)

Nichiren emphasizes the need for Kingo to remain vigilant and alert at all times on his way to and from work and even at home. He considers every possible place where assassins might conceal themselves, including under the floor or in the space above the ceiling. Having weathered numerous persecutions, the Daishonin himself had suffered attacks on his person, both major and minor. From firsthand experience, he knew how important it was to be extremely careful. Buddhism is ultimately a teaching for achieving victory amid the harsh realities of society.

Nichiren was always urging Shijo Kingo to exercise great caution. He writes: "Determine to take every possible precaution. Those who hate you will be increasingly vigilant in watching for a chance to do you harm" ("On Recommending This Teaching to Your Lord and Avoiding the Offense of Complicity in Slander," WND-1, 461); "As I have said before, be millions of times more careful than ever" ("The Hero of the World," WND-1, 839); and "Be even more careful than usual" ("Nine Thoughts to One Word," WND-2, 731). And when, at a later date, Kingo emerged unscathed from an ambush by hostile forces, Nichiren cited his disciple's "usual prudence"[10] as one reason for his victory. Had the Daishonin only taken the trouble to warn Kingo once about being careful, then this victory might never have been realized. Also, had Kingo not faithfully followed Nichiren's instructions, it is quite possible he would have been killed in that attack.

Next, the Daishonin mentions the "night watchmen of Egara" (WND-1, 849), whom he also later refers to as the "four night watchmen" (WND-1, 850). Apart from their job description, which indicates they were responsible for evening security patrols, no detailed information is known about them. Nichiren writes, however, that they had their dwellings confiscated by Lord Ema because of their refusal to recant their faith in Nichiren Buddhism.[11] If Kingo is on friendly terms with these night watchmen and they frequently visit his home, the Daishonin further states, it will deter attacks from enemies, who do not wish to be seen (see WND-1, 850).[12]

Although Shijo Kingo and the four night watchmen were all Nichiren's followers, relations among them seem to have been strained. Nichiren counsels Kingo on this point as well. Fortunate is the disciple who has such a concerned and caring mentor.

He urges Kingo to be cordial toward the four night watchmen. He says, "However disagreeable it may be to you, you should associate with them amicably" (WND-1, 849–50). In other writings, too, he advises Kingo on how he should behave toward his fellow practitioners or his brothers. He writes: "Even if they have their faults, if they are only minor ones, just pretend you do not notice them" ("Nine Thoughts to One Word," WND-2, 731); and "You must be on good terms with those who believe in this teaching, neither seeing, hearing, nor pointing out anything about them that may displease you" ("Unseen Virtue and Visible Reward," WND-1, 907).

Rather than viewing this guidance as directed only to Shijo Kingo, we should take it as an eternal guideline for all practitioners of Nichiren Buddhism. To be on good terms with everyone, to treasure our fellow practitioners—these principles also apply to the SGI. When solidly united, we can overcome obstacles and negative forces and make great strides forward for kosen-rufu. Devilish functions constantly seek to sow division. If fellow practitioners engage in petty infighting, they will only undermine one another, making it possible for devilish forces to gain advantage. As Nichiren writes, "Should you fail to act in harmony, you will be like the snipe and the shellfish who, because they were locked in combat with one another, fell prey to the fisherman" ("Brothers One in Mind," WND-2, 914).

And in a letter to another follower, he says, "All those who keep faith in the Lotus Sutra are most certainly Buddhas" ("The Fourteen Slanders," WND-1, 756). Accordingly, he indicates that to slander and malign one's fellow practitioners is to commit the offense of slandering a Buddha.

The role of leaders of kosen-rufu, in particular, is to warmly embrace and support everyone. That's why leaders have to cultivate a broad and expansive state of being. This is what the call for a leadership revolution in the SGI is all about.

I can imagine Shijo Kingo persevering through adversity while calling to mind the noble countenance of Nichiren Daishonin, who was the epitome of such a humanistic leader.

Behavior Infused With Respect for Others

But since you are hot-tempered by nature, you might not take my advice. In that case, it will be beyond the power of my prayers to save you.

Ryuzo-bo and your elder brother plotted evil against you. Therefore, the heavenly gods so contrived it that the situation would develop exactly as you wished. Then how can you now dare to go against the wish of the heavenly gods? ... You must hurry and talk with these four men and report to me how the matter goes. Then I will fervently pray to the heavenly gods for your protection. (WND-1, 850)

Having suggested various courses of action, Nichiren Daishonin returns to his earlier theme: "But since you are hot-tempered by nature, you might not take my advice. In that case, it will be beyond the power of my prayers to save you."

Throughout his writings, Nichiren makes the point that unless he and his disciples are united in purpose and resolve, their prayers, their goals and aspirations will not be realized. Probably no other follower had put his life on the line to protect Nichiren to the extent Shijo Kingo had. But if Kingo gave in to his temper and acted rashly, forgetting all about his commitment to act in a spirit of oneness with his mentor, he would wind up again foolishly ruled by deluded impulses. In that case, Nichiren says, no matter how fervently he prays for Kingo, it will be to no avail.

I'm sure the Daishonin's repeated warning about not being quick-tempered must have prompted sober reflection on Kingo's part. It is especially interesting to note that he reiterates this immediately after advising Kingo to be on good terms with the night watchmen. This points to the fact that the ultimate foundation of Buddhist practice lies in the solid unity of fellow practitioners and the oneness of mentor and disciple. It is no exaggeration to say that without this foundation the flow of kosen-rufu would come to a halt.

Having advised Kingo to ally himself with the night watchmen, Nichiren writes: "You must hurry and talk with these four men and report to me how the matter goes. Then I will fervently pray to the heavenly gods for your protection."

This is a key point of personal guidance. The process doesn't just end once the guidance and encouragement are given. The person giving guidance must continue to chant wholeheartedly for the other person's happiness. We see that Nichiren always did precisely that.

The Soka Gakkai is committed to giving responsible guidance. To do so, it is important that we not only strive to impart heartfelt encouragement and clear direction to others but also let them know that we will struggle alongside them—as a team, so to speak. And we must continue chanting until the person achieves a positive result or breakthrough. Because we have advanced with this spirit, the Soka Gakkai has grown into the great organization it is today.

Shijo Kingo had been confronted with many challenges: the displeasure of his lord; slander, false rumors and attacks by fellow retainers; his elder brother's betrayal; discord with his younger brothers; and strained relations with a number of fellow practitioners. Nichiren was concerned about each of these situations and gave pertinent advice on how to deal with them. From this letter, we can sense how much Nichiren cared about Shijo Kingo, supporting and guiding him with an affection surpassing even that which one might expect from a family member.

Indeed, the Daishonin thoroughly treasured each follower. Showing thoughtful consideration to each person is an expression of Buddhist humanism.

The Buddhist scriptures describe how Shakyamuni Buddha freely expounded the Law in accord with people's capacity. In one instance, he encountered a grief-stricken mother with her dead child in her arms. When she begged Shakyamuni for a cure, he told the woman in essence: "If you go into the town and bring me a mustard seed, I will make a medicine for your child. But the seed must come from a home where no one has died." As the mother went around from house to house, she learned that every family had experienced the death of a loved one. Seeking to come to terms with the impermanence of life, she eventually became a disciple of Shakyamuni.[13]

On another occasion, Shakyamuni came across a member of the Buddhist Order named Chudapanthaka, who was crying disconsolately by the roadside. Upon inquiry, he learned that fellow monks had rejected the young man over his inability to memorize even one line of verse. Shakyamuni responded to the effect: "You understand your own ignorance. Therefore, you, Chudapanthaka, are in fact the wisest of all. The most ignorant are those who think they are very smart." Thus encouraged by Shakyamuni, Chudapanthaka went on to become an exemplary teacher who was loved and venerated by countless people.[14]

This tradition of Buddhist humanism—characterized by treasuring and showing the utmost respect for each person—is alive and well today in the SGI. The Soka Gakkai's first and second presidents, Tsunesaburo Makiguchi and Josei Toda, always treasured and respected each person.

Mr. Makiguchi, despite his advanced age, traveled numerous times to distant destinations such as Osaka and Shimonoseki (at the southeastern tip of Honshu, Japan's main island), and even Kyushu (an island lying farther south).

Getting there required long train rides with countless stops and transfers, and it meant being bumped and jostled interminably on the hard train seats. Often he would set out on such a trip to meet just one person or encourage one family. At the homes he visited, he would sometimes also meet with members' families, listen to everyone's worries and explain the principle that faith equals daily life in a way anyone could understand.

Once a week, he also held personal guidance sessions for members at his home in Tokyo's Mejiro area, where he would wholeheartedly encourage anywhere from a handful to several dozen people. This continued right up until his arrest in Shimoda (at the southern tip of the Izu Peninsula) on charges of lèsemajesté and violating the repressive Peace Preservation Law. The prosecutor's indictment cited "giving personal guidance" as one reason for the charges brought against him.

As I related earlier, Mr. Toda conducted similar guidance sessions at the old Soka Gakkai Headquarters branch office, and he treasured each person. By contrast, the priesthood muddied and besmirched its heritage, the once pure stream of faith, through having lost touch completely with this wellspring of Buddhist humanism that accords the highest respect to each individual.

Without doubt, humanism will become the current of the twenty-first century. All the leading intellects I have met have shared this view.

It has long been pointed out that positive, supportive connections among people have become increasingly weak in contemporary society. Also, we have arrived at a crossroads where either we allow the divisions among nations, ethnic groups, religions and cultures to widen further, or we take action to create the possibility of mutual understanding and cooperation. The world now seeks a system of thought or philosophy that can bridge these chasms and provide a basis for treating all people with respect. We of the SGI embody just such a philosophy. We have entered a time when our behavior and actions will be highly acclaimed as the practice of modern bodhisattvas and the conduct of living Buddhas.

The Buddhist concept of "behavior as a human being" (WND-1, 852) constitutes a philosophy of action offering a new model of conduct for the human race. The world is in urgent need of people who practice and base their actions on humanism. The conduct of SGI members in cherishing and valuing each person is being lauded around the globe as a model of humanity for a new age.

This lecture was originally published in the November 2009 issue of the Daibyakurenge, *the Soka Gakkai's monthly study journal.*

NOTES

[1] Ryuzo-bo (n.d.): A Tendai priest who was expelled from Enryaku-ji, a temple on Mount Hiei that was the headquarters of the Tendai school, and later came to Kamakura where he won the patronage of a priest of the True Word Precepts school, Ryokan of Gokuraku-ji, a temple in Kamakura.

[2] Dragon king's daughter: Also, the dragon girl. The eight-year-old daughter of Sagara, one of the eight great dragon kings said to dwell in a palace at the bottom of the sea. According to "Devadatta," the 12th chapter of the Lotus Sutra, the dragon girl conceives the desire for enlightenment upon hearing Bodhisattva Manjushri preach the Lotus Sutra in the dragon king's palace. She then appears in front of the assembly of the Lotus Sutra and instantaneously attains Buddhahood in her present form. The dragon girl's enlightenment is a model for the enlightenment of women and reveals the power of the Lotus Sutra to enable all people equally to attain Buddhahood just as they are.

[3] This phrase appears in Miao-lo's *The Annotations on "The Words and Phrases of the Lotus Sutra."*

[4] Buddha nature manifesting itself from within and bringing forth protection from without: When we activate the Buddha nature inside us, it will cause the protective functions of life to work externally.

[5] Greed, anger, foolishness, arrogance and doubt: These are called "the five delusive inclinations." According to *The Dharma Analysis Treasury,* the five delusive inclinations constitute the most fundamental of illusions or earthly desires.

[6] Translated from Japanese. Kiyoshi Miki "Jinsei-ron noto" (Thoughts on Life: Notes), *Miki Kiyoshi zenshu* (Collected Works of Kiyoshi Miki) (Tokyo: Iwanami Shoten, 1966), vol.1, pp.266–68.

[7] Ibid., 270.

[8] Four virtues: Four noble qualities of the Buddha's life, also known as the four paramitas or four virtue paramitas—eternity, happiness, true self and purity. The word *paramita* means "perfection." *Eternity* means "unchanging and eternal." *Happiness* means "tranquillity that transcends all suffering." *True self*

means "true and intrinsic nature." And *purity* means "free of illusion or mistaken conduct."

[9] Eight winds: Prosperity, decline, disgrace, honor, praise, censure, suffering and pleasure. In a letter to Shijo Kingo, Nichiren writes: "Worthy persons deserve to be called so because they are not carried away by the eight winds ... They are neither elated by prosperity nor grieved by decline. The heavenly gods will surely protect one who is unbending before the eight winds" ("The Eight Winds," WND-1, 794).

[10] In "The Strategy of the Lotus Sutra," Nichiren declares: "It is a matter of rejoicing that your usual prudence and courage, as well as your firm faith in the Lotus Sutra, enabled you to survive unharmed" (WND-1, 1000).

[11] Nichiren writes: "It is even more vital for you to ally yourself with the four night watchmen. The dwellings they had earned by risking their lives were confiscated by their lord because of the Lotus Sutra, and more directly, because of Nichiren" (WND-1, 850).

[12] Nichiren writes: "If they frequent your house, your enemies will be afraid to

attack you at night ... Against those who seek to avoid the eyes of others, there are no warriors as dependable as they are. Always maintain friendly relations with them" (WND-1, 850).

[13] This famous parable appears in the Buddhist writing, *Therigatha Atthakatha* (Commentary to the *Therigatha*).

[14] This episode is related in the *Mulasarvastivada Vinaya*. Translated from Japanese. *Komponsetsu issai ubu binaya* (Mulasarvastivada Vinaya), in *Kokuyaku issaikyo Indo senjutsubu ronshubu* (The Japanese Translation of the Buddhist Scriptures: Works Composed in India), edited by Shinyu Iwano (Tokyo: Daito Shuppansha, 1975), vol.88, pp.601–02.

CHAPTER 12

"THE THREE KINDS OF TREASURE"—PART 3 OF 3

THE ULTIMATE KEY TO VICTORY IN LIFE IS ACCUMULATING THE TREASURES OF THE HEART

> ### The Passage for Study in This Lecture
>
> Over and over I recall the moment, unforgettable even now, when I was about to be beheaded and you accompanied me, holding the reins of my horse and weeping tears of grief. Nor could I ever forget it in any lifetime to come. If you should fall into hell for some grave offense, no matter how Shakyamuni Buddha might urge me to become a Buddha, I would refuse; I would rather go to hell with you. For if you and I should fall into hell together, we would find Shakyamuni Buddha and the Lotus Sutra there ... But if you depart from my

advice even slightly, do not blame me for what may happen...

Do not go around lamenting to others how hard it is for you to live in this world. To do so is an act utterly unbecoming to a worthy man. (WND-1, 850)

It is rare to be born a human being. The number of those endowed with human life is as small as the amount of earth one can place on a fingernail. Life as a human being is hard to sustain—as hard as it is for the dew to remain on the grass. But it is better to live a single day with honor than to live to 120 and die in disgrace. Live so that all the people of Kamakura will say in your praise that Nakatsukasa Saburo Saemon-no-jo is diligent in the service of his lord, in the service of Buddhism, and in his concern for other people. More valuable than treasures in a storehouse are the treasures of the body, and the treasures of the heart are the most valuable of all. From the time you read this letter on, strive to accumulate the treasures of the heart! (WND-1, 851)

***

The worthy man Confucius held to his belief "Nine thoughts to one word,"[1] which means that he reconsidered nine times before he spoke. Tan, the Duke of Chou,[2] was so earnest in receiving callers that he would wring out his hair three times in the course of washing it, or spit out his food three times in the course of a meal [in order not to keep them waiting].[3] Consider this carefully so that you will have no cause to reproach me later. What is called Buddhism is found in this behavior.

The heart of the Buddha's lifetime of teachings is the Lotus Sutra, and the heart of the practice of the Lotus Sutra is found in the "Never Disparaging" chapter. What does Bodhisattva Never Disparaging's[4] profound respect for people signify? The purpose of the appearance in this world of Shakyamuni Buddha, the lord of teachings, lies in his behavior as a human being.

Respectfully.

The wise may be called human, but the thoughtless are no more than animals. (WND-1, 851–52)

LECTURE

"The treasures of the heart are the most valuable of all," Nichiren Daishonin says. "Strive to accumulate the treasures of the heart!"

(WND-1, 851). This is the message he imparted to his embattled disciple Shijo Kinjo. It contains the most vital key for winning in life.

The heart is our unsurpassed treasure in life. It is endowed with tremendous potential and supreme nobility. Its depth and breadth can be expanded infinitely, and its strength can be developed without bound. The French author Victor Hugo wrote, "There is a spectacle greater than the sea, and that is the sky; there is a spectacle greater than the sky, and that is the human soul."[5]

How can we expand the inner realm of our lives, develop inner strength and accumulate treasures of the heart so that we can lead better lives? The answer is found in practicing the Mystic Law.

In the latter part of this writing, "The Three Kinds of Treasure," Nichiren teaches that "the treasures of the heart are the most valuable of all" (WND-1, 851). The ultimate treasure in terms of achieving genuine victory in life is our Buddha nature manifesting from within through faith in the Mystic Law. We must never lose sight of this crucial teaching.

Two months before this letter was written, Shijo Kingo faced the grave crisis of having his estate confiscated by his lord, Ema Mitsutoki. Kingo chose to uphold his faith in the Lotus Sutra, even if it meant losing his estate. The Daishonin praised him for this stance and offered this caution: "However wretched a beggar you might become, never disgrace the Lotus Sutra" ("A Warning against Begrudging One's Fief," WND-1, 824).

In fact, these words are meant to teach Kingo the essential criteria he should follow as a practitioner—that faith (a treasure of the heart) is far more important than his estate (a treasure of the storehouse) or his position as a samurai (a treasure of the body). And, indeed, when Kingo practiced in accord with this guidance—putting faith first—his adverse situation began to brighten. Being called on to treat his lord's illness, he regained the latter's favor. Also, those who had harassed and attacked Kingo experienced negative consequences in accord with the strict law of cause and effect.

In "The Three Kinds of Treasure," Nichiren praises his disciple's faith, explaining that Kingo could take the first step toward victory based on the principle of "manifesting the Buddha nature from within and bringing forth protection from without" (see WND-1, 848). The moment Kingo stood up with unwavering faith, his inner Buddha nature manifested; this activated the heavenly deities—the benevolent functions of the universe—and resulted in external protection in the form of Ema's renewed reliance on Kingo.

But Kingo still found himself in a rather hostile environment. Nichiren offers a variety of detailed instructions and advice to help Kingo solidify his victories achieved thus far. He urges his disciple to remain vigilant against attack, to interact courteously and sincerely with others, and to foster good relations with his brothers and fellow practitioners and make them his allies. The Daishonin also warns Kingo to keep a tight rein on his short temper, sternly pointing out that if he succumbs to an outburst, it could cause a serious rift in his relationships and destroy all his positive progress.

To achieve unshakable victory, we need to challenge ourselves in earnest to change our karma. This is also the practice of human revolution, in which we strive to break through our inner darkness or ignorance. Carelessness is the greatest enemy. If we allow ourselves to grow complacent and lose our fighting spirit, then the shortcomings or negative tendencies that arise from our fundamental darkness will resurface. For that reason, the Daishonin consistently emphasizes the point that faith is life's ultimate treasure.

In this installment, let us once more study Nichiren's teaching that the treasures of the heart are the most valuable of all.

Always Return to the Prime Point of the Oneness of Mentor and Disciple

Over and over I recall the moment, unforgettable even now, when I was about to be beheaded and you accompanied me, holding the reins of my horse and weeping tears of grief. Nor could I ever forget it in

any lifetime to come. If you should fall into hell for some grave offense, no matter how Shakyamuni Buddha might urge me to become a Buddha, I would refuse; I would rather go to hell with you. For if you and I should fall into hell together, we would find Shakyamuni Buddha and the Lotus Sutra there ... But if you depart from my advice even slightly, do not blame me for what may happen. (WND-1, 850)

"If you become deadlocked, return to the prime point"—this was the guidance of first Soka Gakkai president Tsunesaburo Makiguchi.

The Lotus Sutra is based on the spirit of the oneness of mentor and disciple. Nichiren Buddhism, too, is a teaching of mentor and disciple. Our prime point as practitioners, therefore, is our vow to struggle together with our mentor. If we constantly return to this prime point of mentor and disciple, we will never become deadlocked.

In this passage, Nichiren Daishonin reaffirms the incident that became the prime point in his relationship with Shijo Kingo as mentor and disciple. It took place during the Tatsunokuchi Persecution.[6] As Nichiren was being taken to the execution grounds, Kingo gripped the reins of his mentor's horse and declared that he was prepared to die at his side.

In praise of the faith that Kingo showed at that time, the Daishonin goes so far as to say, "If you should fall into hell for some grave offense, no matter how Shakyamuni Buddha might urge me to become a Buddha, I would refuse; I would rather go to hell with you." We find the essence of his humanistic teaching in his spirit to respond to the sincere devotion of his disciples.

If the Daishonin and Kingo—mentor and disciple upholding steadfast faith in the Mystic Law—were to fall into hell, then Shakyamuni Buddha and the Lotus Sutra would also definitely be found there. In that case, Nichiren explains, it would no longer be hell but rather the realm of Buddhahood. This is the principle that "hell can instantly be transformed into the Land of Tranquil Light."[7]

We can manifest the brilliance of the world of Buddhahood anywhere. This is the teaching of Nichiren Buddhism. Our first two presidents, Tsunesaburo Makiguchi and Josei Toda, united by the bonds of mentor and disciple, demonstrated this with their own lives. In a prison cell that he described as "cold to the extreme," Mr. Makiguchi wrote, "Depending on one's frame of mind, even hell can be enjoyable."[8] And Mr. Toda, who accompanied him to prison, remarked: "Even if I should fall into hell, it wouldn't matter to me in the least. I would simply share the correct teaching with the inhabitants there and turn it into the Land of Tranquil Light." This spirit is the very quintessence of faith in Nichiren Buddhism.

As long as Kingo doesn't lose sight of this spirit to struggle together with Nichiren, he can triumph in any place and situation, based on the principle that "hell itself can instantly be transformed into the Land of Tranquil Light." But if he is defeated by his own weakness, losing his temper and lacking consideration for those around him, he will veer from the path of oneness with his mentor. This is why Nichiren repeatedly warns him to be careful. He writes, "If you depart from my advice even slightly, do not blame me for what may happen."

The key to victory lies in aligning our hearts with the heart of our mentor who faithfully embodies and propagates the Law. If we ignore our mentor's guidance and simply base ourselves on our own vacillating minds, we cannot complete the arduous path of Buddhist practice. A sutra states, "Become the master of your mind rather than let your mind master you" ("Letter to the Brothers," WND-1, 502).[9] Only when we practice faith in the same spirit as our mentor can we truly become the master of our minds and attain Buddhahood in this lifetime.

Lamenting Over Our Problems Slows Our Spiritual Development

Do not go around lamenting to others how hard it is for you to live in this world. To do so is an act utterly unbecoming to a worthy man. (WND-1, 850)

Here, Nichiren Daishonin especially admonishes against lamentation and self-pity. This passage gets at the heart of people's readiness to bewail matters that are beyond their control. Everyone is susceptible to doing this. Even Kingo, who was prepared to lay down his life alongside Nichiren at a crucial moment, had trouble with human relations because of his rigidity and single-mindedness. He may have given in to complaining in spite of himself. In advising Kingo not to lament to others, the Daishonin underscores that complaining about one's troubles or misfortunes is the way of life of the foolish, not the wise.

He writes:

> If a man behaves in this way, then after he dies, his wife, overcome with sorrow at losing her husband, will tell other people about the shameful things he did, though she has no real intention of doing so. And that will in no way be her fault, but solely the result of his own reprehensible behavior. (WND-1, 850)

Complaining nurtures one's inner weakness and negativity and becomes a cause for stagnation. Here, Nichiren teaches Kingo that doing away with complaint and instead pursuing his own human revolution head-on is the sure path to victory in life.

***

Become a True Winner in Life

It is rare to be born a human being. The number of those endowed with human life is as small as the amount of earth one can place on a fingernail. Life as a human being is hard to sustain—as hard as it is for the dew to remain on the grass. But it is better to live a single day with honor than to live to 120 and die in disgrace. Live so that all the people of Kamakura will say in your praise that Nakatsukasa Saburo Saemon-no-jo [Shijo Kingo] is diligent in the service of his lord, in the service of Buddhism, and in his concern for other people. (WND-1, 851)

It is rare to be born a human being: The number of those born with human life is "as small as the amount of earth one can place on a fingernail." In addition, human life is as hard to sustain "as it is for the dew to remain on the grass." Nichiren Daishonin thus indicates how irreplaceable our lives as human beings are and how precious every single day and moment is.

"It is better to live a single day with honor than to live to 120 and die in disgrace," Nichiren declares, highlighting the criterion for true merit in life. Our true merit as human beings arises from what we decide to make the purpose of our lives and how we go about achieving it.

Nichiren offers this specific guidance to his disciple out of a wish for him to succeed on a fundamental level: "Live so that all the people of Kamakura will say in your praise that Nakatsukasa Saburo Saemon-no-jo is diligent in the service of his lord, in the service of Buddhism, and in his concern for other people." It implies three particular areas in which Kingo needs to be victorious: rebuilding a relationship of mutual trust with his lord, continuing to make unwavering efforts as a practitioner of the Mystic Law and winning the trust of those around him. The treasures of the heart will shine in all these endeavors. In other words, we are truly victorious when we bring forth the brilliance of our Buddha nature in all aspects of our lives.

Nichiren further teaches us to show actual proof of victory by striving to live in a way that wins the praise and admiration of those around us. This offers an important guideline as to what constitutes victory for a Buddhist. In short, fundamental victory derives from the inner brilliance of our humanity that naturally draws others' admiration. It could also be said that an important part of our struggle for kosenrufu is for each of us to win such trust and respect in society.

The power of our humanity as Buddhists ultimately inspires praise. In other words, the treasures of the heart we have cultivated are what win us people's trust and high regard for our exemplary character. Our Buddha nature manifests as the brilliance of our humanity and touches the hearts of even those who do not practice Nichiren Buddhism. *There's something different about those people, a special glow about SGI members,* people will think. Gaining such trust from others is definite actual proof of the power of our Buddhist practice.

Shijo Kingo's relations with those around him—with Lord Ema and the members of his lord's family, and with his own colleagues, brothers and fellow practitioners—were far from smooth. There were probably instances when his doggedness created problems. Without resolving such issues, he could not become a winner in faith.

That's why Nichiren urges him to constantly work on polishing his character and show actual proof by realizing a great human revolution. It was his wish that Kingo, as the central figure among his followers in Kamakura, would develop into an admirable leader in society and lead a life of profound significance and meaning. This compassionate spirit was no doubt behind the Daishonin's guidance encouraging him to win the praise of the people in Kamakura.

A Thoroughly Polished-Character Is Priceless

More valuable than treasures in a storehouse are the treasures of the body, and the treasures of the heart are the most valuable of all. From the time you

read this letter on, strive to accumulate the treasures of the heart! (WND-1, 851)

The above passage is the most well-known in this writing. "Treasures in a storehouse" indicates material assets. "Treasures of the body" means such things as health or acquired skills. "Treasures of the heart," on one level, means an inner richness, wealth or abundance. On a more fundamental level, it means faith and the brilliance of the Buddha nature polished through faith.

In this passage, Nichiren indicates the order of priority of the three kinds of treasure and sets forth a clear standard of value.

Kingo faced the possibility of losing his estate, which, of course, represented an extremely important source of income for him and his family. But the Daishonin insists that far more valuable than the treasures of the storehouse and the body are the treasures of the heart. The accumulation of these inner treasures, he says, is the basis for all victory.

The fact that Kingo had been challenging his situation based on faith in the Mystic Law corresponds to placing the highest value on the treasures of the heart. As a result, he had been victorious so far. That is probably why Nichiren clarifies this point as a universal and unchanging guideline for victory in all areas of life.

And actually, when we base ourselves on the treasures of the heart, the true value and worth of treasures of the storehouse and the body also become apparent in our lives. In short, we need to make accumulating the treasures of the heart our fundamental purpose in life. If we lose sight of this elemental objective, seeking merely to accumulate treasures of the storehouse and the body, it will only give rise to attachment. Fear of losing such material or physical treasures can then become a cause of suffering. Therefore, what is important above all, what is the correct sense of purpose in life, is to accumulate treasures of the heart.

Respond to Others With Sincerity

The worthy man Confucius held to his belief "Nine thoughts to one word," which means that he reconsidered nine times before he spoke. Tan, the Duke of Chou, was so earnest in receiving callers that he would wring out his hair three times in the course of washing it, or spit out his food three times in the course of a meal [in order not to keep them waiting]. Consider this carefully so that you will have no cause to reproach me later. What is called Buddhism is found in this behavior. (WND-1, 851)

Buddhism does not exist apart from the realities of life.

Nichiren Daishonin was extremely concerned about Kingo's volatile temperament. Saying he would like to relate an "incident that is customarily kept secret"[10] (WND-1, 851), he shares with his disciple the story of the irascible Emperor Sushun.[11] It is a lesson about what can happen when one openly displays antipathy toward others.

Next, Nichiren mentions the great Chinese philosopher Confucius, who chose his words with such care that he thought nine times before speaking. And he refers to the Duke of Chou in ancient China, who was so concerned not to keep guests waiting that he would even interrupt his meals or bath time to receive them. Through these examples, Nichiren underscores the need for prudent thought and sincere conduct in our interactions with others.

"Consider this carefully," he says, seeking to deeply impress this message on Kingo. He sensed that his disciple wouldn't achieve true victory in life if he did not overcome his short temper—a flaw that could bring about his downfall—and did not earnestly accumulate treasures of the heart. Nichiren goes so far as to say, "What is called Buddhism is found in this behavior."

Buddhism finds ultimate expression in our behavior as human beings. Both Confucius and the Duke of Chou demonstrated their personal philosophy and creed through their actions. Likewise, unless our conduct displays the supreme treasure of the heart expounded in Buddhism—the Buddha nature manifesting itself from within—we cannot show actual proof of the power of faith or spread Nichiren Buddhism.

That's why Nichiren, at the end of this writing, discusses the importance of our behavior as human beings.

***

Our Behavior as Human Beings

The heart of the Buddha's lifetime of teachings is the Lotus Sutra, and the heart of the practice of the Lotus Sutra is found in the "Never Disparaging" chapter. What does Bodhisattva Never Disparaging's profound respect for people signify? The purpose of the appearance in this world of Shakyamuni Buddha, the lord of teachings, lies in his behavior as a human being.
Respectfully.

The wise may be called human, but the thoughtless are no more than animals. (WND-1, 851–52)

In concluding "The Three Kinds of Treasure," Nichiren Daishonin states that the Lotus Sutra is the heart of Shakyamuni's lifetime teachings. He says that the essence of the practice taught in the Lotus Sutra is found in the behavior of Bodhisattva Never Disparaging, who is described in the sutra chapter that bears his name as staunchly believing in and venerating the Buddha nature of all people.

Deeply apprehending the truth that—when viewed from the fundamental perspective of life—everyone is a Buddha, Bodhisattva Never Disparaging bowed in reverence to all he met, no matter how he was persecuted and attacked. This is the behavior of one who truly embodies the spirit of the Lotus Sutra.

It is said that the Lotus Sutra explains why Shakyamuni made his appearance in this world. Describing the practice of Bodhisattva Never Disparaging, who embodies the sutra's spirit, it indicates that the purpose of Shakyamuni's appearance in this world lies in his behavior as a human being.

As Nichiren notes when he says, "The Law does not spread by itself: because people propagate it, both people and the Law are respectworthy" (GZ, 856),[12] the greatness of the Law or teaching can only be conveyed and spread when expressed in the humanistic actions and behavior of those who embrace it.

The treasures of the heart may be invisible to the eye. But when these inner treasures are given concrete expression as respectful actions toward others, they demonstrate and prove to others the power of the Mystic Law and the Buddha nature.

Viewing treasures of the heart as the most valuable of all reflects a sense of values concerned with what is most important and precious in life. Showing respect to others in our actions, meanwhile, constitutes the standard for our behavior as Buddhists based on this sense of values.

The universally respectful behavior of Bodhisattva Never Disparaging embodies the teaching of the Lotus Sutra, which expounds the Buddha's true intent of enabling all people to realize their enlightenment. Therefore, Bodhisattva Never Disparaging's respectful behavior toward others is itself the true intent of the Buddha.

The ability to manifest our Buddha nature is a benefit of faith in the Mystic Law. The behavior of those who embody this benefit, which is sure to be characterized by respect for others, can serve as actual proof of the greatness of the Mystic Law.

Let us now reconfirm, based on the sutra, how Bodhisattva Never Disparaging—Shakyamuni in a previous lifetime—lived in a way that was always respectful to others.

At the start of "Bodhisattva Never Disparaging," the 20th chapter of the Lotus Sutra, Shakyamuni explained the principle that those who slander the sutra will incur severe retribution for their offense, while those who are slandered on account of upholding the sutra will gain the benefit of the purification of the six sense organs[13] (see LSOC, 307).

As an example, he introduced the practice of Bodhisattva Never Disparaging, who appeared in the Middle Day of the Law[14] after the death of a Buddha called Awesome Sound King. It was an age when arrogant monks held great power and the correct teaching was in decline. At that time, Bodhisattva Never Disparaging would bow in reverence to the four kinds of believers of the day—monks, nuns, laymen and laywomen—who were overbearingly arrogant, saying to them: "I have profound reverence for you, I would never dare treat you with disparagement or arrogance. Why? Because you will all practice the bodhisattva way and will then be able to attain Buddhahood" (LSOC, 308). This declaration concisely expresses the core Lotus Sutra teaching that all people can attain enlightenment; and it is called the "twenty-four-character Lotus Sutra" [in reference to the number of Chinese characters that make up this passage]. Bodhisattva Never Disparaging's practice solely consisted of bowing to others in reverence and greeting them with these words.

The four kinds of believers, however, being filled with arrogance and contempt, responded to his sincerity with curses and abuse, some even beating him with sticks or pelting him with stones. Through enduring these persecutions, Never Disparaging could wipe out his offenses[15] and transform his karma. The sutra relates how, as he was nearing death, he heard in the air countless verses of the Lotus Sutra that had previously been preached by the Buddha Awesome Sound King. In hearing these verses, he gained the benefit of the purification of the six sense organs, extended his life span by "two hundred ten thousand million nayutas of years" and continued widely preaching the Lotus Sutra for others. He then attained Buddhahood and was reborn as Shakyamuni (see LSOC, 309–10).

In contrast, the four kinds of believers who had persecuted Bodhisattva Never Disparaging underwent great suffering for the immensely long period of a thousand kalpas as a result of these offenses, and when they had expiated their offenses, they again encountered Bodhisattva Never Disparaging and received his instruction (see LSOC, 310–11).

In this way, steadfastly showing respect for others through our behavior has the power to change our lives by transforming our karma and purifying our senses. And by respectfully sharing the teachings of the Lotus Sutra with others as long as we live, we can achieve the fundamental victory of realizing our Buddhahood. Such actions are based on a firm commitment to the principle that all people possess the Buddha nature. By holding fast to this commitment even in the face of hardships, we can embody this principle in our lives. As such, our efforts are part of our own Buddhist practice for attaining Buddhahood. In addition, they are part of the struggle to lead all people to enlightenment by brightly illuminating even the lives of those who slander and harass the practitioners of the correct teaching and awakening the Buddha nature dormant in the depths of their lives.

In short, Bodhisattva Never Disparaging's actions of respect for others constitute the fundamental cause for manifesting our Buddhahood. Such actions are crucial if we hope to gain enlightenment. The aspiration of leading all people to enlightenment would just be a pipe dream unless the Buddha taught the importance of our behavior as human beings. That is why Nichiren asserts that this is "the purpose of the appearance in this world of Shakyamuni Buddha, the lord of teachings."

Nichiren also always demonstrated respect for others through his actions. The Buddha nature will manifest in the lives of those who arouse and maintain faith in the Mystic Law, no matter how evil the times. Their behavior will definitely pulse with the fundamental wisdom of the practical philosophy of respect for others.

Nichiren's practice of *shakubuku,* of rigorously refuting error, is also grounded in compassion for the individual in error and concern for the happiness of the people. It is also an expression of his fervent wish for the peace and security of the land. Shakubuku is a struggle to refute the erroneous and reveal the true out of respect for everyone's Buddha nature.

Because shakubuku in Nichiren Buddhism is based on respect for others, it aims to refute the error of those who disrespect others. Premised on this understanding, Nichiren indicates that, even in the evil and slanderous age of the Latter Day, we need to act prudently and respectfully rather than simply rushing in to refute error.

Fully and unequivocally stating the truth is also shakubuku. The Latter Day of the Law is an age rife with distrust and fear stemming from a society in which people are not respected and life is held in low regard. In such an age, shakubuku means standing up alone and resolutely holding high the banner of respect for human beings and the sanctity of life. This, too, is the courageous practice of shakubuku.

As I am always affirming, resolving the various problems of our planet in the twenty-first century will hinge on focusing on the human being. This is an awareness shared by many leading intellects, peace activists and conscientious political leaders.

How do we transform people's inherent fundamental darkness? How do we expand the solidarity of those dedicated to the cause of good? And how do we construct a society in which harmonious coexistence and humanism prevail?

The SGI is taking action to pioneer a magnificent path of intercultural and interfaith dialogue toward finding answers to those very questions. Transcending all differences, surmounting barriers of ethnicity and nationality, we are constructing a realm of broad and open exchange among human beings. The philosophy of the SGI is based on the Lotus Sutra's teaching of showing respect for others through our actions, as well as the principle that all change begins from within ourselves and from accumulating treasures of the heart.

People around the world have high expectations for the SGI's humanistic philosophy. Our efforts in undergoing our human revolution provide hope to humankind.

We have now entered an age when the sincere endeavors of our members, who are putting into practice the humanistic behavior taught by Nichiren Daishonin, are winning trust and understanding on a global scale.

—With my prayers for the great victory in work and life for the men's division and all our members in Japan and throughout the world.

This lecture was originally published in the December 2009 issue of the Daibyakurenge, *the Soka Gakkai's monthly study journal.*

NOTES

[1] From the *Analects* of Confucius.
[2] Tan, the Duke of Chou: A younger brother of Emperor Wu, the founder of the Chou dynasty (lasting approximately from 1100 to 256BCE). After assisting his brother in overthrowing the Yin (Shang) dynasty and founding a new rule, he became closely involved in the affairs of government. When Emperor Wu died and

his son Ch'eng, who was still a child, came to the throne, the Duke of Chou acted as regent for the young ruler. He has been revered over the centuries by Confucianists as a model of correct government and propriety.

[3] This anecdote is mentioned in *Records of the Historian*. Tan, the Duke of Chou, was so eager to find able persons and anxious not to overlook anyone that he would receive visitors even while washing his hair or during the course of a meal. Nichiren Daishonin cites this example to explain the importance of being considerate, cautious and prudent.

[4] Bodhisattva Never Disparaging: A bodhisattva described in the 20th chapter of the Lotus Sutra. A previous incarnation of Shakyamuni, this bodhisattva would bow in reverence to everyone he met. He was attacked by arrogant people, however, who beat him with sticks and staves and threw stones at him. The sutra explains that his practice of respecting others' Buddha nature became the cause for him to attain Buddhahood.

[5] Victor Hugo, *Les Misérables*, translated by Julie Rose (New York: Random House, Inc., 2008), p.221.

[6]   Tatsunokuchi Persecution: On the twelfth day of the ninth month in 1271, powerful figures in the government unjustly arrested Nichiren and had him led off in the middle of the night to the execution grounds on the beach at Tatsunokuchi on the outskirts of Kamakura, the seat of government. They tried to execute him under cover of darkness, but the execution attempt failed, and about a month later, Nichiren was exiled to Sado Island.

[7]   Hell can instantly be transformed into the Land of Tranquil Light: The world of hell, which is a realm of extreme suffering, can be instantly transformed into the Land of Eternally Tranquil Light where the Buddha dwells, or the world of Buddhahood.

[8]   Translated from Japanese. Tsunesaburo Makiguchi, *Makiguchi Tsunesaburo zenshu* (Collected Writings of Tsunesaburo Makiguchi) (Tokyo: Daisanbunmei-sha, 1987), vol.10, p.285.

[9]   A quote from the Six Paramitas Sutra.

[10]   This incident is recorded in *The Chronicles of Japan*. Presumably it was not referred to openly because it involved the assassination of an emperor by one of his retainers.

[11]   Emperor Sushun: A Japanese emperor who reigned from 587 to 592. He was murdered in a plot masterminded by one of his retainers.

[12]   From "Hyaku rokka sho" (The One Hundred and Six Comparisons); not included in *The Writings of Nichiren Daishonin,* vols. 1 and 2.

[13]   Purification of the six sense organs: Also, purification of the six senses. This refers to the five sense organs—eyes, ears, nose, tongue, body—as well as the mind, which makes it possible to apprehend all things correctly. "Benefits of the Teacher of the Law," the 19th chapter of the Lotus Sutra, explains that those who uphold and practice the sutra acquire eight hundred benefits of the eyes, nose and body, and twelve hundred benefits of the ears, tongue and mind, and that through these benefits the sense organs become refined and pure.

[14]   The Middle Day of the Law here does not refer to the Middle Day after the death of Shakyamuni Buddha, but rather a period following the death of Buddha Awesome Sound King. The categorizations of Former Day, Middle

Day and Latter Day were also applied to other Buddhas appearing in Buddhist scriptures. Accordingly, the teaching of each Buddha has its own Middle Day of the Law.

[15] The line "When his offenses had been wiped out" (LSOC, 312), describes how Bodhisattva Never Disparaging eradicated his past offenses of slandering the Law through undergoing persecution.

www.ingramcontent.com/pod-product-compliance
Lightning Source LLC
Chambersburg PA
CBHW010719300426
44115CB00019B/2954